A Primer in Theatre History

*From the Greeks
to the Spanish Golden Age*

William Grange
with Illustrations by Mallory Prucha

D1606635

University Press of America,® Inc.
Lanham • Boulder • New York • Toronto • Plymouth, UK

Copyright © 2013 by University Press of America,® Inc.
4501 Forbes Boulevard, Suite 200, Lanham, Maryland 20706
UPA Aquisitions Department (301) 459-3366

10 Thornbury Road, Plymouth PL6 7PP, United Kingdom

Library of Congress Control Number: 2010929916
ISBN: 978-0-7618-6003-7

Meinen lieben Freunden

Dr. Thomas Bethge

und

Frau Ulrike Delfs-Bethge

gewidmet.

Contents

List of Figures

Acknowledgments

This book is a result of several years' teaching theatre history at universities, here and abroad. The author has learned more from his students in those classes than he ever imagined possible, and it is high time he acknowledged his numerous debts of gratitude to them. Unable to list them by name, his remaining hope is that they in turn have learned something from him.

But his debts owed do not end with his students. He is profoundly grateful to his colleagues, especially those at the Johnny Carson School of Theatre and Film here at University of Nebraska, but also to those at the University of Cologne, the University of Vienna, and the University of Heidelberg. They have been involved in teaching other aspects of theatre art, furnishing the author with generous insights into teaching which nobody else could have provided. Anyone who attempts to write a book on theatre history is furthermore indebted to his teachers. No one owes more to his teacher, the late theatre historian Dr. Oscar G. Brockett (1923-2010), than does the author of this book.

Individuals who also deserve mention for their help in putting this book together include Dr. Patrice Berger, Professor of History and Director of the Honors Program at the University of Nebraska, Prof. Harris Smith, Dr. Jürgen Ohlhoff and Frau Ulrike Münkel-Ohlhoff in Berlin, Mark Temple and Melita Dionsisio-Temple in Los Angeles, the distinguished theatre historian Dr. Marvin Carlson in New York, the Director of the Johnny Carson School Prof. Paul Steger, Antony Geary and Bettina Hartas-Geary in Wylam, Northumberland.

Lincoln, Nebraska
Summer, 2012

Introduction

History and Time

CULTURAL AND AESTHETIC SIGNIFICANCE

In 1993, a movie titled *Ground Hog Day* opened to good reviews and grossed millions of dollars in ticket sales. Though it won few awards and even fewer critics paid it much serious attention to it at the time. Yet *Ground Hog Day* proved to be popular with audiences because it featured a love story with a time twist. In 2006 the National Film Registry selected the movie for preservation in the Library of Congress because it contained "cultural and aesthetic significance." The movie also impressed those who study history, because *Ground Hog Day* featured one character (played by Bill Murray) who actually had a history. Nobody else in the movie had any memory of yesterday, let alone a sense of history. Murray played a television weather forecaster named Phil Connors, who finds himself assigned on February 2 to file a report from the Pennsylvania town of Punxsutawney, where a celebrated ground hog has for years re-enacted a kind of weather-forecasting ritual that began in medieval Europe. According to legend, the animal interrupts his hibernation on February 2 to inspect weather conditions outside his comfortable burrow. If he sees his shadow or is otherwise bothered, he retreats back into his burrow for another six weeks—which means that humans will have to endure another six weeks of winter. If he remains for a time outside, the forecast is for milder weather, maybe even a shorter winter. In the movie, the forecast of the ground hog is irrelevant, because the movie's plot twist propels weatherman Connors into a time warp. The day after Ground Hog Day finds Connors awakening to the startling realization that it is Ground Hog Day all over again. At first, Connors is terrified to think that he is stuck forever in the town of Punxatawney; then he realizes that he is the only person who has retained any knowledge of the previous day. For some reason, everybody else in the movie has no memory of the day before–not the woman he is trying to seduce (Andie MacDowell), not the officials of the town, not even the groundhog himself. Connors immediately seizes on the opportunity, and he spends several days exploiting his knowledge. He persuades lots of women into bed with him, he tricks town leaders into giving him money, he fools the police into letting him break the town's speed limits, he learns how to play the piano, and he even begins to speak Italian (as a way to impress the one woman he really wants, namely the producer named Rita, played by MacDowell).

What kind of cultural or aesthetic significance could a movie like this have? It seems at first glance to be merely a superficial love story, based on the tried and true plot gimmick of withheld information, a gimmick that playwrights have used for hundreds of years in countless plays. The Bill Murray character is the only one with information that counts; he withholds that information for his own benefit, while everybody else fails to grasp the fact that each day's events are actually repetitions of the previous day's events. The movie exaggerates the inability of everybody to recognize the repetition for the sake of comic effect. The implication of their inability, however, presents a broader perspective on memory, and how the memory of past events serves as a guide to subsequent behavior. Bill Murray's character is capable of manipulating nearly everybody in the film because he has gleaned information from them and then uses that information to his advantage. Andie MacDowell's character ultimately falls in love with him because he seems to know in advance the phrases she likes to hear, the food she likes to eat, or the music she thinks is romantic.

Imagine what it must be like to wake up every morning with no memory. In civilizations with no written history and only an oral tradition, one is like Andie MacDowell in *Ground Hog Day*. Consider the Incas of present-day Peru in the year 1532. Francisco Pizarro, along with 124 *conquistadores*, was able to overcome the vast Inca Empire in Peru because he had written accounts of history on his side. The Incan emperor Atahualpa, his Incan chieftains, and their approximately 80,000 warriors did not. When the Spaniards invaded their Empire, Pizarro had studied the history of the Aztec defeat in Mexico, which had taken place only two decades earlier, only a few hundred miles to the north. Yet the Incas knew nothing about the Spanish conquest of the Aztecs—and even if they did, it was only through hearsay. The Spaniards, on the other hand, benefited enormously (at the expense of the far more numerous yet illiterate Incas) from writing. Written historical accounts allowed them ready access to accurate information about native peoples. Pizarro, like many Spaniards, had read the reports of Hernán Cortes and his conquest of Montezuma II, the Aztec emperor. He implemented the lessons Cortes had learned at the expense of the Incas to disastrous effect.

Recorded History

Written history is, as one historian has noted, a gold mine of experience. It provides a range of experiences and circumstances that no single generation could possibly experience on its own. Reading history is, in fact, far more efficient than experience. It provides the discovery of how often the same ideas and experiences have occurred to others over the centuries. The Incan emperor Atahualpa, for example, did not have the faintest idea who Pizarro was nor of what a European presence in his empire could portend. He did not even realize that Pizarro was a threat until it was too late. He had no experience with, nor had he even heard of such threats to himself, nor to anyone anywhere else. The resulting "gulf of experience," as another historian has written, allowed Pizarro to set his trap and for Atahualpa to fall into it.

We really do not have a choice about whether or not to study history. Some cynics have suggested that history is what you can remember and is full of half-remembered facts. Napoleon Bonaparte (1769–1821) was such a cynic. He stated that history was "A set of lies agreed upon." Almost in rebuttal to Napoleon, the Spanish-American philosopher and teacher George Santayana (1863–1952) observed that "They who cannot remember the past are condemned to repeat it." In a similar vein, the 20th President of the United States James A. Garfield) 1831–1881(referred to history as "the unrolled scroll of prophecy." Garfield and others of his generation believed that history had a didactic purpose, while others such as Karl Marx (1818–1883) viewed history in theatrical terms. He agreed that history repeats itself, "the first time as tragedy, the second time as farce." With that aphorism Marx hoped to convince his readers that certain events in history were inevitable. Inevitable, didactic, or prophetic, the foremost imperative in studying history is its function as the memory of the human race, coupled with the most efficient tool of learning ever invented, namely literacy. Reading history grants the reader power of discernment, and a knowledge of history allows one to avoid falling back into jargon that tries to pass itself off as knowledge in a media age. Human beings have often found themselves bombarded with banality that pretends to comport itself as knowledge. Politicians, religious leaders, and some snake oil salesmen have long known how to exploit historical ignorance for their own benefit, usually at the expense of those paying attention to them. The study of theatre history in particular offers some defense against such exploitation, perhaps because theatre functions as the "abstract and brief chronicle of time" (to paraphrase Shakespeare). The study of theatre history is also helpful in avoiding a *"Ground Hog Day* syndrome" of gullibility and overweening credulousness. That is at least one reason why theatre over the centuries has often dealt with subjects of lasting interest to human beings. Among those subjects are fate (as in *Oedipus Rex* by Sophocles), gossip (as in *Much Ado About Nothing* by Shakespeare), education (*The School for Wives* by Moliere), success (*Death of a Salesman* by Arthur Miller), sexual power (*Venus in Fur* by David Ives) and many, many others. Studying theater history is by no means the only or even the most effective defense against gullibility, but it does offer substantial amounts of cultural perspective.

We should remember, however, that recorded history itself is a recent development. Theatre history is even more recent. History, as far as we can tell, began when people began to farm crops and domesticate animals instead of hunting and gathering food. The advantage of farming over hunting and gathering is the acquisition and storage of surpluses over the uncertainties of nomadic wandering in search of nourishment. Food surpluses are nice, but they also require defensible storage facilities and ultimately they require some form of inventory procedure. Most historians believe that alphabets developed from the need to assess the amount of food in storage. Alphabets did not emerge the purpose of writing poetry, plays, or reports about conquests (as in the case of Hernán Cortes). The creation of theatre is a fortunate by-product of civilization and the written word, but then art itself is a by-product, and "the beauty one can find in art is one of the pitifully few real and lasting products of human endeavor," according to the art collector and patron J. Paul Getty (1892–1976). Theatre was one of the many conspicuous of such products among the ancient Greeks about 2500 years ago. There had been many civilizations before then, with walled cities, food surpluses, and alphabets. None of them, however, invented theatre. Why not?

The Greeks are commonly acknowledged as the founders of democracy, and some observers (such as the philosopher Aristotle) believed there might have been a connection between democratic values and the creation of theatre. The Greeks, especially the Athenians, chose rulers not always on the basis of heredity but elected by ballot. Most tribes elected their leaders, but the Greeks exceeded tribal peoples by creating the concept of citizenship, based on political criteria rather than kinship. The Greeks practiced republicanism rather than democracy anyway, since they limited the electoral franchise to a small number of citizens and excluded vast numbers of citizens on the basis of class distinctions. Greek city states such as Athens, Sparta, and Corinth were therefore more concerned with the community than with the individual. Individual "rights" as we have come to know them in modern democracies were subordinated to the community's needs. Those needs defined and shaped individuals with a focused goal of social cohesion. In the modern world, as opposed to the Greeks, we tend to shape social goals for the benefit of individuals or narrowly defined groups of individuals.

An emphasis on community, however, does not explain why the Greeks invented theatre when they did, namely in the 6th century BC. It is difficult in any case to imagine how long ago 2500 years really was. For many people, even imagining how long ago World War II took place is a struggle. Some even use the term "history" as an insult: "My boyfriend? He's history!" is often heard in college dormitories and cafeterias. Colleges have long been places where "history" is a required course, though often dismissed among students as the study of "just one damn thing after another." Such attitudes probably derive from high school history courses, where students are often required to memorize important dates such as July 4, 1776, December 7, 1941, or September 11, 2001. Those dates have historical significance, but dates alone say little about history. Among peoples with no alphabets, history is sometimes referred to as "a long time ago," or "a very long time ago," or "so long ago nobody here can remember."

Time and history are different. History implies something recorded and subject to interpretation. The word "history" itself comes from a Greek term meaning investigation, indeed one that concludes with a narrative to explain what took place is usually part of most history books—or even broadcasts on the History Channel. "Historiography" is the process of writing history, which involves assaying the significance of events included in the "historical record" of the past. Most observers have concluded that the Greeks created historiography, just as they were the ones who created theatre and drama. The first among them were Herodotus (484–425 BC) and Thuycidides (460–395 BC). Those men are thought to have developed a methodological approach to history, examining events from the standpoint of human motivation rather than divine intervention. They believed that such an examination of the past could provide guidelines for future generations. Subsequent scholars of Greek culture noted that the Greeks were so convinced of history's importance that their mythology gave the study of history the protection of a muse, named Clio. She, along with the muses of tragedy (Melpomene) and comedy (Thalia), joined other muses who inspired the creation of music, poetry, dance, and astronomy. The emergence of Clio in Greek mythology is perhaps a sign of how important the writing of history had become, because it helped the Greeks to acknowledge their "past." They realized, at least 2500 years ago, that "the past is never dead," as an American novelist once wrote. "It's not even past."

The Greeks were among the first to recognize that the past, if investigated and interpreted dispassionately, could provide readers with fairly accurate portents for the present and the future. The writers of the Old Testament arrived at similar hypotheses somewhat earlier, though their interpretations had overtly religious admonitions to succeeding generations of readers. To the ancient Hebrews (especially those taken in captivity to Babylon in the 6th century BC), God had a divine plan for them and they strayed from it at their peril. He had his eye on them, and their progress as a chosen people they could actually chart according to their obedience to laws and commandments. The Greeks, on the other hand, often saw history repeating itself in cycles. So did the Chinese, and for that matter so have many Western historians. Regardless of "cyclical" or "linear" interpretations, however, the attempt to decipher history remains an ongoing enterprise. The past is, as noted above, still with us, though it often appears as "a foreign country," according to one historian. "They do things differently there."

Chronology and Geology

Time, on the other hand, is a perception, much like height, width, or depth. "Chronology" is a term that means the study of time, but it requires much less speculative effort to decipher it. Chronology is a listing of events as they occurred during the passage of time, and human beings are acutely aware of time's passage. Humans have over the years developed numerous devices to help them "tell time," that is, to become more aware of time's passage. Time in general, unlike that tiny fraction of time we call "history," is subject not so much to interpretation but to distinct scientific inquiry. Albert Einstein, for example, discovered that time is subject both to gravitational forces and to speed. Time slows down in the presence of gravity (which is actually a function of what he called the "time-space continuum." Time also observes certain physical laws; the Second Law of Thermodynamics states that time is irreversible. That Law also states that heat is released as time moves through the universe. The Law traces its origins to the French physicist and philosopher named Nicolas Carnot (1796–1832), who theorized that the Second Law of Thermodynamics requires everything to move towards entropy, disorder, and decomposition. The Second Law posits that entropy increases with time in any closed system, and that the process furthermore cannot be reversed. For example, when someone drops a teacup on a concrete floor, heat is released if the teacup shatters. It is impossible to recover that heat. Yet humans are often able to feel time passing in the form of events, faces, seasons, and devices for smaller sections of time; humans are likewise singular for their ability to remember the past and to speculate upon it. They have historically speculated on the future as well, largely because they cannot see it. But most people realize you cannot go backwards in time—unless you are in a movie titled *Back to the Future* with Michael J. Fox.

Time is a function of human perception, and only human beings perceive time's dimensionality. Other creatures perceive time—chimpanzees, elephants, tortoises, fish, even mosquitoes—but they perceive time, along with nearly everything else, in terms of their immediate survival or the continuation of their species. Only humans are able to deliberate on time and ponder its significance. The aforementioned *Back to the Future*, for example, is a deliberation on time and its significance for human beings making the trip backwards through it. In the movie, Marty McFly actually meets his own mother back in the 1950s when she was a teenager. Such a meeting is a scientific impossibility, but it gives both Marty, his mother (played by Lea Thompson), and audiences something interesting on which to speculate. Prior to the security food surpluses offered, humans had little incentive to speculate about time. Like other creatures, they were mostly trying to survive. Some individuals since the advent of civilization have wondered what time was like before the creation of the universe. Someone asked St. Augustine (354–430 AD) in the 5th century that very question. "What was God doing before creation?" St. Augustine is reported to have responded with a theological conundrum: "Preparing hell for people who ask such questions!"

Pondering the significance of time is a luxury which only civilizations can adequately provide. Civilizations provide not only food surpluses, organized protection, but also a sense of permanence, and respites from labor that grant time for things like rituals and performances. Civilizations also provide time and energy for artists. Civilizations have likewise been instrumental in formulating devices for dividing time into smaller, more efficient sections. Among these devices have been sundials, hourglasses, and clocks. In the later 18th century, portable clocks allowed sailors to divide the earth into speculative sections of time called longitudinal co–ordinates; they appeared as vertical lines on a global map and helped explorers to define their exact location on uncharted oceans. On land, time was generally "unstandardized": noon was when the sun was highest in the sky, midnight was when the sun was farthest from the place you were. Towns fifty miles apart might have differing time recordings from one another, separated by ten or fifteen minutes. In the mid-19th century, British train companies established "standard" time throughout Great Britain, and in 1888 the American railroad industry standardized time in the United States by creating four speculative "time zones" (Eastern, Central, Mountain, and Pacific). Those time zones remain in use to this day.

Just as history is a minuscule slice of time, we may divide time itself into various geological eras, beginning with what scientists believe may have been the Earth's formation about 4.5 billion years ago. These eras are likewise speculative, but the following chart may help provide a better grasp on the lengths of time that have led ultimately to civilization.

- *Precambrian* (5 billion – 4.5 million years ago): This era constitutes more than 80% of Earth's history. Turbulent volcanic activity worldwide; earth grossly inhospitable to any form of life; glaciations followed by more volcanic activity. Primitive marine life, e.g. sponges, mollusks, flatworms may have emerged. Fossils, if there were any, have not been preserved.

- *Cambrian* (570–435 million years ago): Seas cover continents three times, then recede; some land exposed for periods of time. Marine invertebrates appear, first snails, then lichens and mosses in lowlands. Fossils preserved for the first time.
- *Silurian* (435–410 million years ago): Uniform climate throughout the world; sharks, stingrays, and other cartilaginous animals evolve; scorpions the first known land animals.
- *Lower Carboniferous* (360–300 million years ago): Lush vegetation in middle to equatorial latitudes, later form the lower basis of massive beds of carbon, which remain in the form of coal and other fossil fuels. First known reptiles and other amphibians evolve; more land animals emerge.
- *Upper Carboniferous* (300–290million years ago): Earth warms in upper latitudes; more vegetation creates upper beds of enormous coal, oil, and natural gas residues. Cockroaches and thousands of other huge insects appear.
- *Permian* (290–240 million years ago): Aridity in many areas, glaciers in others. Climate extremes cause extinction of many life forms, specialization of others; soft woods develop.
- *Triassic* (240–205 million years ago): Mild climate in many areas, some flooding over vast areas of emerging continents, some volcanic activity. Clams, reptiles, and some dinosaurs appear.
- *Jurassic* (205–138 million years ago): Named for geological formations in the Jura Mountains, not for the movie *Jurassic Park*. Seas invade contents as global warming takes place, dinosaurs dominate, deciduous trees, grasses, and cereal plants develop.
- *Cretaceous* (138–65 million years ago),climate starts to cool off; mountain build up in the Americas; marsupials and placental mammals appear.
- *Paleocene* (65–55 million years ago): Large asteroid strikes earth, resulting in vast die-off of many life forms, including all dinosaurs and many other reptiles. Some small mammals survive, and early primates emerge.
- *Oligocene* (38–24 million years ago): Alpine and Himalayan mountain ranges form; seas cover much of Europe. Rodents, camels, mastodons, archaic monkeys, beavers emerge.
- *Miocene* (24–5 million years ago): Climate cools, and Bering Straight land bridge forms between Asia to Americas. Spread of grasslands fosters development of grazing mammal species. Primate ancestor common to both humans and chimpanzees emerges in Africa.
- *Pliocene* (5–1.6 million years ago): Continents as we now know them align. Winters increasingly severe. Australopithicenes (subhuman primates) populate Africa. Asian animals migrate across land bridge to Americas. Archaic human beings such as *Homo erectus* and *Homo ergaster* leave Africa around 2 – 1.3 million years ago and find their way to northern Asia.

- *Pleistocene* (1.6 million to 400,000 years ago): Enormous glaciers cover most of Europe and North America, as Great Lakes form. Variation in climates cause extinction and specialization. Mammoths, sabre-tooth cats roam North America. *Homo ergaster* descendent, *Homo heidelbergensis*, may have left northern Asia and reached Europe around 300,000–400,000 years ago and became the progenitor of Neanderthals, who then inhabited much of Europe.
- *Holocene* (300,000–100,000 years ago): beginning of the "youngest" period in geologic time: glaciers continue retreat; climate stabilizes somewhat Anatomically modern human beings *Homo sapiens* form nomadic tribes and hunt herds of mammals with stone weapons.
- *Paleolithic* (Old Stone Age, 70,000–60,000 years ago): *Homo sapiens* replace Neanderthals in Europe, others populate Asia, the Caucasus, and perhaps part of the Americas.
- *Mesolithic* (Middle Stone Age, 60,000–50,000 years ago): Glaciers return, though not to the extent as in the Pleistocene Age. Behaviorally modern *Homo sapiens* emerge with ability to communicate using language; they also utilize fire, stone tools, and painting while living in caves as tribal groups. They carve figurines from soft stone, make tools and implements from animal bone.
- *Neolithic* (New Stone Age, 50,000–10,000 years ago): Glaciers retreat, cereal grains cross-fertilize with wild grasses in Mesopotamia; agriculture begins as plants are cultivated; humans begin animal and plant husbandry.
- *Bronze and Iron Ages* (10,000–present): Humans build walls around settlements to protect food surpluses; they develop alphabets, legal codes, textiles, and highly formalized rituals. They create bronze made by alloying copper with tin; written dialogue in performance, 534 BC; iron smelted and used for tools, weapons, and plows. Ice cream invented in 1904 AD.

It is sometimes convenient to have an account like the one above for "at-a-glance" reference. But no record or account can provide readers with a sense of how long ago, for example, the Miocene Era really was. A more useful presentation might be the following, which presents the creation of earth (4.5–5 billion years ago) up to the present time within the confines of one calendar year:

> *January 1 – November 20*: earth's crust taking shape, oceans and atmosphere forming; a lifeless and hostile world
> *July 30*: some microscopic forms of life appear in the oceans
> *November 21 – December 15*: some plant and animal life appears on some areas of land and in some oceans, the more complex forms by mid-December

December 16: dinosaurs appear

December 27: by early morning the last dinosaur has died (65 million years ago), and early mammals begin to expand their territorial range

December 31: 11:15 PM: human beings appear; 11:59:30 PM: recorded history begins

11:59:55 PM: civilization begins; 11:59:57: Thespis steps out of dithyrambic chorus and assumes a "character" with written dialogue

Note that the study of theatre history focuses on the last three seconds before midnight.

Conceiving of time: Creation of earth fused into our comprehension of one twenty four-hour day:

12:01 AM - 8:00 PM: oceans, land masses in an uproar, with earthquakes, tidal waves, surface fissures, and a beclouded atmosphere

8:01 PM: the turbulence of the earth's surface has settled to the point where some "life" forms emerge as one-celled entities

9:00 PM: ancient life forms emerge in sea and on land

11:00 PM: dinosaurs appear

11:30 PM: early mammals expand their territorial range

1 second before midnight: human beings appear

1/200th of a second before midnight: for the first time "history" is recorded and civilization begins in cities with walls, food surpluses, and hierarchical elites

1/500th of a second before midnight: theatrical energy, written down and rehearsed, is exchanged between actors and a live audience

Note that theatre history comprises that last five-hundredth of a second.

If you still wonder how long ago the world came into being, and by inference how recently civilization emerged from the process, consider taking a walk around the Earth, using Lincoln, Nebraska (approximately the center of the United States) as a starting point. Turn around and imagine that with each step you go through 100 years. With the first step you're still in Lincoln, in about 1910, a town with a population of about 40,000. With the second step, you're in grassy prairie, with little human habitation in sight; Lewis and Clark's exploration is still five years away. Now walk around the earth three times and end up back in Lincoln to go backwards completely to the formation of the earth. You will have taken approximately 450 million steps, 100 years per step. The Greeks invented theatre less than half a mile from where your circumnavigational journey ends.

Still can't get your head around this kind of time/distance measurement? Try perceiving time in billions of seconds: One minute has 60 seconds; one hour has 3600 seconds; one day has 86,000 seconds; one year 31,557,600 seconds. One billion seconds was 32 years ago, and Ronald Reagan had become President of the United States; Margaret Thatcher was prime minister of Great Britain; *Raging Bull* won the Academy Award for Best Movie of the Year; gasoline cost about $1.30 per gallon; *Evita* won the Tony Award as Best Musical on Broadway, and "Don't Stand So Close to Me" by Sting and The Police was the #1 one pop song in America.

One billion minutes ago it was about 101 AD and the Roman Empire dominated all of Europe and the Middle East; Christianity, then a Jewish sect, faced terrible persecution in Rome; Emperor Trajan was "the man." One billion hours ago totals about 924,650 years, when subhuman primates may have occasionally lifted their knuckles off the ground and briefly walked around on two legs. One billion years ago some life forms perhaps appeared in the primordial oceans. Approximately 1,335,460,400 minutes ago, theatre was invented.

Theatre, Civilization, and the Fertile Crescent

That "history" is a tiny fraction of time (about 9,000 years ago to the present day) does not gainsay its importance. A major reason for its importance is not so much when history began but where and why. The bronze age in Mesopotamia and its spread through the "Fertile Crescent" was not significant just because people started making and using bronze. They also started keeping track of things in writing, a means of communication far more efficient than things recorded in the oral tradition at the local tribal level. The memories of tribal elders were important, because they passed important information on to younger generations. Written records are, however, more accurate. The recording of history indeed requires writing in order to develop historical concepts, which are functions of authority beyond a form of "collective memory."

Before any civilization can begin writing down its history however, members of that civilization must possess what historians have termed a sense of "permanence and confidence." Otherwise they will not believe their cultural endeavors worth the effort. Nomadic tribes in most cases have little time for the creation of artistic artifacts. They must order their lives instead around communal movement, in most cases following a food source. Settled civilizations, on the other hand, are more inclined to possess the sense of permanence and confidence needed to create inventories, legal codes, and artifacts that celebrate or at least document the central concerns of the civilization. Some tribes have painted on cave walls, and all tribes have developed rituals of some kind to appease deities or forces beyond their control. The first civilization to create play scripts for that purpose, as we have noted, were the Greeks, beginning in the 6th century. They had earlier created artifacts such as non-portable sculptures, immobile structures, site-specific paintings, and other evidences of the process a civilization goes through in constructing a record of a collective consciousness of itself. All such artifacts emerged in cities protected by defensible walls. Those walls did much more than protect than food stocks, however. They also imparted cultural security to the city's inhabitants, a sense of security maintained and encouraged by the hierarchies that ruled the civilization.

At the same time however, we should recognize that many great civilizations and empires (e.g. Egypt, Persia, the Qin Dynasty in China, the Aztec in Mexico, the Inca in South America, among many others) did not produce theatre. Such civilizations had abundant rituals, dances, or chant exercises that were theatrical, but they were not of themselves theatre. There are various credible reasons for theatre's absence, but the most singular of them is the requirement for a theatre culture to promote literacy within its midst and competition among its performing artists. Only then can a civilization make the leap from dance and sung ritual to what Aristotle called *mimesis*, the imitation of an action. Making that leap is rare. As noted above, the 5th-century BC Greeks did it; the classical Sanskrit civilization of 4th- to 5th-century India did it; so did 13th-century China and 14th-century Japan.

Some anthropologists have noted that it is fairly easy to figure out why tribal civilizations did not develop theatre. Hunter-gatherer societies live by foraging, usually maintaining a subsistence-level way of life. Some seasons bring an abundance of food, but other seasons bring nothing. There is as a result little sense of permanence, though many hunter-gatherer tribes had complex rituals to implore gods or other powers to provide good results before the hunting season; such tribes also had numerous customary practices and observances of gratitude, which were sometimes elaborate. There are numerous records of ceremonies among tribal societies to solemnize rites of passage, marking and/or celebrating birth, circumcision, menarche, marriage, or death. There is little record of the performers in such ceremonies having memorized lines of dialogue. There is also little doubt that some performers were talented, often in song or dance. But they were not actors performing theatre.

Many historians date the rise of alphabets to about 8000 BC among Sumerian settlements in Mesopotamia (a Greek word that means "between the waters," namely the Euphrates and Tigris Rivers in present-day Iraq). The Sumerians also developed a numerical system, based on clay amulets to count foodstuffs and materials they had made. They kept such amulets in containers which were sealed and assigned a symbol for the amulet inside the container. That symbol may have begun to denote a numerical quantity, which some anthropologists believe may have been the beginning of numerical systems. In succeeding millennia, many observers conclude that the result was a numerical system based on 10, probably because humans have ten fingers and ten toes. Meantime several alphabetical systems likewise developed, beginning with pictographs in China, a system of drawings that contain meaning by virtue of their similarity to objects. Such symbolic writing is making a comeback, thanks to computers, advertising logos, and traffic signs.

The Sumerian civilization spawned many innovations and developed many others, mostly in what is today called the Fertile Crescent. That term was one an American archeology professor named James Henry Breasted (1865–1935) at the University of Chicago formulated in 1906 to describe an arch-shaped stretch of territory in western Asia, ranging from the Persian Gulf and arching northward through Mesopotamia into what is today Turkey, then heading southward along the Mediterranean seacoast and into the Nile Delta. That area is not very fertile today, because most of it is desert. But around 9,000 years ago it had forests, grasslands, herds of animals for "domestication," (genetic alteration), and a mild climate that afforded farmers three growing seasons (fall, winter, and spring). Its dry summers afforded time for innovations in the domestication of both cereal grains and animals as food stocks. Its rich soil had developed wild species of both wheat and barley found nowhere else in the world. Farmers had genetically altered those species to produce an abundance of seed pods that remained on the stalk. Those seed pods became the grain which was stored, dried, and ground into flour.

The Fertile Crescent ultimately produced six of the top dozen food crops still farmed and harvested today. The abundance of such high-protein grains in cultivated fields allowed for enormous surpluses to develop—and some of those surpluses were significant by virtue of their capacity to yield alcohol content. Farmers figured out that the increasing carbohydrate content in their grain stocks could produce enough sugar that, when combined with yeast and then cooked, resulted in enough beverage alcohol sufficient to withstand fungal decay and provide food protein through periods of drought or low production. The stuff was indeed "liquid bread" and it was an important contribution to civilization as we know it. It is not, however, to be confused with the pasteurized and carbonated liquid called "beer" available in bars that seem connatural to areas where American colleges and universities are located.

Farmers in the Fertile Crescent were known not only in their domestication of grains but also for their adaptation of breeding techniques developed elsewhere. The dog had been domesticated, it is estimated, by about 15,000 BC in several locales around the Earth. Its ancient ancestor was the gray wolf, and the dog became valuable to early human settlements. The cow, pig, goat, and sheep were all developed in Asia by about 6000 BC and became significant not only as food but, like the dog, also as draught animals (sometimes picturesquely termed "beasts of burden"). These animals remain today five of the world's six most important domesticated mammals. The horse was domesticated in the Ukraine sometime around 4000 BC and made its way to the Fertile Crescent soon thereafter. The following chart provides further information about the importance of livestock domestication in settlements beyond the Fertile Crescent, such as the Andes. Remember that domesticating an animal is vastly different from simply taming it. For centuries, people have tamed elephants; nobody has ever domesticated one. Killer whales perform magnificent tricks in theme parks; lions and tigers do the same in circuses—but forget about domesticating them. If the time and mood is right, they'll eat you. Domesticating an animal species means genetically altering it by selective breeding, so that it will naturally form a dependent relationship with human beings. Domesticated animals likewise are unable to return to the wild.

Chieftains, kings, and their bureaucrats maintained alphabets and calculation systems, as noted earlier, to keep track of domesticated animals as they became increasingly valuable to the civilization as sources of dietary protein. Bureaucrats subsequently developed an expertise in tax collection, overseeing the construction of granaries, ceremonial buildings, bridges, and walled fortifications, allowing them respite from the arduous work of food production. Their absence from production work is thought have granted them time and opportunity to accumulate status, power, and influence. In nearly all such civilizations, positions of status and power were occupied by males—an important developmental factor in the history of theatre as well. There are several reasons for male dominance in human civilization, i.e., in those civilizations with fortified city walls, civil chieftains, military warlords, a priestly class, and bureaucracies. Discussions of those reasons follow in this volume, but suffice it to say at this juncture that even at the tribal level descent

Table 0.1.   Approximate Dates for Evidence of Domesticating of Mammals

Species	Date B.C.	Geographical place
Dog	15,000	Southwest Asia, China, and North America
Sheep	8,000	Southwest Asia
Goat	8,000	Southwest Asia
Pig	6,000	China, Southwest Asia
Cow	6,000	Southwest Asia and India
Horse	4,000	The Ukraine
Ass	4,000	Egypt
Water Buffalo	4,000	China
One-hump Camel	2,500	Arabia
Two-hump Camel	2,500	Central Asia

through the father's line ("agnation") was the most common form of tracing one's lineage. Matrilineal societies trace descent though the mother. Matriarchal societies are those in which women hold power and dominion over men—but no true matriarchal society has ever been discovered or recorded. In most known instances, men hold power and control resources. Matrilineal societies are rarer than patrilineal societies, but they exist all over the world. Males within civilizations turned their attention towards attaining positions with high prestige, status, and power. In a similar pattern they directed women towards positions accorded respect, e.g. maternal activity, maintaining hearth fires, and work with fabric. In very few cases were women allowed to compete directly with men for positions of high status.

One of the major reasons that civilizations outside the Fertile Crescent did not achieve the same magnitude of those within it is protein, mineral, and vitamin content in cereal grains. That content was comparatively abundant in ancient wheat and barley; both contained between 12 and 15 grams of protein; barley (a grain similar to wheat, though with slightly less protein content) had the additional benefit of sprouting readily and providing malt sugars that ancient brewers used to make a preservable "liquid bread." Wheat and barley also provide generous amounts of minerals necessary for the human diet. China had rice, and the New World had corn (maize). But both brown (unmilled) and white rice provide only about 8 grams of protein per 100 grams of grain. The Aztecs recognized maize as important enough to have a god (Cinteotl) named after it. Unfortunately, maize of the New World variety yielded even less than rice in the way of adequate food value, only about 5.6 grams of protein per 100 grams of grain. Maize, with its small amount of protein, has the additional disadvantage of wearing down human teeth, especially when consumed uncooked from the cob. Mayan and Aztec natives used hot water to soften it, but the process caused some important nutrients to leach out, while other nutrients remained unconverted as indigestible carbohydrates. The protein of maize was also insufficient for maintaining a subsistence diet. The Fertile Crescent meanwhile also developed beans with twice the amount of protein in wheat, which also contained abundant vitamins and minerals.

As a result of such advantages, civilizations in the Fertile Crescent historically outpaced and outproduced civilizations elsewhere around the globe. The Fertile Crescent's weather is similar to that of southern California, South Africa, Chile, and southwestern Australia. Those locales also possess soils similar in consistency, but they had no domesticated animals except for the dog. Turkeys were abundant as wild food sources, but like the buffalo, deer, and fish they required elaborate skills for effective capture. The Andes had both the llama and alpaca—both relatives of the camel—but the camel functioned more effectively as a pack animal.

Literacy

Writing as a medium of poetic expression, or even communication, developed much later after its original purpose was filled, namely to keep track of food surpluses. The first use of alphabets for mytho-poetic expression is thought to have developed around 2600 BC. Among the first known literary works was *The Epic of Gilgamesh* in a Sumerian language, composed about 2200 BC. But literacy has never been universal; it arose only in specific locales and was developed only among individuals who needed to use it. Even the recent history of alphabets provides ample evidence that alphabets are intentional, invented for a specific purpose. Literacy furthermore does not follow in due course once an alphabet is invented. It takes centuries for literacy to develop, largely because alphabets require a lot of effort. During the Qin Dynasty in China, learning an alphabet became state policy. The most well known alphabet today is the Latin variety, developed among ancient Romans from characteristics of the Greek. Bishop Ulfilas in the 4th century AD adapted this alphabet for the purposes of missionary work among the Gothic peoples, thought largely to have occupied present-day Bulgaria. Ulfilas abandoned the runic alphabets used among the Goths and created a Gothic alphabet based on 20 Greek and five Latin letters to translate both the Old and New Testaments, allowing many illiterate Germanic tribes a form of entry into the intellectual world of the Greeks and Romans. Later missionaries did the same thing. St. Cyril, for example, invented an alphabet that is named for him, the "Cyrillic" alphabet, for his Slavic converts. It remains in use throughout Russia and parts of Eastern Europe. But the presence of an alphabet does not automatically confer literacy. Today, nearly all Japanese are literate, but 150 years ago only 40% were. In Iraq, where alphabets and literacy began, only 65% of the population is literate. The United States at one time was among world leaders in literacy. Today, the United States Census Bureau estimates an 86% literacy rate. In the nation's capital, Washington, D.C., the literacy rate among adults is about the same as Iraq's. In cities such as Detroit, Michigan, it is estimated that only 45% of the population can functionally read and write.

The mutability of literacy reflects the fragility of civilization as a whole. Civilization is indeed fragile, largely because it takes so much effort and time to establish one. Literacy solidifies and extends a civilization's knowledge of itself and the world around it. Literacy enables knowledge that preceding generations have collected and cultivated to be passed on. Writing compresses thought and is far more accurate than oral transmission; writing promotes cultural permanence in a way that oral traditions do not, and writing allows societies to store knowledge far more accurately and efficiently. Writing promotes navigation across the "gulf of experience" among generations within a society, and writing solidifies "cultural identity." Those who master writing often attain higher status within a civilization because they are perceived to have greater knowledge and as a matter of fact, they usually do have greater knowledge. Writing unleashes power within the mind and allows it to think in abstract terms.

Theatre, as it emerged in 5th-century Athens, was a highly abstract form of ritual based in the written word. Ritual, as noted, is a tribal activity. All tribes develop ritual as a means of educating their young about gods, the earth, the weather, the cycle of life and death, the seasons, and other topics of concern to the tribe. The Greeks, however, were the first to institutionalize ritual as theatre. Literacy made the "imitation" of action among mythic characters far more accurate and feasible, largely because the actors eschewed impersonation. They instead imitated a character's action and embodied a character's motivations. But the development of theatre in 6th-century Greece did not simply and suddenly appear. It had several cultural antecedents.

Greek culture as a whole had numerous significant aspects, including the rule of law, philosophical thought, mathematics, physics, and others the too numerous to list here. Chief among them for our purposes is their invention of theatre. Some historians believe that "invention" is an inappropriate term, and there are dozens of arguments about what actually took place around 534 BC in Athens that resulted theatre. It is fairly clear that what occurred around 534 was an act of separation. What had occurred previous to 534 had included ritual dance and movement, story telling, or choral odes publicly sung in honor of Greek gods and heroes; what happened after 534 was altogether different. It was *mimetic*, as Aristotle termed it, the imitation of an action. Imitation can be a fairly dangerous proposition in many civilizations, since it presupposes a knowledge of motivation. The men who wrote what came to be known as drama (a word that means "man in action") were prone to present characters familiar to Athenian audiences, and many of those characters engaged in actions that reflected the contemporary leadership of the city.

Let us therefore consider some social, political, religious, and cultural facets of Greek civilization, particularly in Athens, which in large measure made theatre possible. Among the traditions in Athens that contributed mightily to the creation of theatre and to city's rise to preeminence was freedom of speech. The Athenians actually had two words for free speech: *isegoria,* which was the right to address political assemblies, and *parrhesia,* the right to speak freely and boldly. That freedom was generally absent in the world that surrounded ancient Greece. The Greeks were unique, according to playwright Sophocles, because they were "free men with free tongues." This kind of freedom led to new military tactics that involved small property owning citizens who voted for and then fought their own battles. The tactics they employed have come to be called "hoplite" battle techniques (derived from *hoplon*, a Greek word for "shield;" free citizens were individually responsible for procuring their own shields, swords, and spears). It involved phalanxes keeping in tight formation as they collided with enemy soldiers. Before hoplite strategies began to emerge in the mid-8th century, armies sought encirclement strategies. Hoplite armies sought open flat fields, where it was easier to advance and stay in formation. Opponents often claimed (as they do in *The Persians* by Aeschylus) that Greeks always sought Greek geography as an ally. Rough terrain made it difficult to maintain a steady line and would have defeated the purpose of employing the use of a phalanx. Thus Greek warriors sought open ground and flat plains on which to confront each other. Greek tribes frequently fought each other, and many scholars have argued that war was a primary factor in actuating tribes and clans to band together in fortified cities to become *poleis*, or city-states. Hoplite formations locked shields together as second rank soldiers projected their spears over the front rank. When in combat, the whole formation consistently pressed forward trying to break the enemy formation. The close order of the Greek phalanx meant each man occupied a slot equidistant from another. That placement of a Greek warrior in combat is thought to have mirrored his place in the assembly hall, in which many male citizens of city-states held the same right as another. Greek geography was also mirrored in the makeup of the phalanx, as farmers from small holdings, not large estates, formed the phalanx. Many formations consisted of friends, neighbors, and relatives. It was a deliberate organization which provided an incentive to fight intensely and offer no quarter to an enemy.

The most famous of all Greek soldiers were the Spartans, but Athens, Corinth, Lebedos, Argos, Chalcis, Carystus, and many others boasted notable warriors and officers. Nearly all became superbly adept at using hoplite formations and strategies. The Athenians used the foot drill as an exercise to instill discipline. Athenians did not see such drills as oppressive but rather an exercise in egalitarianism, bringing soldiers from varying backgrounds into a uniformly clothed, armed, fluid-moving single body. In close-order drill maneuvers, individuals temporarily gave up their private identities and forswore individual status. Athenian actors I the 5th century did likewise, sacrificing their individual identities in the act of *mimesis*, though as actors they directed their efforts not for the sake of Ares, the god of war, but for the god Dionysus. The sacrifice of individual identity in hoplite formations allowed Athenians, like the Spartans and other Greeks, to confront an enemy face to face in broad daylight, eschewing sneak attacks or ambushes, with the intent of destroying enemy formations without mercy. Even if the enemy were to retreat, hoplite strategy was to chase down departing formations and kill them all. Battles of Egyptian forces, by contrast—or armies as a whole from the Fertile Crescent for that matter—were not hoplite shock collisions of armed foot soldiers in formation. They were instead encounters among horsemen, charioteers, and bowmen. Military historians have noted that Athenians in particular were more willing to endure terrific infantry collisions, since shock alone proved an economical method of battle that allowed conflicts to be brief, remorselessly violent, and brutal. But they were usually winnable, allowing Athenians to return home and resume "normal" life after the battle. Athenian civilization fostered and contributed to this "civilized" way of warfare, just as it fostered a civilized polity called democracy and civilized performance we know as theatre. By no means was the merciless butchery of an opponent more "civilized" than the nomadic style of warfare, which was based on looting, raiding, and perhaps a chance to kill the un-armed while seeking the surrender or at least the retreat of enemy forces. Yet the Athenian tradition of civic militarism, free will, free speech, discipline, dissent, freely-voiced critique of freely elected leaders, free inquiry, and the free dissemination of knowledge allowed Athens, particularly in the 5th cen-tury BC, to assume the greatness for which it remains recognized to this day.

CONCLUSIONS

The fragility of civilization has been for years the subject of innumerable books, newspaper and magazine articles, movies, sermons, lectures, and col-lege courses. Warnings have come from near and far that civilization as we know it is about to end. It will collapse because we do not live in harmony with the environment, or because we fail to respect our elders' teachings, or because we all watch too much television, surf far too long on the internet, eat too many French fries, or consume far too much refined sugar. Rarely does one hear warnings about how very recent a development civilization really is. No one knows precisely when our species *homo sapiens* first ap-peared. Some have guessed that anatomically modern humans appeared about 200,000 years ago; about 50,000 years ago, behaviorally modern hu-mans (using spoken language to communicate) made their entrance. There seems to be agreement that "pre-civilizations" (i.e. hunter-gatherer clans and tribes) long predated civilizations with their ample food stocks and defen-sible cities. Anthropology tells us we still need many thousands of years into the future if we ever hope to match the hunting-and-gathering survival record of our forbears. Those forebears inhabited the earth for millennia as kindred bands long before anyone began to record history. Since theatre is a tiny fraction of recorded history, we are wise to study it in historical context. The study of plays, the study of how to perform plays, and studying the history of plays in performance is therefore much more than simply a course or set of courses in a college or university. The study of theatre is a way of life. Theatre holds the mirror up to nature, as actors become the brief and abstract chronicles of their times.

Even the study of theatre's absence from previous civilizations can dem-onstrate how important theatre is to an understanding human existence.

Scholars have debated for years the fact that theatre was non-existent prior to the Greeks, while others have argued that religious ceremonies, rites of passage, public story telling, or other enactments of a public nature were, and in the minds of many still are, analogous to theatre. Such arguments attempt in some cases to revise cultural history, usually for the purpose of rehearsing a political or ideological agenda of one kind or another. Yet theatre violates the "duck test," thought to have originated with the humorist James Whitcomb Riley (1849–1916). Riley presumably observed, in effect, that if something "looks like a duck, swims like a duck, and quacks like a duck, then it is probably a duck." Some literary critics believe likewise that if something resembles theatre, is performed like theatre, or is in some other way theatrical, then it probably is theatre. Theatre fails the duck test. Theatrical ways of dressing, idiosyncratic behavior, extravagant makeup, or memorized dialogue do not of themselves constitute theatre. What then is theatre, and where did it come from? Such questions we shall consider in the following chapter.

Chapter One

The Origin of Theatre in Athens

In some ways, the development of theatre in Athens resembles the development of aforementioned hoplite battle techniques because it raises several anthropological questions. Nearly all human societies have developed ways of defending themselves; they had to, if they wanted to survive. Only the Greeks developed the highly efficient and deadly techniques of hoplite formations. Theatre's roots are in ritual, but all societies have rituals. Nearly all rituals involve some form of sacrifice, usually with a shaman or priestly figure and to oversee the ceremonies. The early Greeks had such ceremonies, and Aristotle believed that actors descended culturally from such shamans and their sacrifices. The difference among the later Greeks which Aristotle observed was that the shamans were actors, and they sacrificed their identities instead of making blood sacrifices. Regardless of the ancient origins of such ceremonial endeavors, only the Greeks developed theatre. And among the Greeks, only the Athenians institutionalized theatre as a civic form of ritual and sacrifice.

Most of what we call "Ancient Greek Theatre" is actually "Fifth Century BC Athenian Theatre," since the plays that remain known to us are nearly all of Athenian origin. Athens had been a city with defensible walls and food surpluses for at least 2,000 years before it rose to prominence among other Greek city-states. Her fortress heights, called the Acropolis (meaning "sky city"), provided a superb vantage point from which to defend the city against invaders from both land and sea. Athens was dominated by a series of tyrants in the 6th century BC, though those leaders (particularly one named Peisistratus) laid much of the groundwork for her subsequent development as a cultural center. Peisistratus ruled Athens from about 546 to 527 BC and is best known for his institution of the Great Dionysian Festival, which by the 5th century became the foremost venue for the premieres of tragedies and comedies. The Athenians began experimenting with democracy as a form of government in the latter part of the 6th century, and many believe (including Aristotle) that democracy was a positive force in the motivation of artistic expression that came into full flower during the 5th century. Athens benefited from outstanding soldier-statesmen, who led Greek armies and navies against Persian invasions. The "Persian Wars" lasted 50 years and the Greek victories in them instilled an abundance of permanence and confidence among the Athenians.

Chief among the Athenian soldier-statesmen was Pericles, who was largely responsible for the building of the Parthenon atop the Acropolis and whose name many historians have invoked to describe the "Golden Age" of Greece. That incomparable period, from the Battle of Marathon in 490 BC to the death of Aristotle in 322 BC, marks a time when some of the most magnificent minds and talents in human history were active. Not only did those decades produce Aeschylus, Sophocles, Euripides, Aristophanes, and Menander in theatre; Athens also bore philosophers Socrates, Plato, and Aristotle; the physician Hippocrates; historians Herodotus and Thucydides; the sculptor Phidias; and many others less well known.

The Athenian-Spartan civil conflict, called the Peloponnesian War, began in 431 BC and concluded in 404 BC with Athens' defeat. In 411 some prominent Athenians overthrew the democratic government, and after the Spartan victory over Athens in 404 another oligarchy called the "Thirty Tyrants" ruled the city. That oligarchy the Athenians overthrew a year later and restored democracy, and Athenian theatre production continued to flower through the 4th century. We do well to remember, however, that this was the Athens rife with plague and corruption, the same Athens that executed Socrates and allowed Phidias to die in prison on trumped-up charges. The illustrious 5th century in Greece was filled with bloody, violent conflict. Some of those conflicts show up in the plays we continue to study. The oldest surviving Greek tragedy is *The Persians* by Aeschylus, a dramatic treatment of Xerxes'defeat at the Battle of Salamis. *Oedipus Tyrannus* (429 BC) by Sophocles is, among other things, about the effect of plague on a large city, probably reflecting the plague besetting Athens between 430 and 426 BC. *Lysistrata* by Aristophanes is, in contradistinction, a comedy about attempts to end the Peloponnesian War.

These and other plays were presented at the Great Dionysia in Athens, foremost among all dramatic festivals in Greece. A smaller rural Dionysian festival took place in what we would today call December. It seems to have been a solstice festival, celebrating Dionysus as the god of wine. It also honored deities of fertility such as Artemis (the goddess of women in childbirth), Priapus (he of the permanently erect penis), Eros (primordial god of sexual love), and even Gaia, the primordial Earth Mother. There is some report that plays performed at this rural festival honored Dionysus as a fertility god, emphasizing the phallus (though not necessarily his own) as a comic sight gag. Plato wrote that this festival featured troupes of traveling actors, which was unusual; most acting in ancient Greece was performed by amateurs with "day jobs." Another festival, the Lenaea, occurred in what would today be January and took its name from a cult who worshiped Dionysus as a youth. It is thought that Aristophanes may have premiered many of his plays at this festival. The Anthesteria festival took its name for the new moon in late February or early March celebrating new wine and newly wedded couples. Most historians believe that drama was not a part of this festival, largely because the Athenians scheduled the Great Dionysia soon after it.

The Great Dionysia was an initially an Athens-only event. In the 5th century it became an inclusively Greek festival to which members of the Athens-led Delian League had been invited and were expected to attend. Athenian leaders had formed the Delian League in 477 BC, including 150 other Greek city states in alliance against the Persian Empire. Notable for her absence in the League was Sparta, whose leaders probably that Athens was using such extravagances as the Dionysian Festival to showcase herself as leader of the Greek-speaking word. The rift between Athens and Sparta ultimately resulted in the Peloponnesian War beginning in 431 BC. War, first with the Persian Empire from 499 to 449 BC, and thereafter with Sparta from 431 to 404 BC, formed a bloody and violent backdrop against which one should regard the great achievements of Athens in the history of theatre. Victorious in the first and defeated in the second, it is remarkable that Athens could find the time, let alone the dedication required, to present a civic festival dedicated to theatre every year throughout the tumultuous 5th century.

GREEK TRAGEDY AND ITS ORIGINS

The inauguration of the Dionysian Festival in the 6th century was part of Peisistratus' attempt to solemnize the idea of Greek culture among all Athenians. In addition to founding the Festival (and the invention of drama that took place within it), Peisistratus is also thought to have commanded that Homer's epic poems *The Iliad* and *The Odyssey* be formally committed to writing. Yet Aristotle had doubts about Peisistratus and his place in the process of exalting the idea of "being Greek." Drama emerged, he believed, not from the exertions of some politician hoping to make himself look good with voters. Aristotle stated the drama had emerged on its own from choral oratorios (called *dithyrambs*) sung in honor of Dionysus. He inferred that no politician or political leader could ever have enough knowledge about the actual workings of a culture to order up innovations like stepping outside the dithyrambic chorus and start a conversation with it. Culture and artistic innovation in any society is local in character. Thus drama did not result from top-down efforts; it occurred instead spontaneously through the actions and interactions of priests, devotees, singers, audiences, dancers, poets, and several others who experimented with practices and customs developed over the decades. They kept the ones they liked, or that audiences enjoyed, or that seemed to have had an interesting effect. They also rejected innovations that did not effectively function in performance. The process by which the ancient Athenians created performances was probably incremental, evolutionary, and decentralized.

Some authorities down through the years nevertheless believe that Peisistratus brought dithyrambic choruses to the festival with instructions for one member to step out of the chorus and assume the persona of *hypokrites*, or "answerer" to the chorus—but such asseverations are difficult to confirm. It is commonly acknowledged that Thespis won the first prize at the first Great Dionysia, a prize bestowed in recognition of written drama. Little is known about Thespis, but we can conclude that he was literate; so were members of his chorus, and they had memorized their lines. The competition among them and other theatre troupes for presentation of their works in the Great Dionysia is fairly certain, and so is the nature of the audience for such festivals.

By the time Athens instituted democracy in the late 6th century, the region of Attica (named for the peninsula of which Athens was the major city) was reorganized into ten "tribes" who were to compete with each other in the Great Dionysia. Members of the "ten tribes" formed a large proportion of the audience. Ten judges sat in adjudication of the competition, and the winner of the competition was awarded a goat.

A goat? Why a goat—and why not money, olive oil, or wine? Goats had associations with sexual potency and before that with ritual sacrifice. Festival participants drank wine from goat skins and performed "goat-like movements" (such as dry humping and other pelvic gyrations) according to some observers, sometimes even wearing goat skins. Goats have a long anthropological history of association with ritual sacrifice. In the Greek language the term tragedy (*tragos* and *ôde*) literally means "goat song," perhaps because the connection between ritual in the development of tragedy. Since Aristotle flatly stated that tragedy derived from ritual, the Great Dionysia was probably for many an act of devotion. Actors devoted themselves to a full year of unpaid effort prior to the Festival, and the playwrights received only enough funds to get their plays rehearsed and presentable before an audience. The plays' direct connection with sacrifice is less clear, though in historical retrospect the act of sacrifice takes place every time an actor imitates the action of a character, sacrificing his own identity. *Tragodos* came to mean "member of tragic chorus" but several language scholars also believe that *tragodos* simply meant "goat," which in any case was a species associated with rituals in honor of the god Dionysus since the beginning of the 8th century BC.

COMPETITION AND THE STRUCTURE OF ANCIENT GREEK DRAMA

Competition was intense at the Great Dionysia. As the festival's reputation grew through the 5th century, it added a competition for "satyr plays" (short parodies presented after tragedies) and comedies. Other Greek city states began to institute their own festivals. Troupes of actors are thought to have competed for prizes in these festivals, though the only plays which remain extant today are those which won competitions in Athens. Our conceptions about Greek theatre and drama as a whole are thus dominated by seven Athenians: three tragic playwrights (Aeschylus, Sophocles, and Euripides), two comic playwrights (Aristophanes and Menander), and two theorist/critics (Aristotle and Plato). The tragic playwrights competed with each other, as did Aristophanes with his contemporaries and decades later, Menander with his; Aristotle took delight in competing with his teacher, Plato. The Greeks had long prized competition as a means of producing excellence. They had begun staging "Olympic" athletic competitions as early as the 8th century, according to many scholars. The ancient Greeks were avid tradesmen, farmers, seafarers, and merchants—all competing with each other for crop production, entrepreneurial success, money, and status. Many Greek competitions like the Great Dionysia had religious overtones. The Olympic Games were held in honor of Zeus, just as later the dramatic competitions were held in honor of Zeus's son, Dionysus.

The significance of Dionysus and his numerous cults in ancient Greece has been a matter of intense discussion, especially since many of his cults were themselves suspect at the height of the Great Dionysia's renown. Dionysus was the god of wine, wine-making, and wine-induced ecstasies, especially ecstasies of the sexual variety. He was thought to have had thousands of devoted followers, who gave themselves over to orgiastic celebrations. Dionysus was born of a virgin mortal named Semele, whom Zeus seduced and impregnated. Hera, the wife of Zeus and according to legend a jealous defender of women and marriage, discovered their affair and planted the idea in Semele's mind that she wanted to see Zeus "arrayed in all his glory." Semele announced her desire to Zeus, an announcement he greeted with considerable dismay: no human could withstand such a vision, he knew. Semele would be vaporized in the process—but as "king of the gods" he felt himself compelled to grant her wish. The result was a kind of thermonuclear explosion, leaving no trace of Semele but allowing Zeus at the appropriate instant to rescue the fetus in her womb. He placed the child in his thigh, near his life-giving testicles. Dionysus was later born and grew to manhood as a kind of messiah figure, one who initiated his devotees in the mysteries of wine—but he was rarely accepted among rulers of locales, who found the idea of orgiastic worship somewhat hazardous. They often killed him, but after a brief period in the grave he rose again to redeem those who believed in him. Some theologians have noted similarities between the cult of Dionysus and early Christianity, citing the use of wine in symbolic worship, the exaltation of Dionysus as a son of god, the virginity of his mother, his suffering at the hands of non-believers, his death, and his later resurrection. There is little evidence of orgiastic, wine-induced celebration among early Christians—though suffering and martyrdom became important themes in Christianity just as they did among devotees of Dionysus. The sufferings of a god-like man or woman—or perhaps the aspirations of a man or woman to appear somehow "more" than human, leading to a kind of transcendental recognition—is likewise a significant aspect of many ancient Greek tragedies.

There were over a thousand tragedies written and performed for the Great Dionysia during the span of its existence in the 6th and 5th centuries. Of them, only 33 remain extant. They are as follows, in alphabetical order: *Agamemnon* (Aeschylus), *Ajax* (Sophocles), *Alcestis* (Euripides), *Andromache* (Euripides), *Antigone* (Sophocles), *The Bacchae* (Euripides), *The Choephori* (*The Libation Bearers*, by Aeschylus), *The Cyclops* (a satyr play by Euripides), *Electra* (Sophocles), *Electra* (Euripides), *The Eumenides* (*The Furies*, by Aeschylus), *Hecuba* (Euripides), *Helen* (Euripides), *Heracleidae* (*The Descendents of Hercules* by Euripides), *Heracles* (Euripides), *Hippolytus* (Euripides), *Ion* (Euripides), *Iphigenia in Tauris* (Euripides), *Iphigenia at Aulis* (Euripides), *Medea* (Euripides), *Oedipus the Tyrant* (Sophocles), *Oedipus at Colonus* (Sophocles), *Orestes* (Euripides), *The Persians* (Aeschylus), *Philoctetes* (Sophocles), *Phoenissae* (*The Phoenician Women* by Euripides), *Prometheus Bound* (Aeschylus), *Rhesus* (Euripides), *Seven Against Thebes* (Aeschylus), *The Suppliant Maidens* (Aeschylus), *The Suppliant Women* (Euripides), *Trachinaie* (*The Women of Trachis* by Sophocles), and *The Trojan Women* (Euripides).

About 25 fragments of plays attributed to Sophocles also remain, as do about 15 by Euripides. The significance of such fragments remains in question, given the questionable status of authorial identity. Some of the full-length plays also have dubious origins, especially those attributed to Euripides. Some scholars have also wondered why the extant tragedies of Euripides outnumber those of Aeschylus and Sophocles by a ratio of more than three to one. The most historically viable reason seems to be their use school curricula after the 4th century in Greece and Greek-speaking territories. In ancient Rome they became well known because the Roman playwright Seneca translated many plays by Euripides into Latin and later adapted several of them for his students, one of whom was the Emperor Nero. Those adaptations came to have enormous influence on writers in 16th and 17th centuries, one of whom was an Englishman named William Shakespeare.

In many ways it is astonishing that any tragedies survived at all. The scripts—as well as poetry, historical accounts, along with everything else legible—had to be hand-written. One may assume that playwrights wrote "sides" of a script (consisting of lines each character spoke) for the purposes of memorization among the actors and chorus members, but we have little way of knowing how scripts were in circulation at any one time—or even if they were accurate copies of the originals in the first place. In any case, it is good to remember that the "golden era" of great playwriting was brief. It lasted only from the 490s BC, when Aeschylus began competing for the top prize in the Great Dionysia, to the end of the 5th century when the last of Euripides' tragedies had their debut in the competition. Playwriting and the competition at the Great Dionysia continued well into the 4th century, though we know of few playwrights and even fewer plays written during that time period. *The Grouch*, a situation comedy written by Menander sometime in the 4th century is extant, and the numerous historical references to Menander indicate that theatre retained its cultural significance at least until about the 1st century AD, by which time Athens and all of Greece had become Roman protectorates.

The playwrights used blank verse in their plays, both in tragedy as well as comedy. Why? What is the purpose of blank verse—why indeed did the Greeks employ an elevated form of dialogue in their plays instead of an idiom spoken and understood by everyone in everyday life? The best explanation is two-fold: the first from the standpoint of architectural reality and the second from the ritual nature of theatre carried over from earlier centuries, when liturgical celebrations of the god Dionysus were taking place. The architecture of the early Greek theatre was temporary and fairly simple: the space for the audience consisted of wooden benches, probably in an amphitheatrical configuration. Amphitheatres provide far more available seating space, and it is thought that attendance at many performances may have exceeded 17,000. The lighting had to be sunlight, since nothing else was effectively available. Yet how do actors capture the attention of that many people at dawn (when most performances started), and more importantly, how did actors maintain audience attention over a span of about five hours? Recent research in the neurological sciences indicates that they did so via the biological action of poetic verse working on the human brain.

Anthropologists have noted in their study of rituals among numerous peoples the sing-song nature of many liturgical or shamanistic idioms; incantations by priests or shamans have a tendency to capture the attention of hearers, precisely because the incantation differs so markedly from everyday speech. People are forced to listen more closely. And when they do, the incantation has a kind of hypnotic effect; listeners are swayed first by paying closer attention to utterances of the priest or shaman, and then by the hypnotic action of rhythmic utterance. The blind poet Homer in 8th-century Greece was said to have possessed (among his many other gifts) an ability to write and then memorize dactylic hexameters uniquely suited to ancient Greek in spoken form. Given the enormous distractions around him as he recited and sang his sagas about heroes, villains, gods, and goddesses in the *Iliad* and the *Odyssey*, he is thought to have employed a means by which his audiences would pay attention. In effect, he hypnotized them. So apparently did Aeschylus, Sophocles, and Euripides by using a variety of rhyme and meter schemes when composing their plays. Some of the scenes are in what linguists consider a formal, old-fashioned Greek (especially when the chorus sings or chants), while others are less formal and more direct (especially in scenes between two characters, or between the chorus and one character).

The comedies of Aristophanes possess a similar hypnotic property; they also feature choral singing and chanting as do tragedies. They are distinctively different from tragedies in several ways, however. First of all, they are organized around thought, whereas tragedies (particularly those of Aeschylus and Sophocles) tend to emphasize plot as an organizing principle. The subject matter of Aristophanes is satiric and his approach is didactic. Though comedy "developed late," according to Aristotle, deriving from phallic songs and fertility rites, Aristophanes was no less talented than the tragic playwrights, according to Plato. His songs, furthermore, "interrupt" the action and in effect "break the hypnotic spell" his verse had held over the audience. Doing so allowed him to make oblique commentary on contemporary personalities, situations, or dilemmas. Chief among such dilemmas was war, which is the predominant topic in four of Aristophanes' comedies, particularly his most well-known, titled *Lysistrata*. Aristophanes' comedies were possible in a political atmosphere of which only Athens could boast, namely an unrestricted democracy, oblivious to political correctness and sensitivity to hurt feelings. Aristotle said that such freedom was the key principle, both in politics and art: "a man should live as he pleases. This, they say, is the mark of liberty, since not to live as a man wishes is the mark of a slave" (*Politics*, Chap. 6). Nobody was excepted from the satirical lash of Aristophanes, who offended almost everybody. That fact may be the most readily available reason for Aristophanes' failure to win first prize for any of his comedies at the Great Dionysian Festival. Many of his plays (he wrote over forty, of which eleven are extant) remain furthermore almost incomprehensible to modern readers. They also largely disappeared from public performance, once democracy had been suppressed in the later 4th century.

The "satyr play" became a requirement of competitors in the Great Dionysia at the beginning of the 5th century. Satyr plays were somewhat similar in structure to tragedies, though they often included indecent language and obscene gestures. Such dramas plays were often performed after a lengthy trilogy at the Great Dionysia, and many believe they were designed to provide "comic relief" for audiences who had just sat through a trilogy of tragedies. Of the hundreds of satyr plays written, only one (*The Cyclops* by Euripides, based on the episode in Homer's epic *The Odyssey* in which Ulysses and his men trick the eponymous one-eyed giant and escape from him) remains extant. A fragment of Sophocles *The Trackers* also remains, and like *The Cyclops* it features a chorus of satyrs. Satyrs were the bestial accomplices of Dionysus, and the plays in which they appear seem often to have been burlesques of some myth or legend familiar to audiences.

In the 4th century, another form of comedy supplanted the choral comedy of Aristophanes. That form of comedy has some become known as "new" comedy in place of the "old" choral style, but differences between the two were far more noteworthy than which came first and which came later. "New" comedy was actually situation comedy, using recognizable character types who faced superficial, decidedly non-political dilemmas. Minor characters such as cooks, pimps, petty thieves, maids, and mothers-in-law figure prominently in the cause of comic effect, though such characters are largely one-dimensional. There is no chorus in "New Comedy," and what usually made the plays funny was a character's quandary in attempting to cope with a situation (e.g., debt, unruly adolescent children, sexual desire, a planned marriage gone awry, etc.) over which there was little effective control. Situation comedies in Greek are usually identified with the playwright Menander, who had close ties with the men who ruled Athens in the 4th century. His plays were politically harmless, as were those of his contemporaries Philemon and Diphilus. Menander's only extant comedy *The Grouch* (discovered in 1957) is one of more than a hundred he wrote, though numerous fragments of his and those of other playwrights are extant. Menander's subsequent influence on Roman comic playwrights is what makes him important. Roman playwrights copied Menander relentlessly, and the situation comedies they wrote remained popular centuries afterward. They were an important source for the commedia dell'arte in Renaissance Italy, for Shakespeare and Ben Jonson in England, Moliére in 17th-century France, and most notably for television "sitcom" writers such as Neil Simon and Larry Gelbart in the 20th century.

The structural features of Greek tragedy and comedy are notably different. All ancient Greek tragedies have either history or myth as their basis. They usually begin with a prologue by a single character, providing information about events leading up to the play's opening. That information is crucial, because all the tragedies feature a climactic structure with a late "point of attack." That means the events leading up to the beginning of the play have already taken place. Presented in performance are the results of those events, leading to conclusive decisions on the part of the leading characters. The entrance of the chorus follows in most cases, and it is fairly elaborate. The scene is then set (though with very little scenery) for a series of episodes, separated by choral odes, in the development of main action. The action usually involves recognizable plot developments involving both reversals and recognition, providing new truths to one or more of the characters. In the best tragedies, there is a recognition that suffering is an inevitable part of human existence and new insights are granted. Contrary to what many people think, not everybody dies at the end of a Greek tragedy. In many cases, death represents a profound conclusion (which Aristotle called a "catharsis," or cleansing), but not always. At the conclusion of the play, chorus and characters make their exits—not together, but separately.

In choral comedy a prologue likewise sets the scene, followed by the entrance of the chorus. The chorus then begins a discussion of the play's dominant idea or ideas, as the chorus weigh the merits of the ideas under discussion. A decision is usually reached to make an attempt to realize the practical aspects of the dominant idea. A series of loosely connected scenes follow, showing the results of implementing the idea. The final scene concludes the play with reconciliation and departure of all characters and chorus members to a feast or celebration. In situation comedies, the standard practice is to present a recognizable, contemporary character who has a happy, stable life. A situation or dilemma soon develops which he must resolve, usually with a rapidly approaching deadline. He involves other recognizable contemporary characters, with mistakes, misunderstandings, overheard conversations, and other comic devices complicating the hoped-for solution. By the play's end, problems are resolved and stability is restored.

The Importance of Aristotle

The philosopher Aristotle (384–322 BC) did not experience at first hand the "golden age" of Greek tragedy during the 5th century, which had begun decades before his birth. But like his teacher Plato (424–348 BC), he was fascinated with the theatre in Athens because it represented, to him, a unique manifestation of Greek outlooks on the world. The Greeks used theatre to make sense of their world, he believed, a world without media to which the modern world has become accustomed. He wrote a number of treatises which were collected under the general title *Poetics* that reveal his thinking about the subject. As noted earlier, Aristotle believed that tragedy had developed somehow from religious practices long familiar to the Greeks, especially to those devotees of the god Dionysus. These practices involved the praise of Dionysus, often concentrating on his suffering. Few gods suffer much in the Greek pantheon, but this one was different. Dionysus came to dwell among mankind in an effort to draw mankind closer to the gods on their Olympian heights. His presence, his devotees believed, diminished the traditional adversarial relationship between gods and humans. He was rejected and persecuted by humans in power and whose interest was served by continuing the adversarial relationship; according to his cult followers. In many of the legends surrounding him, he often suffered death, but afterwards he rose from the dead to preach his gospel again and to win new devotees. They worshiped him in ecstatic frenzy, not through solemn oblation.

Such ideas intrigued Aristotle, and he pondered at length how this religion could have become the basis for theatre practice. The fundamental basis of theatre, he realized from his teacher Plato, was something called *mimesis*, or "imitation." For Plato, this term was pejorative. He believed that human beings lived a kind dualistic existence, one in the "real" world (he called it the *phenomenon*) and one in the "ideal" realm (called the *noumenon*). These two realms exist alongside each other in human consciousness simultaneously, Plato believed. We perceive "reality," that is, the phenomenal world, through the senses. That world is, however, an imitation of the non-sensate noumenal world, and we make sense of "reality," according to Plato, by means of "ideality." For example, you see a woman and she strikes you as beautiful. Why is she beautiful? Because in your mind there are inborn standards of womanly beauty, said Plato, and the woman you are seeing right now manifests something in her appearance that corresponds with your idea of beauty. The same may be said of other ideas, such as justice, love, morality, right, wrong, art, vacations, or edible fruit. Most human beings have standards by which they judge, or at least try to make sense of, the world around them. Plato felt that theatre, based on mimesis, was an imitation of reality and thus bogus. It was an imitation of an imitation. He drew a parallel of theatre's phoniness with magnetism, citing the Lodestone of Heraclea as a genuine source of inspiration. Iron rings successively attached to the lodestone also become magnetized. If the lodestone is a metaphor as the ideal (noumenon), then the first ring in the chain is the real (phenomenon). All other rings get their magnetism from the first ring, and have no direct connection to the lodestone. They are, in effect, imitations of an imitation. Theatre was one such ring, so he banned actors, playwrights, and others involved in theatre from his ideal republic.

Aristotle, as many good students will often do, questioned the validity of his teacher's convictions—then used his teacher's ideas to formulate a new conviction. Aristotle said that *mimesis* was actually a good thing. Imitation does not bespeak a lack of genuineness, as Plato had insisted, but instead it was a means by which human beings can understand the world better. After all, the word *theatron* was the "seeing place" in a Greek theatre, and theatre offered a new way to see the world. It also offered a new way to experience something communally, Aristotle said. Have you ever seen a movie or a play that you really liked, then met a person two or three years later, whom you don't know at all, and he or she liked the movie or play as much as you did? You feel a kind of bond with that person. Not a deep bond, but a sense of something shared; when you are in the audience, you share a communal experience. That temporary bond unites a group of human beings—and it helps them realize their common humanity among each other. This kind of shared experience is the basis for theatre in general. Only human beings, Aristotle noted, can imitate. Children do it all the time, he said. He did not mean "mimicry" the way a parrot speaks nor does it mean merely pretending. By *mimesis* Aristotle meant the things all of us did as children: we really believed (however momentarily) that our bicycles were horses or that a baby doll has really wet its diaper and needed changing. Children have a wonderful quality called "childlike" belief in their play, and Aristotle noted that as children "we delight in doing it," and as adults we "delight in seeing it done."

Aristotle thus made a complete break with Plato, because he argued that *mimesis* had social value—not because theatre had a lengthy background in religious observance, but because it offered participants in the "seeing place" a democratic experience. Aristotle went on to describe certain aspects of tragedy, and his influence on what we today term "drama theory" remains immense. It is impossible in this space to provide a comprehensive account of Aristotle's observations and then evaluate them accordingly. But let us consider the following aspects, which will serve as guidelines for future reference.

First, an "imitation of an action," which is at the basis of everything Aristotle subsequently enunciated about the theatre as an art form. "Action" is best described in Aristotelian terms as "motivation," that is, what a character in a play wants, and what he or she is willing to do to get what he or she wants. When that character's motivation runs up against and conflicts with another character's action, the result is dramatic tension. Dramatic tension is what holds the audience' attention. But it must be a "serious" action, says Aristotle, and it must have a certain magnitude if an audience is to remain attentive. It must also be complete in itself, he says, with a beginning, middle, and end. By no means is theatre, or the dramatic tension that fills it, to be considered an act of story telling. A play's plot may have some similarities to a story, but story in Aristotle's mind is "narrative," which is suitable for epic poetry, not for dramatic performance. The play's incidents, when organized properly, arouse human emotions, and most important among them are fear and pity. "Pity" is not the same as "feeling sorry" for somebody, however. The word Aristotle uses is *eleos*, originally meaning "mercy," but in his use it is closer to "empathy." The significance of these words is Aristotle's demand for "identification" with the character. If audience members identify with a character's dilemma, they are far more likely to pay closer attention to the entire performance. These feelings must, in a good play, build through the performance and result in *catharsis*, or cleansing of those same feelings. Aristotle believed that a good play leaves you "drained," a feeling you have probably experienced at the end of a good play or movie. It doesn't always happen, however. While the audience ideally goes into a kind of "trance," that is, entering completely the "world of the play," many plays and movies simply cannot carry the freight.

Suffering

Yet that feeling of catharsis is worth striving for, because if everyone in the audience has a shared experience, we will notice that fact. We will have entered the theatre as individuals but will leave it with some sense of community, having identified with the protagonist's struggle. The Greeks placed value on struggle and suffering because, as Aeschylus notes in *Agamemnon* when the chorus intones that man is fated to suffer: "Suffering comes first, then after awareness." Many Greeks believed that man learned only through struggle or suffering. They believed that human beings realized their fullest measure of humanity when faced with insurmountable suffering—and yet struggled onward, even if the struggle was futile. One of the reasons for continued struggle and suffering is the attainment of "heroic" status. Becoming a hero often involves an immense struggle to discover one's "identity" or "individualism," an idea that dates at least from Homer's *The Odyssey* and proceeds through Sophocles' *Oedipus to* George Lucas's Luke Skywalker to J.K. Rowling's Harry Potter.

The discovery of one's individual identity is crucial to the understanding of Western conceptions of the heroic in terms of Western man's economic, technological, medical, and even spiritual development. Eastern philosophies often place emphasis on identity with a group; one defines oneself in Eastern thought by one's similarity to others in the group. The West, on the other hand, emphasizes identity that makes one different from others. You have probably heard in grade school how you are like a little snowflake: there's nobody else like you. That may be genetically true, but in terms of social interaction, most successful efforts are group efforts. We often praise and glorify the individual in Western history nevertheless. We especially praise those who have made significant discoveries, who have won noteworthy battles, written great plays, found cures for diseases, or invented industrial processes. Why else do we celebrate Christopher Columbus as the discoverer the New World, when the Vikings actually discovered Newfoundland in 1000 A.D.? Why are the discoverers of vaccines (e.g. Edward Jenner and Jonas Salk), the inventors of light bulbs (Thomas Edison), flush toilets (Thomas Crapper), or magnates of enterprise (John D. Rockefeller, Henry Ford, or Steve Jobs) remembered? It is usually because they are highly individualized, because they struggled to realize some vision they had, some dream, often suffering in a struggle against forces who resisted them. As a result, many such individuals attain "heroic" status, and sometimes even "tragic" status, in the case of Julius Caesar, Abraham Lincoln, or perhaps Martin Luther King, Jr.

To the Greeks, at least, such individuals possessed heroic dimensions, not only because their tribulations elevated them to a higher level. Characters like Prometheus, Ulysses, or Antigone were worthy of emulation. To Aristotle, their actions were worthy of imitation, probably because the spectacle of a human being subject to the whim of the gods, yet who strives often to flout the gods was essential to the dynamic process of self-definition. Aristotle, unlike his teacher Plato, saw human beings a process; Plato tended to see them as a product. They defined themselves in theatrical performance by means of the choices they made, according to Aristotle. Human beings are able at times to act independently of gods or cosmic forces, even though there is a terrible price to pay for such independence. Humans may even seek to defy those forces, and in so doing embrace complete destruction. But the power of choice remains, and making such choices makes a person god-like or at least able to annoy the gods. That may be, Plato would have replied, but in doing so they arouse emotions within the audience which are fervent and offer no release. Quite the contrary, Aristotle would have answered his teacher; audiences are themselves transformed in the process, for they have witnessed a kind of sacrificial offering, yet one that offers more than just a blood-soaked spectacle. It can also provide, as it does at the close of many Greek tragedies, a form of redemption.

The Six Killer Apps of Theatre and Drama

Aristotle is thought to have written dozens of treatises, of which 31 have survived. Among them are three with *Ethics* in the title, along with others titled *Physics*, *Logic*, *Rhetoric*, *Physics*, *Politics*, and for our purposes his treatise titled *Poetics*. Most of Aristotle's treatises (and *Poetics* is no exception) are similar to lecture notes or drafts intended for further development. He was famous for his polished prose style, yet his treatises do not often manifest it. But they provide excellent insights into his thinking as the "Father of Logic," and the curiosity that led him to classify human knowledge into distinct disciplines—many of which are still in use today. One of the best ways to approach Aristotle is through his belief in *causality*, since the cause-to-effect relationship is so significant in Greek drama. Aristotle's definition of *mimesis*, the "imitation of an action" as the distilled essence of dramatic art is a result of his interest in the actual vs. potential state of things. "What causes a character to kill his mother?" in the *Oresteian Trilogy* is a good example. "Why does fate have such a hold on a character's actions?" in *Oedipus Tyrannus* is another. In Aristotle's observation, there were four causes. They were the material cause (the substance of which a thing is made); the formal cause (its design); the efficient cause (its builder); and its final cause (its purpose). An analysis of causes could explain, he thought, most things. In a parallel effort to understand drama, he noted that plays consisted of what we might today call six "killer apps:" 1.) *mythos* (plot), which is the organization of the action and incidents; 2.) *ethos* (character), the human agent of action and emotions in tragedy; 3.) *dianoia* (thought), the ideas behind the drama; 4.) *lexis* (speech or diction), the words used in a drama; 5.) *melos* (melody), the music or sounds the words make, or by extension the melodies heard along with all sounds in the production; and 6.) *opsos* (spectacle), which Aristotle does not define specifically, but in Greek the word means "optic," the visual usually associated with spectacle elements in a play.

Aristotle raised causality to the status of aesthetic principle. If the plot's events did not have a cause-to-effect relationship, the plot was weak. Many people remain to this day convinced of the same thing; if a movie or play is not "believable," the result is an inferior product. It does not matter even when the plot runs backwards (as in the film *Pulp Fiction*). If the action makes sense, audiences will be more likely to accept it. They are also more likely to accept it if the other constituent parts, such as character and speech support the plot and each other. A wealthy insurance executive, for example, rarely appears in torn or ratty clothing. The lines of Shakespeare's *Romeo and Juliet* seem at first inappropriate when Leonardo DiCaprio and

Claire Danes speak them; you get used to it after a while, however. In fact the language seems to "elevate" the characters, making what they do seem more important. Character, language, plot and other constituent parts contribute to unity, and unity is a prime requisite for Aristotle's idea of quality in drama. Plot, for example, is more than just a chain of events. The plot must also have reversals, scenes of recognition, and exposition to hold our attention. Some plots, Aristotle complained, have too many incidents; a good playwright knows how to limit the number that is believable, he said.

Aristotle also recommended believability in characters. Simplistic characters were inadequate, and the "arousal of emotions" did not occur when "a good man" merely suffers adversity, nor when an evil one lands inexplicably in the lap of prosperity. Believable characters are "neither perfect in justice or virtue," nor do they "fall into misfortune through vice and depravity." Most effectively, characters make choices. In doing so they often miscalculate, and miscalculation (*hamartia*) has become a famous misnomer in Greek because it sometimes gets interpreted as a character's "tragic flaw." Adding to the confusion is the appearance of *hamartia* in the New Testament (the Gospels of Luke and John particularly) as the Christian sense of sin. But in Greek drama, miscalculation is neither flaw nor sin; it is often the result of a motivation to do good, such as Oedipus' desire to find the killer of his father Laius, leading to his own indictment. It also appears in *The Oresteian Trilogy*, as Orestes' desire to avenge his father's death leads to his own indictment for the murder of his mother. Agamemnon makes numerous miscalculations in Greek drama. He miscalculates most severely in Euripides'*Iphegenia in*

Aulis, creating a tissue of lies in a good cause, namely keeping the Greek army pacified before they depart for Troy. Creon in Sophocles' *Antigone* completely underestimates the motivations of his prospective daughter-in-law, which results both in her death and that of his son. Pentheus makes a gruesome miscalculation about his cousin Dionysus in Euripides' *The Bacchae*. The result is death and dismemberment, as Pentheus' mother brings home the head of her son, mistaking it for the head of a lion she thinks she has killed in the forest. Such miscalculations, mistakes, and errors of judgment make the characters in Greek drama more human. Rarely are they mere figures on stage, speaking in poetic abstractions.

Aristotle devotes much less discussion in *Poetics* to the remaining categories he has outlined, though he admits they are important. They are not as important as plot and character, but he nevertheless insists that ideas behind the incidents "should speak for themselves, without any kind of verbal exposition." Speech rightfully belongs to the art of delivery and inflection, since they make the words of the play spoken among characters and chorus members comprehensible. Music and spectacle are the least considerations of Aristotle in *Poetics*, but that likewise does not mean he considers them superfluous. Music and spectacle provide vivid sensual pleasures unavailable while merely reading. Thus we see that Aristotle intended to create a hierarchy of applications for the enjoyment and understanding of drama (plot, character, thought, speech, melody and spectacle), but that each of those applications is important for the overall unity of the performance.

Actors and Acting

In nearly all productions at the Great Dionysia, the same actor played several roles within one trilogy. Thespis in most cases gets credit for creating dramatic structure by inventing the first actor (called *hyprokrites*, or "answerer") in the 6th century. But about all that actor apparently did was speak and otherwise interact with the chorus. Aristotle credited Aeschylus with creating theatrical structure by inventing the second actor, allowing dialogue scenes (called *agon* or "manly debate") to take place. From the word *agon* come our words protagonist and antagonist, the two figures who most vigorously engaged each other in said debate. Later, according to Aristotle, Sophocles created painted scenery and added a third actor, allowing performers to play several different characters. Simply adding another actor seems obvious. What did not anyone think of it before? The answer is they probably did, but Aeschylus was the first prize-winning playwright to have done so.

Actors in any case were amateurs, or at best semi-professionals; the Athenian *archon*, or elected ruler, awarded a chorus of actors to three playwrights for the Great Dionysian Festival. Those playwrights then worked with and taught the actors how to play their parts over a period of about a year before actual performances took place before an audience. Men played all the roles, since performing in the Great Dionysia was considered a "high status" activity and women were expected to engage in "high respect" activities, generally stipulated by the cult of Hera, Zeus's wife and goddess of the hearth. Actors wore masks whether they played women or men, and costume conventions in all likelihood helped identify the characters as well.

In a theatre space like the one created for the Great Dionysia, with outdoor seating for thousands, there was likely an emphasis on the voice in performance. Scholars at one time believed that the masks contained some kind of megaphone device within the masks, but that theory has fallen into disfavor. The plays, both tragedies and comedies, demanded intense vocal work in three kinds of delivery: speech, recitative, and song. Actors projected their voices in outdoor amphitheatres and were understood by thousands, particularly when delivering their lines in blank and rhymed verse forms on which the audience (as noted earlier) had to concentrate. Of equal consequence was the actors' movement, about which little is known. In later centuries, actors used high-platform footwear called *kothurnoi* to enhance their stage presence, stiffening and formalizing their gait onstage. Since facial expression was set and static, the actor was constrained to use elaborate "body language" which today would seem extravagant and utterly unrealistic. But the Greek theatre was anything but realistic. For example, the *kothurnoi* were thought to have added about four to five inches to an actor's height, but more importantly they restricted flexibility in the actor's knees. Such footwear supposedly had insteps made of solid wood—though it remains conjectural if actors in 5th century BC productions wore *kothurnoi* or not. Likewise conjectural are questions about the masks worn in the original productions of Aeschylus, Sophocles, Euripides, or Aristophanes. It is thought that the "complexion" of masks depended on the type of character: light skin for heroes, dark skin for villains, servants, or messengers. Heroes had dark hair, slaves had yellow hair, and so on. There are also reports of actors dressed in a "tragic robe" of some kind, but there is little evidence for specific costumes conventions among character types.

There is substantial evidence, however, that the actor's status rose in the 4th century BC, largely because professionals began to replace amateurs. The reputation of individual actors also grew, resulting in prizes given to performers at the Great Dionysia. The Theatre of Dionysus in Athens by 325 BC had been completely renovated and literally set in stone by the beginning of the 3rd century BC, while acting troupes had begun touring prize-winning productions throughout the Greek-speaking world. Some built for themselves "pan-Hellenic" reputations, allowing them (and presumably the troupes which accompanied them) to book themselves in far-flung venues from the coast of Asia Minor to the Levant, from cities and towns along the North African coast to territories in Macedonia.

The conquests of Alexander the Great (356–323 BC) made the "Hellenistic" world and its cultural assumptions a reality. Alexander and his armies created a Greek-speaking empire that stretched from the original boundaries of Greece on the Aegean, down to Egypt and across the Fertile Crescent, the former Persian Empire, deep into Afghanistan and India. Scholars apply the term "Hellenistic" both to the territories Alexander conquered (and subsequently "Hellenized") as well as the time period succeeding that of the Greek Classical Age. Hellenes built cities, libraries, and theatres, spreading Greek culture nearly everywhere they went. Their empire did not last long, but its cultural legacy endured for centuries. One may see this influence by the number of theatres still in existence, and most entertainingly in a movie titled *The Man Who Would be King* (1975) starring Sean Connery and Michael Caine. In it, inhabitants of the fictional "Kafiristan" imagine that Sgts. Daniel Dravot and Peachy Carnahan (Connery and Caine respectively) are descendants of Alexander the Great. Dravot and Carnahan imagine the Kafiris want to make them kings. Connery's character runs afoul of the Kafiris when he decides to be more than their king. He wants additionally to be their god. Alexander himself suffered similar delusions, and in many plays about him after his death he takes on posthumously divine characteristics.

In the Hellenistic world, performers of tragedy and comedy became institutionally professional, having sometime during Alexander's reign formed a guild which called itself the "Artists of Dionysus." This organization incorporated not only actors and chorus members but ultimately playwrights, musicians, costumers, mask-makers, shoemakers, and other craftsmen in-

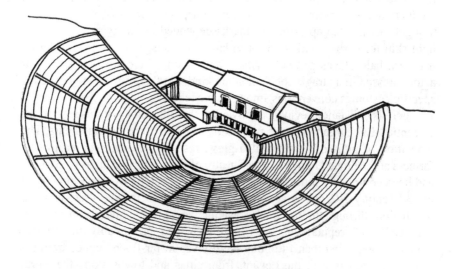

Figure 1.1.   Structure used for Hellenistic theatre performances.

volved in theatre production. It promoted the welfare of its members and acted as an agency for booking troupes into festivals, cities, and towns which presented plays throughout the year. The Hellenistic theatre was thus far more prolific than its Athenenian progenitor, which presented plays only at specific times during designated seasons. It also developed a theatre architecture that was distinct from that of Athens.

Conjectural Performance Spaces

The amphitheatrical performance spaces in ancient Athens are thought to have consisted of four major architectural features. The "playing place," called the *orkestron*, was circular and measured approximately 60 to 75 feet in diameter. Access to the playing place was through the choral entryway called the *parados*. Through this passageway the chorus made its stately entrances and exits. The actors in most cases came into the playing space the main entrance of the scenic façade called the *skene*. Some plays required actors to enter through the *parados*, but mostly they used the *skene*. Other plays indicate that actors went from the *skene* into the *orkestron* and performed around an altar or other scenic structures, often interacting with the chorus. The "viewing place," called the *theatron*, was where Aristophanes marveled at "the hosts of thousands of people sitting here!" Those hosts of thousands consisted of Greeks from all over the Greek-speaking world, who had come to celebrate with the Athenians and, after the defeat of the Persians, to celebrate the greatness of the city herself. They sat, in all likelihood, on wooden (or at least temporary) benches during the first two centuries of the Dionysian Festival. In the 6th century they had seated themselves in the *agora*, or central gathering place of Athens at the base of "sky city," the Acropolis. Around the beginning of the 5th century, performances began to take place on a southern slope of the Acropolis, looking out on the city of Athens below. There is generally good evidence that performances began at dawn and continued into the afternoon. In the latter part of the 4th century, the city built an amphitheatre made of stone. In the beginning years of the Dionysian Festival each audience member received a coin with his seat number on it. Later in the 5th century, a policy of free general admission had been instituted, though citizens with influence usually were allowed to sit in front rows.

It is important to note a few of the most significant architectural features in the classical Athenian theatre, because those architectural features bespoke certain cultural assumptions among the Athenians. First among them was the complete separation of performers from audience. Each occupied separate areas entirely, giving each a discrete role in the enactment of events. The size of the event made the proceedings logocentric, that is, "word-focused." As a result, there was emphasis on acoustics and an acting style based in ritualistic declamation. The performances furthermore constituted a civic forum, in which Athenians saw and heard a distinctive form of public deliberation on topics of communal concern: patriarchy and justice (*Oresteian Trilogy*), religious traditions (*The Bacchae*), fate (*Oedipus Rex*), Greek identity (*Medea*), the significance of "heroism" (*Iphegeniea in Aulis*), among others. This was of course an age before newspapers, radio, television, or the internet. The Dionysian Festival was one the few occasions anywhere in the world where controversy, dissent, accusation, debunking, disparagement, satire, and demystification were allowed full public disclosure.

It is also instructive to consider architecture's impact on the plays' composition. Athenian playwrights were adept at creating the exquisite timing required of actors for entrances and exits, the rhythmic criteria for compelling choral passages of both song and dance, and the poetic exchanges between the actors and the chorus. The architecture of amphitheatrical performance also necessitated an absence of illusion and an understanding of what was theatrically effective. There is some mention in historical records of Sophocles' painted scenery, but his was a kind of "suggested spectacle" that complemented his verse, which remains some the best verse ever written. Architecture's impact on performers was even more profound because it required, as noted earlier, a big, loud, and strong voice able to project and enunciate the memorized word throughout a space filled with thousands of people. Those actors had also to demonstrate a proficiency and versatility in movement, since the *orkestron* was large. Actors needed likewise to possess an appreciation of mutual cooperation with each other along with a comprehension of the play as a whole, since they usually played more than one role. Theirs was furthermore a "presentational" style of acting, one that acknowledged the presence of the audience and eschewed entirely the concept of "intimacy" between or among characters. There were no furniture, no curtains, and no lighting except from Apollo as he coursed in his fiery chariot across the heavens.

The Hellenistic theatre space, in contrast to that of classical Athens, featured a raised stage in front of the *skene* that gave more focus to the individual actor. That platform was called the *proskenion*, a word from which our "proscenium" derives. Some theatres provided access to the *proskenion* by means of a ramp, according to some authorities; others indicate the use of a step unit from the orkestron up to the proskenion. The Hellenistic theatre also featured in some locales a two-story *skenion* with openings for entrances and exits. There also seems to have been wider use of scenery in the Hellenistic theatre, probably using the *periaktoi*, or three-sided scenic posts, along with painted backdrops against the *skenion*. There is also evidence that actors wore padded costumes (especially in comedy) to allow for more gymnastic-style movement), headdresses and thick-soled boots (especially in tragedy) to lend movement a sense of solemnity to the proceedings.

CONCLUSIONS

Because ancient Greece is pivotal to our understanding of civilization, one must make critical decisions about the interpretations of what we actually know about the Greeks. One of the major problems in studying Greek theatre is the reliability of dramatic manuscripts. Many believe that the earliest intact manuscripts date from about 900 AD. Medieval scribes made copies by hand of those manuscripts, and subsequent generations completed hand-written copies of those copies until the invention of the printing press in about 1455. At that point, scholars began to edit and distribute published manuscripts, consulting with each other for accuracy and authenticity. That process greatly expanded the tendency to interpret texts and conditions of performance, a tendency that continues to this day. One recent trend in interpretations of the Greeks, and of theatre cultures as a whole, is the practice of "intertemporal abstraction." The practice of applying such abstractions has, however, facilitated judgmental approaches to the study of history. For example, the Greeks owned slaves, kept concubines for their pleasure (as Pericles gladly noted), sequestered respectable women, and disallowed all performances by females. Such behavior we find misogynistically abhorrent, but we are not in the position to pass moral censure on the Greeks. Yet many condemn the Greeks anyway on the basis of moral equivalence, and in doing so promote invidious comparisons based on the way "things ought to have been" rather than the way things were. Such misuse of historical analysis creates what one historian has called "a zero sum concept of the world," in which the gains of one culture mean losses for other cultures. Such were the "Afrocentric" arguments in the 1990s, for example, which maintained that the Greeks had "stolen" most of their ideas from African cultures. Such approaches often seek to create a therapeutic victimhood mentality, in which the achievements of one culture is a grievance to be prevented or avenged in another. As the English novelist Hilary Mantel (1952–), has advised, "Learn to tolerate strange worldviews. Don't pervert the values of the past. Women in former eras were downtrodden and they frequently assented to it. Generally speaking, our ancestors were not tolerant, liberal, or democratic. None of them read the Guardian, and very likely believed in hellfire, beating children, and hanging all manner of malefactors. Can you live with that?"

Theatre provides a stimulating means to live with that, while opening a unique window onto the world as we see it. It is the most immediate and ephemeral of arts forms, largely because it is tied so closely to the time in which it exists. Some few plays survive the times in which they appeared before their first audiences, but almost all plays are forgotten soon after their premieres, lost to history and vanished into the mists of time they so faithfully reflected. If only there were an archive or library somewhere to which all theatre artists could send their scripts, costume drawings, set and costume designs for safekeeping! But history demonstrates that such a repository would probably not survive the passage, much less the test, of time. That we have so many extant plays from ancient Greece (33 of them!) bears a time-less testimony to the origins and achievements not only of theatre, but also of civilization itself.

Chapter Two

Rome

Republic and Empire

Rome was the most significant of all the cities in the Mediterranean basin which bore the influence of Hellenistic culture. Centuries before Greek influence began to spread, however, Rome was merely a settlement town along the Tiber River where Latin-speaking peoples had settled. Rome languished in the shadow of the much stronger Etruscans, who inhabited the northwestern portion of the Italian peninsula called Tyrrhenia—a district roughly similar to contemporary Tuscany (Toscana), of which Florence later became the capital. In the centuries prior to Rome's "hellenization," the Etruscans held sway. Then, in 509 BC, the Romans overthrew their Etruscan ruler (named Tarquin) and established themselves as a republic. Tarquin attempted to regain his throne, but the Romans defeated him and the armies he had assembled. The Roman republic proved to be the most enduring and exemplary city-state in the ancient world; her leaders were renowned for their incorruptibility, sense of civic duty, belief in the rule of law, and loyalty to the Roman Senate. After the defeat of Carthage in the Punic wars from the 3rd to the mid-2nd century, the Roman military had become the most formidable of any, known for its hoplite strategies and its genius in civil engineering. Rome's influence had by then spread far beyond Italy, into North Africa and large portions of Spain. By 146 BC the Roman republic had conquered Athens and extended its reach to most of the Hellenistic empire of Alexander.

Many Hellenistic cities (of which Rome remains the best known) adopted "foundation myths" to enhance their reputations. Among the Romans at least, such myths helped to justify their aggressive expansion throughout the Mediterranean basin and beyond. Like many Greek city states, the Romans touted a "unique relationship" among themselves, with certain deities which granted them ancestral rights, and with heroes from whom they claimed to have descended. The Romans alleged they had descended from a set of twins named Romulus and Remus. The former became their city's namesake. The twins themselves were said to be the heirs of Aeneas, a Trojan prince and son of the goddess Aphrodite. Aeneas was (according to Homer in the *Iliad*) saved from death in the fall of Troy, largely because the god Poseidon said he would survive, but also because his father was a son of Zeus. Any man so blessed of the gods made for good "founding father fodder" in the ancient world. That is exactly what Aeneas was in the 1st century BC Latin epic *The Aneid* by Virgil. In that poem of nearly 10,000 verse lines he emerges as the "authentic" founder of Rome. Aeneas' bravery (he actually went up against Hercules in a hand-to-hand matchup, according to Homer), his piety, humility, resourcefulness, and the favor he enjoyed among the gods gave Romans a way to reformulate history in their favor, especially as they proceeded to build an enormous empire. The Roman Empire, in fact, is what remains in the minds of most people rather than impressions of the Roman republic.

The Roman Empire emerged after numerous civil wars that plagued Rome in the 1st century BC. The wars culminated, many classical scholars believe, in the conflict between Julius Caesar (100–44 BC) and Pompey the Great (Gnaeus Pompeius Magnus 106–48 BC). Caesar emerged victorious in that conflict and was awarded unprecedented dictatorial powers "in perpetuity" by the Roman Senate. Caesar famously suffered assassination at the Theatre of Pompey on the "Ides of March" (March 15) in 44 BC, an event which set off another civil war and a frantic scramble for ultimate and absolute power in Rome—though the concluding battles took place in Greece. On one side were the assassins, led by Brutus and Cassius; on the other were Caesar's protégé Marc Antony and Caesar's great-nephew Octavian. The armies of Marc Antony and Octavian defeated those of Brutus and Cassius in 42 BC at Philippi (northeastern Greece). Marc Antony and Octavian then squared off against each other eleven years later in the naval Battle of Actium (31 BC), off the southwestern coast of Greece. Octavian emerged victorious and Marc Antony later committed suicide in Egypt. These events appear most theatrically in two of Shakespeare's finest tragedies, *Julius Caesar* and *Antony and Cleopatra*. There have subsequently been numerous movies about the Romans and their empire. Those movies, such as *Julius Caesar* starring Marlon Brando, *The Robe* (1953) starring Richard Burton, *Ben-Hur* (1959) starring Charlton Heston, *Spartacus* (1960) starring Kirk Douglas, *Cleopatra* (1963) starring Elizabeth Taylor, *The Fall of the Roman Empire* (1964) starring Christopher Plummer, *Gladiator* (2000) starring Russell Crowe, the HBO television series titled *Rome* (2005–2007), along with numerous others, have established in the public mind a popular notion that the Romans were ruthless, slave-owning, greedy, patriarchal, decadent, haughty, and unoriginal. All of those attributes apply to the Romans in some ways at certain times. But we should remember that Rome at her beginning had about 10,000 people within its city walls; by the time she became the capital of a far-flung empire she had a population of over one million inhabitants and was the largest city anywhere in the world. As one historian has noted, the Romans were also practical, frugal, and plain-spoken. They possessed endurance, a vast knowledge of construction methods and materials, and a strongly imbued sense of duty. They admired Greek intellectual and philosophical attainments but dismissed the Greek inability to form a unitary state. While each Greek city-state had its own idiosyncrasies, the Romans built an enormously effective apparatus that collected taxes, built infrastructure, precisely defined its own territory (and effectively defended it for centuries against invaders), minted coins, and educated its citizens. "All roads lead to Rome" was no empty phrase; it was a metaphor containing the solid conviction of Rome's greatness, especially in the minds of her contemporaries.

The study of history enables us to make intelligent comparisons. We may thus find among the Romans a patriarchal inclination to be sure, but unlike women anywhere else, Roman women could own land, write their own wills, and testify in court. Women could hold no public office in Rome nor serve in the army. Yet before we condemn the Romans for their lack of "progress in gender affairs" we should compare them with Africans, who regularly performed female genital mutilation, or the Chinese who bound and crippled the feet of women for cosmetic purposes. In India the practice of *suttee* (self-immolation) for widows was well established. Such traditions and customs were never tolerated in Rome nor anywhere under Roman dominion.

The Roman Empire is, as one historian has written, an instance of history in which "unworthy vessels are the bearers of great human goods." Ancient Rome witnessed gladiators hacking each other to death—sometimes on a daily basis—and cheered as enemies of the state were crucified. The Romans fed live Christians and other dissenters to wild beasts. They worked slaves to death in mines and aboard sea-going galleys. In Rome, the barbaric easily comingled with the cultured and civilized. Within the city walls there were over two dozen public libraries, all of which had books which any citizen could check out and read at his or her leisure. Book shops were numerous, and anybody wealthy enough to do so built a library in his or her home. No home of any substance, said Seneca, lacked a library "with shelves of rare cedar wood and ivory from floor to ceiling." At the height of her empire, Rome's paved highways led from northwestern England to southeast of Jerusalem, more than 3,700 miles. Roman sea lanes, protected by the Roman navy, provided unprecedented safety for ship voyages throughout the Mediterranean world. The Romans created their port of Ostia by dredging and building an artificial harbor only sixteen miles from Rome's center. Rome's Colosseum accommodated over 50,000 people, the largest outdoor arena anywhere until the 20th century. They built other public buildings larger than the Capitol in Washington, D.C., without the benefit of iron or steel framing. They constructed baths, gardens, libraries, and recreation centers throughout Europe, all open for a small fee to citizens. In the 1st century AD, Romans developed the codex in replacement of the scroll, which had for centuries been the primary format for reading and disseminating the written word. The codex format is still in use today: it is a collection of sheets (in Roman times made of papyrus or vellum, today the material is paper) bound together between two covers. It was far more convenient and economical than a scroll, because there was writing on both sides of the sheets; scrolls had writing on only one side. The codex was the most important medium of written knowledge until the invention of printing in the 15th century. The Roman poet Marcus Valerius Martialis (best known for his witty and often obscene epigrams) was the first on record to praise the hard-bound book because he could carry it and erotically amuse himself with it everywhere. By the 6th century AD, hard-bound books had almost completely replaced the scroll throughout what was then becoming western Europe.

Rome remains celebrated for her public personalities. Marc Antony in Shakespeare's *Julius Caesar* claimed that Brutus was the "noblest Roman of them all," but Marc Antony's observation was ironic. His mentor Caesar had earned that title long before his death, and to this day Julius Caesar putatively remains the most familiar name among all the Romans. Caesar was in fact a superb general and political reformer. His writings, which have come down to the modern age almost nearly intact, reveal that he was talented with the stylus as well. His *Commentaries* on the Gallic campaign and the civil war he later initiated contain arresting points of commentary, providing succeeding generations all over the world with readable accounts of the Roman worldview.

Caesar, however, was not an historian. The Romans Livy (59 BC–17 AD), Tacitus (55–116 AD), and Suetonius (AD 69–140) deserve that title, for they often follow in the exalted Greek footsteps of Thuycidides (ca. 460–ca.395 BC). They were "political realists," and they provide gripping accounts of characters from Roman history, and those characters often assume a life of their own within those historical accounts. Many of them later became characters in plays among "neo-classicist" playwrights of the 16th and 17th centuries. Among the greatest writers in Rome were rhetoricians, that is, men whose command of Latin (particularly in public speaking) was persuasive, trenchant, and often provocative. Perhaps the greatest of Rome's rhetoricians was Cicero (106–43 BC), essentially a cultural historian. His wit, irony, and profound skepticism about public figures such as Marc Antony were based on his personal experience with such unscrupulous individuals and his knowledge of Greek philosophy and culture. For students of theatre history, Quintilian (Marcus Fabius Quintilianus (35–95 AD) offers worthy insights into the connection between rhetoric and public performance. Quintilian was among the first Romans to write a treatise on the subject of public performance and many believe him to be the first advocate of "method acting," which has come to mean bringing the character in the play together with the experience of the actor in life. Quintilian was the first to insist that actors and/or speakers base their work on "their own natures." Such a performer, he noted, "should get to know his own peculiarities and… consult not merely the general rules of technique, but his own nature as well with a view to forming his own delivery." Quintilian was speaking mostly about orators and oratorical skills, yet he enjoyed the status of an authority on the subject even in his own time as well as in the Renaissance. He was born in Spain and taught rhetoric in Rome during the reign of the Emperor Vespasian, who awarded him a yearly salary and made him a consul. His magnum opus *Institutio oratoria* (Institutes of Oratory) is a survey of rhetoric in twelve books.

Plutarch (AD 46–120) was perhaps the greatest of all the Roman biographers—though he was not really a Roman and he wrote in Greek. But his subject matter was a comparison of Greeks with Romans, which Roman readers found irresistible. His *Parallel Lives* consisted of 46 biographies arranged in pairs, allowing readers to compare lives of Greek and Roman notables. Among the Roman intelligentsia (all of whom could read Greek) Plutarch's *Lives* was a bestseller. In subsequent centuries, particularly the 16th century in England, Plutarch's influence was enormous. That was particularly true in the case of Shakespeare, who took events in his plays *Timon of Athens*, *Coriolanus*, *Antony and Cleopatra*, and *Julius Caesar* directly from Plutarch. Not all of Plutarch's *Lives* is accurate, but the author's ability to "get inside" a character and study his motivations and his moral inadequacies place him within the top ranks of Roman writers.

Rome, with her many roads and paved avenues, became herself a thoroughfare for values, technologies, expertise, theology, and wisdom throughout what was to become the Western world. The Romans developed and improved concrete, glassblowing, construction cranes, bridges, aqueducts, dams, water pumps, grain mills, heated baths, and dozens of other technologies adapted from cultures they encountered on their way to conquest. They did the same thing with when they encountered theatre during the Punic Wars. Their court system and body of law is reflected to this day in much of Europe. Without Rome, we would know little about the Greeks and the values undergirding Western Civilization as a whole. Absent Rome and its empire, we would probably regard the Greeks today as we do the Qin Dynasty of China or the Mauryan Hegemony of Ashoka in the subcontinent of India: curious footnotes among the myriad cycles of human history.

Chapter 2

ROMAN THEATRE PRACTICE

Rome was heir to Hellenistic theatre conventions by virtue of its encounter with Greek theatre in southern Italy. The Romans saw performances there during the Punic Wars in the 3rd and 2nd century BC and found the idea of *mimesis* amusing, if not profound in the Aristotelian sense. When they destroyed the nearby Greek-speaking kingdom of Epirus in 167 BC, the Romans brought over 150,000 slaves to Rome. Those slaves were often far more well educated and cultivated than were the Romans themselves. The city of Rome was a more rough and tumble place than were most of the Greek city states—especially Athens—which may help to explain why the Romans preferred entertainment values in their theatre over profundity. In Rome, most historians estimate the average life-span at about 25 years. Emperor Augustus lived to be 75, but he was privileged enough to have three meals a day and a job that required no heavy lifting. Only about four men in 100 lived beyond 50—and almost no women did. Pregnancy and infancy were fraught with mortal danger, and a 50% death rate for babies in their first year of life was common (as it was in most parts of the world). Women perished in childbirth at a lower rate than did their offspring. They, like men, had no access to anaesthetics, pain killers, antibiotics, serums, or immunizations. Women could avail themselves of folk medicines to induce labor, though such medicines often proved ineffective. Perhaps due to overcrowding and poor sanitary conditions (though they had ample fresh water by way of their aqueduct system), the average Roman was exposed to death and disease in ways that today are found mainly in the most "underdeveloped" (i.e., primitive) parts the world. During periods of plague or highly infectious contagions, it is estimated that about 2,000 people died every day in Rome.

For the Roman population to grow in such conditions, a Roman woman had to produce at least five children during her brief lifespan. Not all women could bear children, and a small majority of children lived past their first year of life. Many Roman women, therefore, had to bear more than their "share" of children. Religious practices in consequence developed rituals, practices, and even doctrines that emphasized fertility. The Romans, and for that matter most other religious groups at the time, placed extraordinary value on reproductive power. The Old Testament commandment "be fruitful and multiply" the Romans had never read, but they certainly agreed with it in principle. They were similar to other pantheistic peoples in that they worshiped numerous gods and goddesses who promised fortune, long-lasting fame, and veneration to women who generously peopled the earth. As a result, there was an insistence that pregnancy was absolutely indispensable. If a woman could be pregnant most of the time until she died, her value as wife and mother rose accordingly. As a result of such concerns with fertility, the Romans celebrated numerous fertility festivals. The most well known among them was *ludi*

Florales in honor of the fertility goddess Flora. Events in her festivals included mime shows called *fabula ricinata* in which actresses and prostitutes performed nude; there was a tradition in Roman lore that Flora herself had actually been a prostitute before she became a goddess. The *fabula ricinata* over the years became increasingly popular with Roman audiences, and not only because of naked performers. In the 3rd century AD the emperor Heliogabalus decreed that sex acts in the mime shows were to be performed live and non-simulated.

General knowledge and practice of medicine in ancient Rome remained guesswork for the most part, and high mortality rates, particularly among women and children, may explain in part why Romans preferred plays—especially comedies—that emphasized sexuality, fecundity, prostitution, pregnancy, seduction, young love, the phallus, and physical attractiveness. Those kinds of comedies already existed in Greek, as we have noted. The work of Menander was widely imitated among Roman acting companies, nearly all of which were professional touring companies. The *fabulae Atellanae* (Atellan farces) were first seen near Naples, and they later made their way to Rome. The Atellan farces were known for their stock characters, such as the old man type, the braggart warrior type, the obese glutton, the lusty servant, and a type who had some kind of physical deformity such as a limp, hunchback, or stutter. Other dramatic forms from southern Italy arrived in Rome, and when they did they encountered robust competition for audiences in the form of Etruscan entertainments. Some historians maintain that these entertainments included "Fescennine Verses," which were a form of vulgar dialogue exchanges. Roman theatre audiences were for the most part possessed of vulgar taste; they rarely saw theatre as a civic forum the way Athenians did.

The Romans inherited from Etruria their most spectacular pastimes, namely blood sports. Roman audiences subsequently became notorious for their taste in *spectaculae* (non-dramatic spectacles). These merriments included gladiatorial contests, chariot races, boxing matches, dog fights, sword swallowing, fire-eating, bull baiting, and many others less notorious. Later, a form of Greek mime called *phylakes* became the most popular entertainment of all—though blood sports tended to attract the largest crowds, most infamously at the Colosseum. The mime shows were usually presented on temporary stages, often featuring obscene burlesques on the adventures of gods and goddesses. Such entertainments the poet Juvenal grouped under the rubric *panem et circenses* (bread and circuses) to lament the decline in taste among the Romans by the 2nd century AD. Juvenal's objections may have been a response to the Emperor Trajan's stagings of numerous spectacles, presenting fights to the death among over 10,000 gladiators he had hired. It is reported that at the end of the festivities, over 11,000 wild animals had also been killed, either from fighting with each other or in combat with human opponents.

Competing for spectators with the Colosseum in Rome were numerous smaller amphitheatres, the Stadium of Domitian (completed in about 86 AD) and the gigantic Circus Maximus. Construction of the Colosseum had been completed in 80 AD on the site of the Flavian amphitheatre. The Colosseum retained its original name *Amphitheatrum Flavium*, even though it was the largest of its kind anywhere. The Stadium of Domitian seated about 30,000 fans, while Trajan rebuilt the Circus Maximus (a large horse- and chariot-racing track, not a stadium) in 103 AD to accommodate over 150,000. The Circus Maximus occupied an enormous plot of what had been sacred ground in Rome, where chariot races of both the four-horse and the two-horse variety had taken place for centuries. Numerous religious festivals had begun there in about the 6th century BC, along with ceremonial games called *ludi*. *Ludi circenses* were those dedicated to horse racing; *ludi venationes* were artificial hunts, often featuring humans and wild animals in elaborate and grotesque predator-prey relationships. Republican administrators and later imperial rulers had several times improved and enlarged the Circus Maximus. The Theater of Pompey, meanwhile, had been built in 52 BC, the first "permanent" (i.e., made of stone) theatre in Roman history.

The Theater of Pompey was intended for *fabula palliata* (comedies based on Greek characters), *fabula togata* (comedies with Roman subjects), *fabula*

Figure 2.1.   Stage space for Roman performance.

crepidata (straight dramas based on Greek precedents), and *fabula praetexta* (straight dramas with Roman subjects). Pompey the Great, the theatre's namesake, was an outstanding military leader who had initiated construction to commemorate his numerous victories abroad. Those victories had generously expanded Roman dominion throughout the Mediterranean world and had brought unprecedented wealth to the city's municipal coffers. The Theatre of Pompey was an enormous structure, accommodating about 25,000 people. It was intended not only to glorify its namesake but also to promote the idea that legitimate drama had an important—and permanent—place in the cultural life of Rome. The structure included not only a huge performance space but also a sacred grove in honor of the goddess Venus, a temple in her honor, and a shopping center. Pompey had once been Julius Caesar's political ally and son-in-law. He later became Caesar's enemy in the civil wars to determine who ultimately would rule the republic. In 44 BC, Caesar was assassinated in the Theatre of Pompey; when Caesar's heir Octavian later became "Caesar Augustus," he ordered the Theatre of Pompey transformed into a vast public toilet.

Roman Audiences

Many scholars have retrospectively compared Roman audiences with their counterparts two or more millennia apart in the United States and have found similarities between the two. The embrace of trivial entertainment, the popularity of violent sporting events, the fascination with sexual titillation, and the apparent need for farcical diversion are all roughly comparable. So was (and is) the tendency to become easily distracted from one form of amusement to another. Several accounts report that Roman audiences quickly vacated one entertainment venue for another when they heard that next door something more interesting may have been going on—just as Americans often practice "channel-surfing" when they watch television. Also like Americans, Romans briefly embraced star performers and then discarded them, avid in their search for "the next big thing" in show business. Unlike Americans, the Romans were more interested in how things worked and less in probing the philosophical ramifications of why things worked the way they did. The Greeks had already covered those questions, many Romans believed. That is one reason why the Romans amalgamated Greek gods and turned them into their own. It was more practical to adapt existing deities. Zeus accordingly became Jupiter, Aphrodite became Venus, Poseidon Neptune, Artemis Diana, etc. Roman borrowings from Greek theatre practices generally excluded any serious exploration the human condition, as the Greeks had done. Roman theatre practice was like Roman sculpture or architecture (much of which was also borrowed from the Greeks): grandiose, impressive, or diversionary.

Theatre performances were almost always part of a larger celebration of a god or goddess. The Romans placed no limits on the number or kind of gods to be worshiped. As a result, the number of festivals grew, and along with them so did employment opportunities for actors and their troupes to provide the kinds of entertainment thought to please the gods. By around 78 BC, 48 days each year were set aside for festivals. By 354 AD, Romans dedicated 175 days each year to festivals, of which 101 featured theatrical performances and /or spectacles (by then called *ludi scaenici*).

Romans were what might be termed the original party animals, with toga parties all day, and all of the night. They were also very superstitious. The Roman habit of reading portents in the skies prompted them to build their holiest shrines on Rome's Capitoline Hill, the highest in the city, therefore the one closest to the sky. From there they could see more clearly what the gods had portended for them, as they sought auguries from lightning or the movements of planets, comets, and shooting stars. They also sought omens in the entrails of certain animals; the liver was thought to contain the most significant information. They believed spirits inhabited stones, that no one should enter a house with the left foot (the Latin word for "left" is "sinister"), and owls always brought bad luck. Chickens, however, could be harbingers of good fortune if one could recognize the right signs. Bees always meant good luck, even if they stung you. Actors have long been noted for their superstitions, especially with regard to certain plays; Roman actors were no different. They were never to whistle nor use real coins on stage, nor to do anything that might annoy the deity to whom their performance was putatively dedicated.

Roman Playwrights

There are numerous playwrights on record in Rome, but few of their works remain extant. The ones whose plays have survived into the modern era (and thus are most familiar to readers) are comedies by Titus Maccius Plautus (254–184 BC) and Publius Terentius Afer (known as Terence, 195–159 BC). Both men were active and popular in the Republican period. Plautus is thought to have written over 100 plays; of them, 20 have survived. Terence was far less prolific, with six plays to his credit—yet all of them remain extant. The comedies of both have antecedents in Greek New Comedy, eliminating the chorus completely and providing music that was crucial to the performance. There is ample pictorial evidence that an onstage flute-player accompanied the shenanigans which the characters perpetrated in these comedies, marking in the comedies of Plautus and Terence a distinct similarity to American musical comedies. The action of their plays always takes place on a street, bordered by houses or structures of some kind, all of which featured doors opening onto the street. The principal plot devices were eavesdropping and exposition.

Tragedies were also popular, though the plays of only one Roman remain known: Lucius Anneus Seneca (4 BC–54 AD). There is no record of Seneca's plays having been publicly performed, yet nine of them remain. Seneca is best known for his role as Emperor Nero's tutor and later his advisor. Nero (37–68 AD, reigned as emperor 54–68 AD) later ordered Seneca to commit suicide, and the playwright complied. Nero appears in the first circle of hell in Dante's *Inferno*, and he remains a popular figure in many video games. Seneca's plays were intended to be read before a select audience—presumably Nero and the imperial family—and were generally considered unstageable. They remain difficult as vehicles for performance and are today infrequently performed—but they were enormously influential on Shakespeare and other Elizabethan playwrights. One of the reasons Seneca's plays remain extant is their superb versification in Latin. Though based largely on Greek models, Seneca's plays adhered to the formal demands of a five-episode structure with choral interludes. Seneca's long-winded speeches by characters under emotional duress later became a model for Elizabethan playwrights, as did his practice of presenting violence onstage, including disembowelment, impaling, and cannibalism. Seneca created characters who were obsessed with turbulent passions, which likewise prompted emulation among succeeding playwrights in the 16th and 17th centuries. His expositional devices such as asides and soliloquies were also widely imitated by English playwrights such as Shakespeare, Marlowe, and Webster; the use of the Senecan confidante (a character in whom the leading characters confide) among French playwrights is also conspicuous. While thought to be more influential than actually performed, Seneca's preoccupations with blood, cruelty, humiliation, and the bizarre finds easy resonance in American "slasher" movies. We may conclude that Seneca is one of the most influential of all playwrights in history.

Equally influential, though not as a playwright, is Horace (Quintus Horatius Flaccus (65–8 BC), one of the most authoritative poets of the so-called "Augustan Age." The "Augustan Age" refers to the Emperor Augustus, named for Julius Caesar's heir Octavian, who became known as Caesar Augustus during his reign between 63 BC and 14 AD. In 18 BC Horace composed his *Ars Poetica* (*Art of Poetry*), which became a guide for poets and playwrights in the Renaissance and in Elizabethan England. In *Art of Poetry*, Horace insisted that poets and playwrights should "delight" and "instruct" their audiences, adding a moralistic dimension to drama which had only in the works of Plato appeared previously. Horace stated that "the marvelous and offensive" (i.e., ghosts and murders) be kept offstage and handled through narrative. Such demands obviously had no effect on Seneca, who provided both ghosts and murder onstage in abundance. Horace also believed that tragedies should contain five acts, and those divisions were allowed by the playwright to be arbitrarily demarcated. Gods, however, should appear only when required to resolve the action. From this proscription derives the famous *deus ex machina* (gods appearing from the machine) convention of the Renaissance and the neo-classical period. Horace also deigned no more than three speaking characters on stage at any one time. Why? It was inappropriate, he said, and it was also "unrealistic."

Rome also produced one the most remarkable medical minds (for his time) in the person of Claudius Galenus (129–200 AD), known as Galen in English. Galen was heir to the traditions of the Greek medical philosopher Hippocrates, who was among the first to assert that diseases could not be attributed to gods. Galen added substantial clinical proofs to anatomical knowledge with his work in the dissection of mammals and primates. He was also instrumental in developing ideas about the human brain, which he claimed (correctly, as it turns out) had control over muscles in the human body and muscular movement by means of the nervous system. Rome also produced remarkable historians, such as Cato the Elder (234–139 BC), the first historian to write in Latin. Livy (Titus Livius, 59 BC–17 AD) was perhaps Rome's most prolific historian, composing a monumental work in 142 volumes (of which only 35 remain) titled *Ab Urbe Condita Libri* (Books on the Founding of Rome, but generally translated as *The History of Rome*). In these volumes, Livy traced Rome's mythopoetic beginnings with Aeneas up to the death of Drusus the Elder, brother to Tiberius. Livy's accounts are highly readable, though sometimes unreliable. He attempted what today might be called "historical fiction." Tacitus (55–ca. 116 AD), on the other hand, is perhaps the most accurate of the Roman historians, best known for *Germania*. In that book, Tacitus gives a positive depiction of the Germanic tribes to the north of the Danube and east of the Rhine, whom the Romans were never able to subdue. He praises the Germans for their valor in battle, their modesty, honesty, and domestic stability. Often in *Germania*, the Germans appear as the opposite of the Romans, especially the Roman leadership which Tacitus found wanting. Suetonius' accounts of Roman leadership, especially in his *De Vita Caesarum* (*The Lives of the Twelve Caesars*, 69–71 AD), was devastating. He portrayed the Julian line (those emperors who traced their lineage back to Julius Caesar) as utterly corrupt and posited the idea that their devotion to the theatre was a good example of their decadence.

Actors in Rome remained members of the Artists of Dionysus, though during the imperial period the Latin term *histrione* came to encompass all manner of performers. *Histriones* had originally meant only those performers who did spoken drama, while *mimus* referred to those who performed silently in degraded spectacles that came to feature nudity and obscenity. During the latter part of the Republic and well into the Empire, actors of spoken drama prospered. The names of some have come down to us as particularly accomplished. Roscius (131–63 BC), for example, was raised to the nobility and accumulated substantial property. Mime actors on the other hand, were largely slaves and subject to all manner of abasement. Only among the mimes were women allowed to perform, a reliable indication of the low status under which the *mimus* languished. Star performers such as Roscius, however, had followings in many cities under Roman influence. They and the troupes with whom they performed were apparently in great demand wherever they went. Their renown as the years unfolded during the Empire, however, was supplanted by a less glamorous kind of performer, among whom were jugglers, gymnasts, strippers, transvestites, catamites, and castrati. Such performers were equally versatile as their more legitimate counterparts, for they generally performed without masks. Mime performers were also required to possess an aptitude in improvisation, since none of their shows had written dialogue.

Decline of Rome

The "decline of Rome" has attracted almost as much attention among historians down through the years as has the "rise of Rome." Stories of sexual excess, misuse and abuse of slaves, feeding Christians to lions and hyenas, unregulated and violent gladiatorial contests, equally grisly chariot races, and contests pitting man against beast have long been part of Roman lore that has fascinated people since at least the 18th century. In 1776, a notable year for many reasons, an English scholar named Edward Gibbon published a six-volume work titled *The History of the Decline and Fall of the Roman Empire*, a work that spawned many imitators. His principal thesis was that over time, Romans abandoned the noble traits and characteristics which for centuries had made Rome great. Gibbon also believed that Christianity had contributed to Rome's decline because of its insistence on the afterlife. Such wide-ranging speculations have contributed little to a concrete understanding of Rome's transformation in the 5th and 6th centuries, largely because Rome's decline has been greatly exaggerated. In many ways, Rome is still with us, though in an altogether different guise. As one historian has noted, we should consider Rome an enormously luxurious house that a very rich and large family once inhabited. Due to various circumstances over the centuries, the family could not afford the upkeep of the house and so divided it into apartments. The house served the new tenants very well indeed but ultimately the structure disintegrated over the course of time. But its neighbors and the descendants of those neighbors heard fantastic reports of the house and sought to imitate it. This metaphor we find in Paris, Berlin, London, and especially in Washington, D.C., where a number of official structures are distinctly Roman.

Some authorities have even asserted that theatre performances contributed in some way to the decline and fall of Rome. That is especially true of some early Christian church leaders, who began to lump all manner of public performance into a category that included blood sports, obscene mimic displays, even public executions. Church leaders began to assert themselves in Rome after Christianity was legalized in 313 AD under the Edict of Milan. Not only was Christianity permitted, Christians were for the first time openly free to worship and to build churches. These developments immediately followed one of the worst of several persecutions of Christianity in Rome under the Emperor Diocletian (he of the infamous decision in 285 to divide the Roman Empire into Eastern and Western spheres). In 321, Constantine declared the first day of the week (Sunday) an imperial day of rest. In 325, he convened the First Council of Nicea, in which a number of doctrinal disputes within Christianity were resolved. In the decade between 320 and 330, Constantine attempted to re-unify the Roman Empire, though he began and effectively completed his new imperial capital on the site of the Greek city of Byzantium near the Bosporus Straits in present-day Turkey. He named the new city after himself, "Constantinople." There he commissioned the construction of several churches, while in Rome he began to order the razing of pagan temples. In 380, Emperor Theodosius established Christianity as the "official" religion of Rome and her empire. Theodosius was also the last emperor to rule over a nominally undivided Empire. In 395 the division became permanent.

The sack of Rome in 410 AD at the hands of a German Visigoth tribe marked the first time an enemy force had penetrated and conquered the city of Rome herself. But worse was yet to come. In 476, a Teutonic warlord named Odoacer became the first non-Roman Emperor. The Roman Senate gave Odoacer its full consent and cooperation, while Gothic and Lombard tribes soon began to dominate the entire Italian peninsula. These and other Teutonic tribes squabbled over the domination of Italy for centuries, initiating what many have come to call the "Dark Ages," when entire former territories of the Western Roman Empire went up for grabs.

The Eastern part of the former Roman Empire, with Constantinople as its capital, suffered no such indignities. It remained intact for another millennium, known as the "Byzantine Empire." It was the legal successor to Rome as a whole, but it differed substantially from the Roman original. It was fully Christian from its beginning, and over the years became a wholly Greek-speaking enterprise. Because Greek was its *lingua franca*, the numerous Byzantine libraries sheltered and preserved hundreds of documents from the Greek Golden Age, the Hellenistic period, and from early Christianity. At its height, the Byzantine Empire was as strong, rich, and influential as its predecessor to the West had been. Among the most well known Byzantine rulers were Emperor Justinian (483–565) and his consort the Empress Theodora (500–548). Justinian was the last emperor to use Latin, and his were also the most successful of attempts to reconquer the "lost" territories of erstwhile classical Rome. At the height of his successes, Constantinople was beset with bubonic plague, which abruptly halted the expansionary efforts of the Byzantines to "re-connect" with Rome.

The presence of a Theodora, a former actress, as the imperial consort to Justinian has raised several questions about the status of theatre in the Byzantine Empire. Because of its Christian foundation, there is reason to believe that the Byzantine Empire followed the strictures—and prejudices—set forth among early Church fathers in banning or severely proscribing official theatrical activity. Little evidence of theatrical activity in Byzantium has survived, though some historians believe that mime performances persisted on an improvisational basis. Emperor Justinian banned the public subsidy of performances; yet there seems to have been nothing in the way of an outright prohibition of private funding. Indeed the Byzantine Emperors (who were both heads of state and heads of the Church) blessed the spectacles mounted regularly in the Hippodrome. While the actual records of performances in Byzantium remain somewhat cloudy, and no actual play scripts from the Byzantine Empire remain, the historical fact remains that the Byzantine Empire preserved most of the classical Greek manuscripts of which we now have knowledge and benefit. Scholars in Byzantium were possessed of a long-standing admiration for classical Greek drama, philosophy, and literature. When the Eastern empire finally collapsed in 1453, many scholars escaped to Italy with manuscripts that were even at the time priceless in their cultural value.

CONCLUSIONS

The American poet Edgar Allan Poe (1809–1849) coined the phrase "the grandeur that was Greece, the glory that was Rome" in honor of a woman he had known in his troubled childhood. It is an apt phrase when thinking about acting in the ancient world, the kind of acting one almost never sees (except as a parody) in today's theatre productions or in movies. Theatre structures in both ancient Greece and Rome were comparatively large in scale, many of them seating thousands of people. It is difficult for us today to conceive of acting styles so grandiose they could fill spaces the size of a small stadium. Almost all theatre nowadays takes place indoors; there are some outdoor venues for some "festival" theatres, but even there the acting tends to be "small" and the voices electronically amplified. The Roman actor who performed before a crowd of thousands employed conventions with which none of us in the modern world are completely familiar. We have little empirical idea about what kind of acoustics existed in the theatre spaces of the ancient world, though recent experiments undertaken in some spaces have revealed surprisingly good conditions for vocal projection. Yet the scale of the productions remain unknown territory, the dances of the tragic chorus a mystery, and the emotional impact of witnessing poetic utterance as a member of an enormous gathering nearly unimaginable.

The study of Rome is not, however, based on an attempt to emulate the Romans. Western civilization does not regard the ancient Hellenistic world as a kind of Saturnian Age, filled with admirable qualities and artistic abundance, to which we should always strive to return. In many cases, just the opposite is true: many of us in the West prefer to distance ourselves from ancient Rome in our desire to avoid her excesses. Meanwhile we study Rome's architecture, civic planning, military strategies of conquest, rhetorical greatness, and deplorable standards of public entertainment. The Roman policy of keeping the masses distracted with spectacles best described as "rude, crude, and tattooed" is evident almost everywhere, particularly in the United States. Have we Americans reached that stage of decadence which immediately precedes a downfall? Many around the world believe we have already met that pass, and our downfall has been underway for some time.

Chapter Three

The Theatre of the Middle Ages

The frequent attacks leaders of the Roman Catholic Church issued against theatre performance (and performers) are good indicators as to how prevalent theatre remained in the so-called "Dark Ages" (between the 5th and 9th centuries). Since the Church also had a monopoly on the written word, and almost always in Latin, the secular theatre in vernacular tongues during this period left little traces of itself for historians to analyze. Many assume that traveling troupes carried rudimentary scenery with them in an oxcart as they wandered through the countryside in search of an audience. They also, we may reasonably presume, carried with them rudimentary scenarios, largely memorized in the vernacular languages spoken among the inhabitants of former Roman provinces and Germanic territories in "Dark Age" Europe. These performers were largely entertainers, both versatile and resourceful, as they demonstrated their various skills as jugglers, dancers, contortionists, ventriloquists, singers, acrobats, gymnasts, musicians, or animal trainers. The Church regularly issued attacks against such individuals, especially at the councils assembled to clarify old doctrines or to formulate new ones. Councils banned clergy from attending any kind of theatrical performance, just as they forbade the baptism of anyone remaining in the performance business. Monks were not allowed to shelter performers in monasteries, and anyone who married an entertainer faced excommunication. Performers also faced economic pressure to cease and desist from exercising their "profession," since their activity took workers away from "useful activity," and any money earned from performance left with the players' on their oxcart out of town.

One important reason for the Church's anti-theatrical prejudice was acting's continued association with pagan festivals. The Church had its hands full converting heathens in central, northern, and eastern Europe, attempting to convince local tribal members to stop practicing their pagan ways and turn to the Church for spiritual succor. But old ways died hard: seasonal festivals such as the winter solstice (around December 21), the vernal equinox (around March 21), flower festivals (usually around May 1), and many other local observances had deep roots in the worship of pagan gods, whom the Church sought to discredit. The Church thus attempted to expropriate as many pagan festivals as it reasonably could and replace them with Saint's Days, as it had done with Christmas and Easter holidays.

A RENASCENT THEATRE

The Church ultimately embraced theatre as a means of propagating the Gospel message, which amounted to one of the most astonishing 180-degree turns in cultural history. The Church had spent four centuries denouncing and even persecuting the practice of theatre in Europe, yet by the mid-9th century it came to accept *mimesis* as a means of teaching, if not a step on the road to salvation. Some scholars have postulated that the structure of the Roman Catholic mass or other rituals were responsible for the turnaround in Church policy. The re-enactment of the Last Supper, for example, was once thought to have provided the impetus to re-enact New Testament episodes and parables, such as the discovery of Christ's empty tomb, the conversion of St. Paul on the road to Damascus, the return of the prodigal son, or the wise virgins and the foolish virgins. Such episodes and parables, however, are encased in narrative. They offer little in the way of character motivation and action, which are the core values within *mimesis*. The mass itself has been described as ritual based in words. Those words constitute a highly aesthetic process of visualization and commemoration, but they offer little in the way of dialogue. Yet the Church appears to have recognized the need for some kind of dialogue-based mimetic experience, perhaps sometime in the late 7th or early 8th century when it is believed that monks began to experiment with the "service of the hours" that featured antiphonal singing. Antiphonal singing is by its nature a form of dialogue, emphasizing two choirs or even two voices who respond to each other. Experiments with the service of the hours (such as matins, or morning songs, and vespers, which are evening songs) were taking place with official permission by the 9th century, and it is widely believed that the Church endorsed *mimesis* in the use of "tropes." Tropes are short sections of melody in a literary form which were added to the accepted liturgical text. How and why such additions were made is anybody's guess, but they are a sign that Church officials believed some innovation in worship services was appropriate. The oldest trope on record is the *Quem queritis* ("Whom Seek Ye") trope, performed or sung at Easter in many venues throughout Europe.

The *Quem queritis* trope featured the New Testament encounter of women with two angels at the empty tomb of Christ. The trope remained popular for centuries, and it probably spurred numerous imitations or adaptations of other New Testament passages. There are several extant copies of such litur-

Figure 3.1.   Conjectural depiction of space used in church for trope performance.

gical dramas which seem to have been based on tropes, as noted above. Tropes were sung or performed in the choir of a church, the area between the nave and the apse. Lengthier tropes probably led to recognizable liturgical dramas, and as they did the performers moved from the choir into the nave. In the church nave a singularly European form of stagecraft developed for the purpose of eventually staging liturgical drama. This stagecraft has come to be known as the "mansion and platea" arrangement, assembled in the church nave to facilitate the movement of performers. These performers, in all likelihood priests and/or monks, are thought to have worn ecclesiastical garb such as copes, mantles, albs, cassocks, dalmatics, surplices, or other vestments to differentiate or identify them as dramatic characters.

Many students of the Middle Ages also believe that by about the midpoint of the 11th century, a distinct change was beginning to take place in Europe. Some have termed this period a time of cultural blossoming, as seeds planted in earlier centuries began to show forth a distinct unfolding of unprecedented beauty in literature, drama, music, and court entertainment by the 12th and 13th centuries. One of the more interesting footnotes in this development was the work of a north German nun named Roswitha of Gandersheim (ca. 935–ca. 1000), who wrote dramas in Latin based on her adaptations of comedies by the Roman comic playwright Terence. Roswitha's works were utterly ignored for five centuries until their discovery in the early 16th century. Some contemporary scholars regard her as the "first German playwright," but there was no knowledge of her work, no record of her plays in performance, and there were no successors to her efforts in Gandersheim or anywhere else. Yet her work evinces a mastery of Latin, an indication that classical learning was alive and well in Central Europe by the turn of the millennium.

Many of the vernacular languages in Europe meantime began to achieve a maturity in phonetics and orthography that only Latin had heretofore allowed writers to exploit. Such linguistic virtues in vernacular languages played a substantial part in the creation of the great medieval sagas that remain famous. Some examples are *The Song of Roland* (ca. 1100) and Chretien de Troyes' *Perceval, the Story of the Grail* (written between 1181 and 1190) in French and Geoffrey of Monmouth's *History of the Kings of Britain* in English (ca. 1138), all of which marked a distinctive departure from previous efforts. In Middle High German, "minstrel epics" marked further development in courtly entertainments: *King Rother* (1152) and *Duke Ernst* (ca. 1190) were popular pieces of substantial length and poetic mastery, which troubadours publicly performed to music (now lost) before audiences that included both court and citizenry. Perhaps the greatest of all German sagas emerged around 1200: *The Song of the Nibelungs*, recapitulating heretofore emerging European concepts of Christian knighthood, courtly romance and intrigue, legendary chivalry, and proper comportment in battle.

Plays and Performances in Vernacular Languages

The years between 1200 and 1350, perhaps as a result of achievements in vernacular language development, saw a complementary increase in vernacular plays specifically intended for staging before an audience in public. In 1210, Pope Innocent III issued an edict against priests or monks acting, performing, or entertaining in public. Some historians believe the edict forced laymen into the unaccustomed endeavors not only of acting but also of playwriting and staging the plays. As a result, many believe, various trade guilds began producing vernacular plays at sites removed from Church property.

A constituent element of religious and/or didactic doctrine remained in the vernacular plays, however—though not in a strictly ecclesiastical format. The vernacular play cycles of trade guilds often incorporated farcical elements and embraced weird anachronisms that placed saints on the stage, for example, immediately after the birth of Christ. Sometimes farce extended to satire, and personages of respect became figures of fun, such as priests, judges, soldiers, or even bishops and princes. Latin drama in the Church, meanwhile, did not die out. It had continued up to this period and had begun to present the lives of saints, which were Christian episodes to be sure—but not necessarily of scriptural derivation. Biographical plays about saints resembled cycle plays because they took place outside church walls and were performed in a vernacular language. They were furthermore performed by laymen, most of whom were members of trade guilds. Economics played as large a role in the development of vernacular drama as did any other factor. By the 13th century in many parts of Europe, a mercantile economy was emerging, particularly in key merchant towns and cities where commerce and banking were principal activities. In such cities and towns, trade guild members as well as artisans and merchants assumed responsibility for creating and performing plays, which usually featured some reference to a Biblical event. Many towns began staging a long form of vernacular drama centered on the last week in Christ's life, called the Passion. Passion Plays could be elaborate exercises in community effort, often with scores of people in the cast.

Some historians have cited the inauguration of the Church holiday called Corpus Christi in 1261 as an impetus to further outdoor theatre performances in Europe. This feast, or series of feasts, began on the first Thursday after Trinity Sunday (which itself was celebrated on the first Sunday after Pentecost). That time of year usually provided better weather in Europe than did the more well known feast days of Christmas and Easter. Since vernacular performances almost always took place out of doors, and since the feasts sometimes took four days to complete, Corpus Christi afforded ample opportunity for increased theatrical activity, especially as part of local celebrations already taking place. The lengthy nature of the Corpus Christi feasts, in addition to the possibility of good weather during the feast days, may have led to an expansion of cycle plays, presenting Biblical material in chronological order. Numerous plays from cycles remain extant, and they represent some of the most interesting innovations in medieval drama. Some of them included innovations such as staging plays on "pageant wagons." These wagons were extrapolations of the mansion and platea convention, since the self-contained units were actually what we would recognize today as "floats," or mobile mansions designed for one specific show in the cycle. In a "station-to-station" arrangement, the pageant wagons made their way from one point to another in a chronological arrangement of scenes. Audiences for each presentation on and near the pageant wagon occupied most of the outdoor platea. They witnessed the action on the wagons parked near market squares or municipal plazas in the town or city where the cycle was being presented. Whoever wrote these plays seems to have enjoyed a relatively free hand in developing the material, since the plays' humor and character development possess a kind of maturity no one could have foreseen a century earlier.

A late development in medieval drama was the morality play, a form which maintained a didactic purpose while using secular conventions such as literary allegory to gets its message across. Dramatic allegories had begun to appear in German as brief playlets in Middle High German by Konrad von Würzburg (ca. 1230–ca. 1287) by the end of the 13th century. His *The Indictment of Art* (written in about 1250) depicts a Poet testifying at the trial of Largesse (presided over by Justice). The Poet accuses Art of colluding with

Figure 3.2.   Pageant wagon, ready to roll.

Largesse in rewarding unworthy poets. By the 14th century such allegories took on a darker tone, prominently featuring a character named Death. By the beginning of the 15th century, numerous morality plays began to appear, beginning with a "poetic prose dialogue" by Johannes von Tepl (ca. 1350–ca. 1415) titled *Death and the Plowman*. Little is known of its performance history, but it features a lengthy dialogue between Death and a Bohemian farmer who castigates Death for taking his wife from him. In England at about the same time, *The Castle of Perseverance* made its debut, though it is more recognizably a play because it features 36 characters, all of whom are allegorical. At the center of its plot is a character named Mankind, who finds his castle beset with trials, tribulations, and characters named Covetousness, World, Flesh, Penance, and finally Death. The Dutch morality play *Elckerlijc*, attributed to Peter van Diest (ca. 1454–ca. 1507), is thought to be the source for *Everyman*. Many consider *Everyman* the most well known and frequently performed of all morality plays. It featured a title character who strives to avoid Death's summons. The plot is structured as a journey, with various stations used to introduce new characters and ideas. Characters merely personify ideas, and the numerous incidents do not advance the plot. No complications ensue, episodes are not connected, and there are few psychological complexities. Everyman merely pleads with allegorical friends and relatives (variously named Kindred, Cousin, Fellowship, and Goods) to accompany him on his journey to the grave, but only Good Deeds agrees to make the trip with him. The sister of Good Deeds (named Knowledge) agrees to guide him on his path. Confession assists him in his final hours, while Discretion, Strength, and Beauty depart. There is some consensus among scholars that such morality plays served as spurs to wider acceptance of secular drama, since the characters, one-dimensional though they may have been, were distinct from those found in earlier plays with scriptural antecedents.

Another factor in the increase of theatrical activity during the 14th century was the "Babylonian Captivity" of the papacy in Avignon, France from 1309 to 1378. There then ensued a period in which different popes competed with each other for supremacy. During those years the Church's tendency to support measures aimed against actors and other performers waned; local and regional strictures remained in place, many of which had been tightened during the plague years (1347–1351). In some venues, actors were accused of spreading the plague from one performance site to another. The peripatetic nature of their profession had made entertainers immediately suspicious in the eyes of many officials, compounding the numerous complications already in place against them.

One of the best cinematic representations of the rigors entertainers faced during the plague years is *The Seventh Seal* (1957) by the great Swedish director Ingmar Bergman, starring Max von Sydow, Gunnar Björnstrand, and

Bibi Andersson. In this film, a knight returning from the Crusades encounters Death, as if the two were in a morality play. They then play a game of chess to see who ultimately will overcome whom. In the end, Death claims all the film's characters except the entertainers, who presumably are left to help anyone else still alive make sense of it all. The bubonic plague is thought to have exterminated about a third of Europe's population in the 14th century— but no one should infer that theatrical effort in Europe significantly diminished as a result. There were no doubt scores of troupes on the road attempting to attract audiences, just as they do in *The Seventh Seal*. Indeed the breakdown of civil order may have stimulated new directions in theatre activity throughout Europe, even while despair was probably the prevailing mood in many cities, towns, and courts.

The horrors of the "Black Death" notwithstanding, the staging of cycle plays and passion plays continued, sometimes in quite elaborate forms. In parts of Germany, Italy and France, passion plays in particular began to take precedence over most other kinds of public performance. Sometimes passion play productions featured an enormous stage more than 100 feet long, with stadium-like seating around it. There had been "theatres in the round" in the southern English county of Cornwall—but those theatres were circular earthworks and are thought to have featured mansions planted in the audience seating area. The passion plays, along with several cycles of plays, featured mansions set on a horizontal level perpendicular to the audience. They also featured dressing rooms and backstage areas where costume changes could be executed. Since many of the passion plays had scores of characters, it is probably safe to assume that local citizens played multiple parts. The "Paradise" mansion (the abode of God and his angels) was in most cases at one end of the stage; at the other end was an elaborate "Hell" mansion, featuring smoke, fire, and numerous imps with pitchforks, accompanied by sounds of wailing and the gnashing of teeth emanating from within. In between Heaven and Hell were numerous locales from the Bible, all existing simultaneously with each other. There was no thought of changing the scenery, for the juxtaposition of the locales was intended to impress upon audiences the similarity of Bible times to their own. Numerous devices to facilitate astonishing scenography was present in some productions. In one instance, the decapitation of St. Paul allowed his severed head to bounce three times on the stage, and with each bounce fountains of living water sprang up. In another play that featured decapitation, St. Denis of Paris walked holding his severed head in his hands for a distance of about six miles, preaching the whole way. "The first steps were the most difficult," he was reputed to have said. Trapdoors, movable scaffolding, fog effects, fire-breathing monsters, miraculous risings from the dead, angels flying to the aid of Christians in danger, and other gimmicks are thought to have effectively held most medieval audiences spellbound.

The development of more sophisticated vernacular idioms by the 14th century also abetted the growth and proliferation of the urban middle class. Cities and towns throughout the West, particularly in Italy, had increased in number, affluence, and size during the decades previous, and there is a general consensus that cities had largely begun to replace feudal courts as sources of influence upon and income for writers. The middle class and its growing wealth enabled many citizens to commission the writing of passion plays and their staging. Some families had grown so wealthy that they regularly loaned money to kings and emperors to finance their wars. Many scholars contend that the expansion of wealth among the urban middle class led to a new kind of literature, one that de-emphasized courtly ideals in favor of more "realistic" depictions of character, especially as those characters became more individualized. A "cash economy" was rapidly developing by the middle of the 14th century, and cash has always attracted entertainers. The market for live entertainment grew apace as merchants sought independence from feudalism and its regulations. For example, a landless serf could gain his freedom if he could remain in a town or city for a year and a day. Merchants meantime sought to impress each other not only with the ornate houses they built for themselves and the fine clothing they and their families wore, but also by employing a troupe of entertainers at banquets or local holidays.

Some feudal regulations remained, however, sometimes to the detriment of traveling entertainers. One such regulation was a common-law concept of "vagabondage." A "vagabond" was a masterless man, a vagrant with no permanent dwelling or recognized profession. That definition applied to

Figure 3.3. Scenic Structures used for Passion Plays.

some entertainers, particularly those without the funds to pay fees to municipal authorities who demanded cash for permission to perform within their
local jurisdictions. Vagabonds could be jailed for two weeks or more and
fined. In response, many entertainers sought to avoid charges of vagabondage through the patronage of households who could "sponsor" (i.e. protect)
them for a year or more. Such feudal regulations and practices remained well
into the 16th century, though they gradually began to die out as the Protestant
Reformation initiated a widespread abandonment of numerous customs and
laws after 1517. Temporal authorities took sides in this religious conflict, as
whole countries began to ally themselves either with the papacy and the
Church or with Martin Luther and his dissidents. The result was ultimately a
theatre which itself was often forced to take sides, if for no other reason than
to find shelter between warring camps of religious devotees. The warring
camps often seized on theatre as a weapon in their struggle, with the result
that many theatre artists abandoned the performance of plays which had any
kind of religious subject matter. In some cases, rulers issued decrees that
forbade the presentation of religious drama in the hope of preserving peace
within their domains. A large number of cycle plays, passion plays, saint's
plays, and morality plays disappeared. As a result, the amount of secular
drama increased; writers and performers began copying or imitating the plays
of ancient Greece and Rome, as the interest in humanism that had developed
initially in the Italian Renaissance began to spread throughout Europe. The
theatre was forced in many ways to re-invent itself since it could no longer
claim to be useful as religious instruction. It furthermore had to justify its
existence as an activity that was commercially viable. That process of re-
establishment led to some of the most important achievements the theatre has
ever known.

CONCLUSIONS

The "Middle Ages" between the fall of Rome and the beginnings of the
Renaissance covered almost an entire millennium and featured many innovations in and styles of theatre performance. Students of theatre history often
wonder where to begin a serious study of theatre in the Middle Ages, and
often they are content to become familiar with some of the aspects that form
comfortable reference points within their memories. Among those points of
reference are the close relationship between theatre and religion; theatre
could not on its own have wholly survived had not the Church rehabilitated
performance as a teaching method sometime during the 9th century. At the
same time, one should make note of the paradoxical relationship of the
Church with theatre, for Church officials, along with temporal authorities,
could often make life for the touring actor very difficult. The secular form of

drama among the touring troupes, however, is the form that we today find most important for medieval theatre's survival, or at least the one most resonant with our contemporary sensibilities. Rarely do we find productions of saint's plays or ecclesiastical drama, yet the kind of farce performed among troupes traveling by oxcart one may find at the core of many popular television shows and movies to this day.

Chapter Four

The Theatre of the Italian Renaissance

The inception of humanism took place south of the Alps, where the renewal of ancient classical values was underway in the northern Italian cities by about 1350. It proceeded northward into Alpine areas of German-speaking territory, then towards the Rhine and eastward along the Danube, westward into France and ultimately north to England. The reign of Karl IV as Holy Roman Emperor in Central Europe from 1346 to 1378 was instrumental in the spread of humanism, largely because Karl had succeeded in transforming his residential city of Prague into a cultural showpiece using Italianate models as precedents. His 1348 founding of the university that still bears his name in Prague is a good example, and to its faculty Karl invited many of the best minds of Italian humanism.

ARISTOTLE AND HUMANISM

In the musings of two University of Paris professors, Peter Abelard (1079–1142) and Thomas Aquinas (1225–1274) we find the roots of what was to become European humanism. Abelard was among the first in Europe to embrace Aristotle's view of a world that one should observe, analyze, and attempt to understand. Abelard realized that for the previous eleven centuries, Christian doctrine was at its philosophical heart largely "Platonic." That realization did not infer that anyone in the Church mistook Plato for a primordial Christian—but the Church had in its councils and doctrinal disputes espoused the conviction that the world was incomplete, an "imitation" of an ideal, non-sensate realm where God ruled. In such a world, unchanging ideas and immutable forms were more "real" than we anything we could see, touch, taste, smell, or hear in our earthly existence. This ideal realm was one of universals, and in our phenomenal existence there is nothing universal, only anecdotal. Abelard, in contrast, used Aristotle's ideas to argue that things in the earthly world were indeed knowable, not by their universal qualities but by the use of reason and analysis. "The prime source of wisdom," Abelard stated, "has been defined as continuous and penetrating inquiry." Who defined it? "That most brilliant of philosophers Aristotle," said Abelard, "who encouraged students to undertake this task with every ounce of their curiosity... By doubting, we inquire, and by inquiring we perceive the truth."

In Germany, the most significant student of Aristotle was Albertus Magnus (Albert the Great, ca. 1193–1280) in Cologne. Albert was careful to state, "I expound, I do not endorse, Aristotle," yet many sources acknowledge Albert as the foremost Aristotelian in Germany during the 13th century. Several historians of philosophy have granted Albert pride of place as the scholar who was among the first to translate the works of Aristotle into Latin from Greek and Arabic sources, then teaching Aristotelian scholasticism and concepts of inquiry. Through his analytical exposition of Aristotle, Albert is thought to have introduced a pursuit of secular knowledge and wisdom to the Germans. Albert became perhaps best known as the teacher of Thomas Aquinas (Tomasso d'Aquino, 1225–1274), who wrote numerous commentaries on Aristotle's works, using the philosopher's ideas extensively in composing his own *Summa theologiae*. In that work Thomas is thought to have "inferred as much as he derived," giving himself a lot of freedom to interpret on his own. One popular historian has stated that Thomas' writings about Aristotle "intellectualized" Europe by supplanting divine revelation, scripture, and Church canon with human reason, but nobody could have foreseen that in the 13th century.

Humanists became the heirs of Thomas Aquinas because they admired the ability of human reason, particularly as it had manifested itself in the classical world, which they believed was largely responsible for the more notable achievements of the human race. They did not necessarily dismiss the achievements of the Church, nor did they automatically condemn its corrupt practices. They persisted, however, in viewing human excellence and virtue as valuable in themselves. That value was most apparent in this present world as a means towards understanding God's creation, rather than as a necessary qualification for entry to a world beyond human understanding. An emphasis on the next world had characterized medieval teaching before Abelard, Albert, and Thomas Aquinas, an emphasis which has come to be known broadly as "scholasticism." Humanism, in contrast to scholasticism, came to represent the kind of thinking that began to take firm shape in Italy during the 14th century.

The working language of the humanists was Latin, yet a form of Latin the humanists had developed among themselves and the academies they founded to study classical Roman literature. Most humanists felt that Church Latin was corrupt and antiquated, incapable of describing new European interpretations of Aristotle. Humanists began to employ literary terms found in later Roman writers, whose manuscripts they were beginning to read as they became more readily available from Byzantium archives and libraries. Their idiom they called "neo-Latin," which became the *lingua franca* of intellectual life that spread mostly from Florence in northern Italy throughout Europe in the 14th century. As Italian humanism strengthened, diversified, and spread, Florence became its intellectual base. Florence had a population that by 1380 exceeded 80,000; the city's gold florin became "coin of the realm" in many parts of Europe. The University of Florence, established in 1321, became instrumental in the replacement of scholastic viewpoints with humanist thinking throughout European intellectual life, thus making Florence a central focus of a re-awakening of learning that came to be known as the "Renaissance."

The Renaissance and New Conceptions of Space

The term "Renaissance" was of French derivation, meaning "rebirth," yet historians first began to use it only around 1840. The term "Middle Ages" also appeared about the same time, perhaps to signify those centuries between classical civilization and humanist innovations in neo-Latin, perspective drawing, and the renewed interest in Aristotle among intellectual elites who populated learned societies, academies, and Italian universities. There was a sense among many 14th-century humanists that the Middle Ages had indeed possessed a vital cultural heritage, but one which differed substantially from that of the ancient Greeks and Romans. Yet humanists did not simply dismiss that culture as inferior, as many 19th- and 20th-century critics did. The humanists of the 14th century were deeply troubled nevertheless by Church leaders, popes and bishops alike, who attempted to define what knowledge really was. But the ideas of Thomas Aquinas and others began to have an impact on the way knowledge was understood.

One particular instance, however, marked a clear departure from previous ways of thinking, and that departure was the way 14th-century artists began to conceive of space. Filippo Brunelleschi (1377–1446), for example, invented linear perspective. He had already made a name for himself in Florence as a designer of the theatrical machinery used in some saints' and passion plays. His machines allowed saints and angels to descend from Heaven or to fly from one location to another accompanied by fireworks and convincing explosions. Perspective drawing, however, allowed him to create a sense of space by creating artificial depth with pictorial materials. No one can perceive depth in only two dimensions; Brunelleschi was among the first to assume a viewer's distance from an object in a drawing and then to scale that object relative to the viewer. This technique employed what is called a "vanishing point" opposite the viewer's eye, while all lines parallel with the viewer's line of sight receded towards that vanishing point.

Brunelleschi's invention had enormous consequences for the reconfiguration of theatre and the space required in which to perform it. For Italians and others who were familiar with the ruins of Roman theatres strewn about the Italian peninsula, the use of the vanishing point in scenery was revolutionary. The Romans had never used it, nor had the Greeks. There was in fact very little "scenery" at all in ancient Greece and Rome. There was only the *skenion* (in Greek) or *scaenae frons* (in Latin) that formed an optical background to the performance. In Renaissance Italy, the idea was to compress scenery into one full stage picture. Scenery in the Middle Ages required a scenic structure such as a mansion, around and in which actors spoke their lines. Scenery that employed perspective enclosed the performance space and thus created a stage milieu. The humanist theatre thereafter no longer depended upon the spoken word as its primary medium; it combined the stage picture with the actor's presence to create a new kind of experience for audiences. Audiences were meantime no longer merely "auditors" in an "audience," that is, listeners. They were now viewers as well, revivifying the concept of "theatre" in its Greek cognate *theatron*, or "seeing place."

Humanist academies (dedicated to studying and publishing texts on classical literature, art, sculpture, and architecture) were instrumental in spreading Brunelleschi's ideas about a stage milieu within a compressed and artificial space. One of the most important texts they distributed among themselves was a treatise by the Roman architect Vitruvius (ca. 80–ca. 15 BC), who served in the Roman army under Julius Caesar. Vitruvius had devised a wide variety of battle machinery, but his reputation among humanists derived from his *Ten Books of Architecture*, rediscovered in 1414 (though copies of the work had been in medieval libraries for centuries). Humanist research into the unfamiliar Latin terms in these volumes allowed scholars to see Vitruvius with new eyes. They set about copying some of his plans for new structures, and learned academies developed plans to create theatre structures based on Vitruvian models. In the 15th century, the Roman Academy attempted to duplicate Roman staging conventions.

Changeable Scenery

The Roman (though he was born in Bologna) architect Sebastiano Serlio (1475–1554) deserves special mention in this regard, because his was the first architectural treatise to devote an entire chapter to theatre staging, including Vitruvian variations of tragic, comic, and pastoral settings. Serlio, however, additionally incorporated the ideas of Brunelleschi's perspective drawing into his duplications, with an upwardly-sloped stage floor (whence the term "upstage" derives) and scenery created in perspective towards a single vanishing point. In 1579 the Olympic Society of Vicenza commissioned one its members, the architect Andrea Palladio (1508–1580) to build a theatre (enclosed within an already existing building), using Vitruvian principles. It was to be the last commission Palladio received before his death, and the structure remains the oldest of its kind anywhere in the world. The Teatro Olimpico also features what is considered to be the oldest stage set in existence, consisting of five street scenes built in permanent perspective, receding from the three openings in the decorated facade. Each of these scenic constructions featured an identical vanishing point, and each was lit by candles and oil lamps.

The first theatre building with a proscenium arch was the Teatro Farnese in Parma, completed in 1618. There is some debate as to how the proscenium arch developed, but most agree that it was essentially an enlarged opening in the proscenium wall, perhaps based on the architecture used for triumphal arches dating from Roman times. More important than its provenance was its purpose: to hide stage machinery that facilitated changeable scenery. Changeable scenery was already in use by 1618, and the single arch effectively limited the audience's vision to the space within the arch. Designers such as Nicola Sabbatini (1574–1654) exploited the unseen backstage area to deploy machines that created visual effects taking place in full view of the

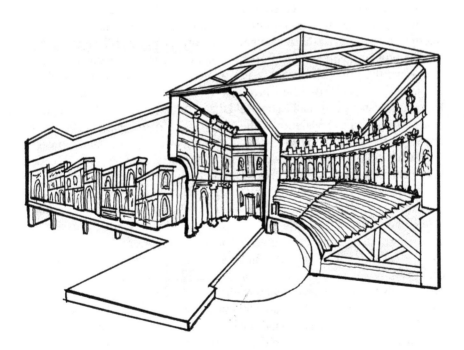

Figure 4.1.   Teatro Olimpico.

audience. Such effects included transforming a scene from indoors to out-doors, creating storms on land and at sea (including lightning and cloud formations), and the use of stage lighting for atmospheric purposes. Among the devices Sabbatini developed were three-sided *periaktoi*, which Sophocles is reported to have invented and which Vitruvius mentions in his *Ten Books of Architecture*. Sabbatini's *Periaktoi* (a Greek word meaning "revolving") turned on mechanical axes that, in turn, suggested three different locales. But they were only suggestions; Sabbatini's sliding upstage shutters were far more representational and visually explicit. They closed together in pairs like sliding closet doors and provided a backstage vista in perspective. He based his *portculli* on the French *portcullus*, or "sliding door," that was the iron grating of a castle that slid along vertical grooves at the sides of a fortress gateway. It prevented the entrance of attacking soldiers. Sabbatini's *portculli* were sliding flats that rose from underneath the stage through slots parallel to the stage apron. His angle wings were panels built on a 90° angle at the side of the stage and presented a scene in perspective by unfolding like pages in a book. Remember that the newly constructed theatres were dependent on artificial light, since they included a closed roof. Sabbatini's use of candles and oil lamps also emphasized the use of perspective, hoping to make the illusion of depth (however dimly lit) more realistic. Rapid scene changes became necessary by the latter half of the 16th century, as *intermezzi* (inter-missions) became popular entertainments between the regular acts of a play. The need to change settings rapidly for the alternating segments of plays and intermezzi encouraged the development of new devices for shifting scenery.

The problem with shifting scenery is that it required so many stagehands to execute the shift that the backstage area could become both crowded and dangerous. Scene shifts often involved at least two sets of side wings, a backstage vista, and usually some overhead "sky borders" which depicted clouds. An ingenious designer by the name of Giacomo Torelli (1608–1678) improved the situation by the mid-17th century when he invented a mecha-nism which one individual could operate under the stage floor. Torelli called his mechanism the "chariot-and-pole" system. By attaching long upright sup-ports (his "poles") through slots in the stage floor to wheeled platforms (his "chariots") running along the floor under the stage, Torelli could rapidly change an entire stage setting. He employed a single winding mechanism called a windlass (originally invented to raise or lower heavy anchors as ships were entering or leaving harbors) to operate the movement of the chariots moving under the stage floor. The advantage of the chariot-and-pole system was to carry flats into view while simultaneously removing flats that had set the previous scene—all without a single stagehand in the wings. Torelli stated that his chariot-and-pole system was so effective, and so easy to maneuver, that an 11-year old boy could operate it with little difficulty. Thus at one stroke Torelli simultaneously increased the number, diminished

Figure 4.2. Teatro Farnese.

the danger, and reduced the cost of crowd-pleasing, complicated scene changes. The windlass could change all scenic elements within three to four seconds, which audiences found akin to wizardry. The best filmic example of a chariot-and-pole scene change appears in Ingmar Bergman's 1975 film of the opera *The Magic Flute* by Wolfgang Amadeus Mozart (1756–1792). In it, we see a woodland daytime scene of rocks, crags, and trees transformed into a nighttime landscape of clouds and foggy shores within about five seconds—all with the original chariot and pole equipment of the Drottningholm Theatre in Sweden.

Neo-classicism: Minturno, Scaliger, and Castelvetro

The aesthetic principles which constituted neo-classicism were nominally part of the initial "re-discovery" of the ancient world. Some critics have asserted that those principles (often called "strictures," "norms," or "ideals") were manifestations of the European search for cultural identity as it emerged from medieval to rationalist ways of thinking, greatly assisted by newly found manuscripts from the ancient world of the Greeks and Romans. Per-

haps a more accurate definition of neo-classicism was its usefulness in efforts
to control and standardize the practice of dramatic performance. Such efforts
were in practice first in Italy during the 15th and 16th centuries, then later in
France during the 17th and 18th centuries. Neo-classicism thus became a cultural movement, a continent-wide aesthetic creed that imposed standards of
artistic quality for at least three hundred years.

Americans are familiar with the practice of standardization. Walt Disney
(1901–1966) was among the first to recognize the merits of standardizing the
county fair of the 19th and early 20th centuries, which in many counties
throughout the United States consisted mainly of a few mechanical rides that
offered thrills and chills to local yokels at harvest time. But Disney saw in the
county fair a communal exercise, something that offered the aforementioned
local yokels a sense of belonging. His creation of the "theme park" was a
grandiose extrapolation on the idea of the county fair. But Disney did far
more than allow the local high school band to come marching onto the fair
grounds, permitting fair operators to occupy tents, and authorizing food pur-
veyors to hawk corn dogs, cheese fries, and funnel cakes to hungry visitors.
At his Disneyland (in California, which opened in 1955) and Disney World
(in Florida, which he planned during the last years of his life), he closely
standardized everything from balloons to toilet paper. All facilities in those
theme parks adhered to a strict code of hygiene, all employees dressed in
approved costumes that conformed to Disney's idea of period authenticity,
and everything was wholesome—just as it had been, or seemed to have been,
when he was attending county fairs as a boy growing up in Missouri. Ray
Kroc (1902–1984) had a similar idea with hamburgers. He was familiar with
the hamburger stands that dotted towns, cities, and roadways during the 1920
and 1930s. Sometimes they offered a juicy burger "with everything" (usually
ketchup, mustard, lettuce, tomatoes, onions, and pickles). Other places simply offered fried ground beef and called it a hamburger, while most other
places offered something in between. Kroc got the same idea as Disney:
standardizing would guarantee the consuming public a product they could
trust, something that was consistently a quality product.

Neo-classicism predated both Walt Disney and Ray Kroc by about three
centuries, but its goal was the same: essentially control and maintain predict-
able standards of the product set before a consuming public. Neo-classicism
had begun as an Italian rediscovery of Greek and Roman theory, but it
continued mostly as reinterpretations of Aristotle and Horace. Among the
most significant individuals who initially advocated neo-classicism was Antonio Minturno (1500–1574), the Bishop of Ugento. He was most concerned
with what should be preserved from rediscoveries of Greeks and Romans, yet
he misinterpreted Aristotle and Horace and stressed instead the need for
"verisimilitude" in performance. Verisimilitude means "similarity to truth,"
but Minturno believed that "truth" was a universally understood virtue; eve-

rybody, he thought, understood it as "reality." If a production depicts kings in tragedy (speaking verse), commoners in comedy (speaking prose), and the humble, mean, or ludicrous (speaking clichés) in satires, the audience will recognize the results as "decorum" in character, and thus true to genre. Truth to genre fulfills preconceived notions of what a play actually "is," and the audiences will be both "taught" and "pleased." Minturno also insisted on fidelity to a 24-hour limit in the play's events, which resulted in an over-emphasis on causality.

Julius Caesar Scaliger (1484–1558) was likewise influential in establishing new rules for drama. He defined tragedy and comedy in terms of content, yet he viewed characters as more important than plot, since moral improvement was the goal of drama. In this regard he differed from Aristotle, defining drama not as imitation but "a delightful instruction by which the habits of men's minds are brought to right reason." Instruction was a very big deal among humanists, and they believed theatre was an excellent means of changing human nature because it was the most immediate art form available for the purpose. They believed that "struggles borne bravely" upon the stage would cause people to bear their own struggles more bravely in real life. Such arguments resemble those of affirmative action advocates today; if audiences view members of approved ethnic groups or women on the stage playing "non-traditional" roles the results will be socially beneficial. For example, if a woman plays a role traditionally written for and assigned to a man, the audience's cultural horizons will widen to include diversity of every sort.

Giambattista Giraldi Cinthio (1504–1573) asserted that tragedy was to set before us the passions we should avoid, while comedy sets before us what is to be imitated, namely temperate feelings mixed with laughter. Such techniques "summon us to the proper way of life," he believed. Lodovico Castelvetro (1505–1571) differed from other neo-classical humanists in his writing about drama, because he downplayed drama's duty to instruct. Teaching was not needed for a learned and aesthetically sensitive audience, he said, yet one must remember that a sensitive audience demands the "unities of time, place, and action." It is not possible, Castelvetro stated, to convince an audience that several days and nights have passed "when their senses tell them otherwise." Castelvetro believed that audiences, even the most learned and sensitive ones, were incapable of accepting the rapid passage of time or a sudden change of place while they were sitting in a theatre. The addition of a subplot might be possible, however, if the playwright is skillful and can somehow make plot twists and turns seem logical. Yet Castelvetro was like other neo-classicists in his insistence upon rules and normative standards. Dramas were not to show murder onstage, he declared. They were instead to be reported by messenger, as the Greeks had done.

The theatre, and the performing arts generally, have suffered for centuries under the good intentions of misguided people who want audiences not to see what they like but what they ought to like. There have been numerous rating systems for motion pictures, television, and popular music down through the years in many Western countries, aimed at regulating what is shown on the stage or on the screen for fear of causing people to act out what they see or hear. In the 1920s a program of self-censorship in films attempted to depict married couples sleeping in separate beds; in the 1930s further attempts kept all nudity off the screen, and the only time a vulgar word such as "damn" was heard was when Clark Gable managed to utter it at the end of *Gone with the Wind* (1939). The 1940s saw a slight retraction of some censorship, as home-coming soldiers were not always depicted as valiant heroes but as psycholog-ically damaged from experiences in combat. The 1950s saw the wide accep-tance of the term "rock and roll" (which had previously connoted sexual intercourse), but Elvis Presley was barred from swiveling his hips on televi-sion. Only in the later 1960s were films allowed to use language that was obscene and to display the human body in its altogether unclothed state. But in the 1970s, new attempts to control audiences appeared: feminists and civil rights advocates wanted "positive role models" on the stage and on screens. They wanted certain words that might cause unease to be banned or at least more "sensitively" used. Sensitivity, in fact, became the new neo-classicism. As more females and members of ethnic groups were included in all aspects of production and performance, the results were supposed to be uplifting and no longer demeaning. What has happened in many societies since the 1970s, however, has been a return to neoclassicism's original premise: control the audience and teach it to respond in appropriate ways.

Commedia dell'arte

A theatrical movement in the 16th century was concurrently taking place in the streets of Italian cities that seemed at first glance to defy neo-classicism. It was an improvisational form of theatre performance called *commedia dell'arte* (which means "professional theatre performers"), featuring touring troupes in popular, non-academic theatre that emphasized the actor, a tradi-tion which thumbed its nose at neo-classicism. Commedia actors usually performed in open air spaces, beginning about 1550, though commedia troupes probably existed long before that time. It was an actors' theatre based upon the actor's physical skill, voice, quick wit, and mastery of the northern Italian dialect. Commedia troupes were unique in that they performed im-provisationally, not from memorized scripts but from memorized routines, sketches, or scenarios. They were direct cultural descendants of the Roman theatre (and thus were fully within the humanist mainstream) by virtue of the stock character types that formed the core of their work. Most scholars agree that the stock characters derived in some way from the plays of Plautus and Terence.

All character types except the lovers in commedia performances wore masks featuring exaggerated facial features. The lovers (called *innamorata*) did not wear masks because commedia troupes emphasized their physical attractiveness to the audience. They were not only attractive but witty, educated, and contemporary, though at times naïve. Other characters included establishment figures, such as the *pantalone*, who was usually a miserly father or a wealthy merchant of some kind; the *dottore*, a learned type such as a lawyer, notary, doctor, or perhaps a music teacher; and the *tartaglia*, a kind of officious civil officer who delighted in serving summonses and arresting people. The *capitano* figure was an obvious derivative of the *miles gloriosus* in Roman comedy, a military braggart who was in reality a coward. The *zanni*, or servant type, was the most numerous and interesting of the stock types in commedia. The *zanni* usually played maids, valets, servants, cooks, or sidekicks who were witty, agile, vulgar, cunning, gluttonous, and bawdy. Among the most well known of them was *arlecchino*, sometimes anglicized as Harlequin, an illiterate glutton who carried a slapstick with which he beat his fellow servants named Figaro, Scapino, Trivellino, Brighella, Scaramuccia, Columbina, Pulcinello (also known for his slapstick), Truffaldino, and especially Pierrot, a servant who takes blame for everything in many scenarios—though he is almost always innocent.

Commedia dell'arte enjoyed extraordinary popularity in northern Italian cities and towns. Troupes such as *I Gelosi* (The Zealous Ones), *I Confidenti* (The Confident Ones), *I Innocenti* (The Innocent Ones), *I Desiosi* (The Desired Ones), *I Fideli* (The Faithful Ones), and *I Acessi* (The Inspired Ones) openly featured actresses playing the roles of women. In fact, one of the actresses from *I Gelosi*, named Isabella Andreini (1562–1604), is renowned as the "first woman on a professional European stage," a distinction somewhat doubtful, though emblematic of commedia's significance as a whole. Commedia troupes were initially all-male, according to many scholars of the subject. Yet their gradual introduction in the 16th century met with overwhelmingly popular approval, especially if at times the actress lost parts of her clothing during a particularly energetic scene. Women participated fully in the organization and performance of commedia scenarios, and indeed Isabella Andreini was so valued that *I Gelosi* disbanded upon her death.

Many commedia troupes remained prosperous until about 1650, when improvised comedy itself went into slow decline. By that time several non-Italian cities, especially Paris and Madrid, became venues where there had developed native variations on what was called "Italian comedy." Italy itself had gone into decline by the mid-17th century, largely because the rest of Europe had imitated, caught up with, and had begun to surpass Italian banking practices. That does not mean Italy was finished as a source of the humanist impulse. A new art form known as opera began in Mantua, where the premiere of Claudio Monteverdi's *Orfeo* (based on the ancient Greek legend of Orpheus) took place in 1607; he later wrote operas based on other Greek precedents and premiered them in Venice during the 1640s. The influence of the papacy had likewise diminished due to the spread of Protestantism, and with it diminished an accustomed ability to support cultural activities as a whole. New avenues and methods of trade supplanted what had formerly been Italian hegemonies. Yet the influence of Italian humanist norms and practices flourished throughout Europe until the end of the 18th century. Italy had been the incubator of an entirely new worldview, where neo-classicism had first established itself and then spread, allowing most Europeans fully to become heirs of the Greek and Roman classical tradition.

CONCLUSIONS

The Italian Renaissance marked a turning point in Western civilization, though there is substantial argument as to when it actually began. There are even differences of opinion about what actually constituted the turning points in various intellectual endeavors and art forms, such as humanist reinterpretations of Aristotle and Horace, the transformation of banking, the discoveries in mechanical engineering, and the innovations in architecture, painting, sculpture, music, and drama. For the study of theatre history, the implementation of perspective drawing in scenery, followed by innovations in changeable scenery, remained fundamental. Those innovations led to further developments in the concept of pictorial scenery, changeable scenery, scenery as a backdrop for acting, and the restraints on actors who formed part of the "stage picture." There was little concern for the optical aspects of theatre before the Renaissance, largely because the actors spoke their lines in front of unchangeable façades. Scenic conventions had emerged in the Middle Ages, but none of them sought to identify the actor within a pictorial space. Touring actors, who mostly performed on portable platforms or the tailgates of their ox-carts, thought themselves fortunate simply to have avoided arrest for performing in public, much less thinking about the scenic features of their presentations.

The Italian innovations in re-interpreting theoretical formats of theatre seem overwrought and hypothetical today, but to many "neo-classicists" of the 16th century the re-thinking of Aristotle and Horace became the intellectual backbone of a new consciousness in the theatre, one based on verisimilitude and the semblance of reality. "Reality" is a slippery term in any case, since its definition changes with time. One generation's reality soon becomes another's artifice. A definition of reality can also become a boundary or even a hurdle, as the demand for reality can quickly calcify into a convention, a convention into a presumption, and a presumption into an institutionalized postulate. Such was the case with neo-classicism, and its postulates remained in place for centuries, affecting scenery, acting, theatre architecture, and the writing of drama.

Chapter Five

The Classical Theatre of Asia

The evolution and expansion of theatre culture in Asia took place on vastly different levels and at dissimilar rates of development. There have been noteworthy theatre cultures throughout the East, from the Indian subcontinent to what we now call the "Far East," but this chapter is limited to the history of theatre in China, India, and Japan. Profound contrasts in climate, geography, language, religion, and political leadership make for fascinating cultural comparisons among those three in any case. It were a consummation devoutly to be wished, to paraphrase Hamlet, that lengthy examinations of each could take place in this chapter. Limitations of space regrettably prevent such, but the bibliography at the end of this book is a good place to begin further inquiries.

CHINA

The experience of Chinese emergence from a tribal existence to what we have termed civilization—with food surpluses, defensible city walls, alphabets, and ruling hierarchies absent patrimonial kinship—resembles to a certain degree the experience of some Western peoples. Like the Greeks and the Romans, the Chinese ultimately had an empire (they had several empires, as it turned out). Like the empire of Alexander the Great and its Roman successor, Chinese empires covered vast stretches of real estate. Centrally administered armies defended conquered territory, enforced tax collection and built enormous walls against invaders. The Roman Empire, however, was heterogeneous, granting Roman citizenship to various nationalities, language groups, and ethnicities, all of whom were allowed a considerable degree of self-rule. Not so the Chinese!

Unlike the Romans, the Chinese demanded and enforced conformity, using a common language as the major instrument in establishing and maintaining conformity among the populace. Most Chinese could understand each other's dialects because they had several important collections of analects and aphorisms handed down to them over the centuries from generation to generation. These collections underwent ongoing redaction and revision, resulting in editions that used "mandarin" ("language of the bureaucrats") as a common idiom. Their *Book of History* dated, according to some experts, to about 3,000 BC, as did the *Book of Changes*; the *Book of Rites* to about the 5th century BC. Scholarly volumes dedicated to the study and interpretation of these tomes number in the thousands. The ideas written down in those volumes have served as a basis for social cohesion within Chinese culture for centuries. The importance of the written word in Chinese culture is best exemplified in the *Encyclopedia of Learning*, which officials of the Ming Dynasty (1368–1644) commissioned in the early 15th century, employing about 2,000 scholars to complete the project. It ultimately totaled 11,000 volumes and was surpassed in the amount of knowledge contained therein, according to the scholar Niall Ferguson, only in 2007 by Wikipedia.

The first great dynasty in Chinese history was the Zhou (770–256 BC), made up of several quasi-independent Chinese kingdoms. One kingdom, the Qin, succeeded the Zhou in 221 BC and established a dynasty that eliminated kinship-based social hierarchies and democratized the army, much as the Greeks had done six centuries earlier. Like the Greeks, the Qin diminished that status of warrior princes like Achilles, Hector, and Ulysses. Unlike the Greeks, the Qin began conscripting masses of peasants, then expropriated the properties of patrimonial landowners and awarded land directly to soldiers (in ways similar to the Romans). The Qin Dynasty established a precedent for subsequent Chinese dynasties, which were essentially unitary states (instead of multi-ethnic empires on the Persian model) with uniform laws, government bureaucracies, standing military forces, and vast accomplishments in education and infrastructure. Unlike Europe, with its compact yet variegated topography of rivers, mountain ranges, forests, lakes, and seas, China's numerous rivers served as unimpeded conduits through vast and often uninterrupted landscapes. The Chinese could thus construct extensive roads, canals, and paved walkways atop defensive walls, such as the one atop the "Great Wall of China," one of the Ming Dynasty's most significant achievements. These thoroughfares allowed for the rapid deployment of armies, as they did likewise in the Roman Empire. The first Qin emperor, Shihuang (259–210 BC) is thought to have standardized written Chinese, a goal which had already begun when the Kingdom of Qin was a state in the Zhou Dynasty. The goal of standardization was uniformity and consistency in government documents. That standardization process subsequently promoted standard usage throughout China, expanding to uniform weights and measures, coinage, calendars, and myriad other aspects of Chinese life.

Chinese Thought

The various Chinese dynasties over the centuries shared the goal of achieving social cohesion and uniformity for the purpose of effective defense against invaders. In the absence of a theistic religion, the aforementioned *Book of Changes* (*I Ching* in Chinese) provided some of the most cherished and influential notions in Chinese thought, especially about the related concepts of harmony and conformity. Among those notions is the dynamic balance of opposites in human existence. *The Book of Changes* provides one of the first discussions of those opposites, known as *yin* and *yang*. Down through the centuries, scholars provided commentary on several aspects of *The Book of Changes*, lending the text a kind oracular authority. A compilation of aphorisms titled *The Way of Life* by Lao Tzu (ca. 600–520 BC) elaborates on *yin* and *yang*, leading to a school of thought called "Taoism." Taoism is a belief system that espouses the necessity of human accommodation to the forces of Nature and harmony with "the flow of natural events." In contrast to Taoism stands Confucianism, which incorporates the thought of Kong Fu-tse (ca. 550–480 BC), known in the West as Confucius.

Confucius is familiar to many Westerners by virtue of his numerous aphorisms. Adherents and/or devotees of Confucius probably organized his teachings in their present form sometime in the 2nd century BC. Confucius was primarily a moralist, one who believed that human beings should live within certain parameters if they were to live in harmony with one another and if human society was to prosper. The ideas of Confucius were at wide variance with Taoism, because the world of Confucius was primarily a material one. "What you do not wish for yourself, do not do to others" is one of his more well known aphorisms. "You may rob the Three Armies of their commander, but you cannot deprive the humblest peasant of his opinion" is another. Confucius remains widely praised as a philosopher of ethics, though his views espoused a strict authoritarianism. He admonished Chinese rulers, "If the people be led by laws, they will try to escape punishment and have no sense of shame. If they are led by virtue, and uniformly seek among themselves the practice of ritual propriety, they will possess a sense of shame and come to you of their own accord." Taoists considered such ways of thinking superficial, recommending instead "the path of wisdom" over the Confucian "path of knowledge."

The somewhat mystical side of Taoism and the practical approaches of Confucianism combined to create a tension within Chinese culture that manifested itself in theatre and drama during the late 13th century AD. Prior to that time, entertainments of various kinds blossomed and faded, seeking audiences both at imperial courts and with the common public at outdoor theatre structures. In both venues performers featured what we might today term "variety acts" that included sword swallowing, tightrope walking, marionette shows, singing, dancing, juggling, and probably one-act comedies featuring some dialogue. Very little evidence of such activity exists until the Han Dynasty, when emperors began actively to encourage it. During the Tang Dynasty from the 7th to the 10th centuries AD, there are records indicating a movement towards training performers in the art of speech, song, and dance. The Song Dynasty (960–1279 AD) witnessed the creation of actual scripts for full-length plays, though few of them are extant.

The Yüan Dynasty

Only after the Mongol invasion of China and the subsequent rule of Kublai Khan (1215–1294, grandson of Genghis Khan) do Chinese playwrights begin to write the dramatic masterpieces that are still performed, in part and in whole, throughout China to this day. In the plays of the so-called Yüan Dynasty (1279–1368), we find the development of numerous conventions in both thought and dramatic presentation which remain distinctive. First among them are the Confucian ideals of family loyalty and second are the Taoist convictions of mystical intervention by Nature. A good example of the latter is *The Injustice Done to Ngo Tzou*, a play by Guan Hauquig. In this play, a pious widow named Ngo Tzou suffers many trials and tribulations as a test of her loyalty. A court sentences her to death for murder. After her execution she returns as a ghost and pleads her case before her father, who has become a court judge. The father discovers discrepancies in the accuser's testimony and sentences him to death. Ngo Tzou remains dead, but is now vindicated. The ideal of Confucian loyalty is embodied in both Ngo Tzou and her father, while the false testimony of her accuser betrays the Confucian ideal of piety and honesty. The appearance of her ghost defies Confucian ideals, but according to Taoism it is fully justified because it re-establishes the dynamic balance of nature, in which all things operate in harmony with each other.

The dynamic balance between Taoist and Confucian ideals appears in several other Yüan plays, of which scholars have estimated there to have been about 700. Only about 170 are extant, but two of them have a curious history in the West. The first was Qi Zhun Xiang's *The Orphan of the Family Chao*, later translated and adapted by the French playwright and philosopher Voltaire (François-Marie Arouet, 1694–1778) in 1755. It proved to be popular among French audiences, but it was rarely performed elsewhere in the West. The idea of an orphan baby who grows to manhood in the household of his family's murderer, then avenges their deaths by arranging to have the murderer's skin flailed off was a novel conclusion to an exciting drama filled

Figure 5.1.   Conjectural depiction of Yüan performance structure.

with intrigue, rescues, and numerous lively songs. Its theme of family loyalty in the face or treachery and brutal violence found wide appeal among the French, but rarely among other audiences. *The Story of the Chalk Circle* had a much longer life in the West, first as *The Circle of Chalk* in 1923 by the German poet Klabund (Alfred Henschke, 1890–1928) and in 1944 as *The Caucasian Chalk Circle* by German playwright Bertolt Brecht (1898–1956). Brecht's adaptation was widely published in several languages and performed in theatres around the world thousands of times during the 20th century. It concerns the dilemma of two women who claim motherhood to a small boy; a drunken and dissolute judge commands the boy placed in a chalk circle and orders the women to pull him out. He awards the boy to the woman who refuses to hurt him.

During the aforementioned Ming Dynasty, which succeeded the Yüan Dynasty, one of the most noteworthy plays to appear was *The Peony Pavilion* by Tang Xianzu, featuring 55 acts and an extremely large cast to depict a young girl who wastes her life in longing for a man she has met only once, and that was in a dream. She dies, but at her gravesite the would-be lover appears. She is miraculously resurrected—but her father has the man arrested and beaten while in custody. The plays is full of adventure, hair's breadth escapes, stirring music, and what the Chinese consider the most exemplary of poetry for the stage.

Ching hsi, the "theatre of the capital"

The most exemplary of all Chinese theatrical forms grew from the precedents set within the Yüan and Ming dynasties. It is popularly known as Beijing Opera, or "theatre of the capital." Beijing became the capital of China in 1421 during the Ming dynasty when Emperor Yung-lo Ti (1360–1424) moved his governmental operations from Nanjing in the south to Beijing in the north. Beijing Opera as a distinct art form, however, did not appear until the 18th century, by which time the conventions it presently employs had become firmly established. It emphasizes the actor's skill in performance, particularly singing, acrobatics, stage combat, speech, and symbolic gesture. There are hundreds of plots used for productions of Beijing Opera, most dating from the Yüan and Ming dynasties. Other plots derive from Chinese folklore, history, and fairy tale.

Most significant in beginning to understand Beijing Opera are the stock characters which populate the operas and the costumes such characters traditionally wear. Principal among them are the *sheng* role, a male who sings falsetto and is highly skilled in acrobatics; the *dan* role, a female character usually played by a male performer. The *jing* role features elaborate face makeup and forceful vocal technique; there are thought to be over a thousand variations on this role in the Beijing opera repertoire. The *chou* role is a clown, known for his quickness both in his thinking and his fighting skills. Costumes in Beijing opera are elaborate and make use of wildly contrasting colors. There are few realistic props in performance, so the weaponry and special effects have symbolic value. One of the more intriguing of recent film treatments about Beijing Opera training and performance was the 1993 *Farewell My Concubine*, directed by Kaige Chen. The film was nominated for an Academy Award in 1994; it chronicles the lives of two boys enrolled at a Beijing Opera school whose training techniques can charitably be described as brutal and sadistic. The film follows their development as performers over decades and presents a stunning tapestry of techniques and conventions inherent to this remarkable form of theatre.

INDIA

Indian civilization putatively began with the immigration of Aryan tribes from somewhere south of Russia in the Caucasus (at the border of Europe and Asia, between the Black and Caspian Seas) in about 1900 BC. The Aryans moved through present-day Afghanistan into the Punjab, or "Land of Five Rivers." Those and many other smaller rivers have their origin in Tibet and flow southward to form the Indus River, which empties ultimately into the Arabian Sea. When the Aryan tribes encountered the Dravidian-speaking natives of the Punjab and the Indus Valley, the usual battles for territory, grazing land, livestock, and other resources ensued. The Aryan tribes were victorious, and they perhaps began composing the Upanishads thereafter. The Upanishads are presumably best understood in the West as holy scriptures, orally transmitted among the Aryans and based on the evolving Brahminic religion the Aryans had presumably brought with them from their Caucasian origins. This set of religious beliefs represented a significant departure from traditional veneration of one's genetic ancestors, which most tribes in the Indian subcontinent traditionally practiced. The beliefs of the Aryans instead embodied a cosmological system that took in the whole of natural existence. Such a religious system distinguished India from China, which remained largely non-theistic and, under the influence of Confucius, remained fiercely devoted to honoring one's parents and forebears. Brahminic practices focused instead on a transcendent world, but access to it only the Brahmins could provide. Within the Brahmin hierarchies were several sub-hierarchies, the function of all was nevertheless to generate ritual prayers and practices in Sanskrit. These prayers and practices constituted the *Vedas*, which over the centuries evolved into poems and narratives of various lengths, along with hymns, charms, chants, incantations, and spells. The *Vedas* became so influential in India that religious practice superseded all other political, economic, and legal concerns.

The infamous caste system in India grew out of religious practice, though some Western observers believe that religion in India was like religion everywhere else: an elaborate system of excuses for material interests. The material interests of the Brahmins, Karl Marx and others have argued, involved the perpetuation of their hegemony over other castes. The Brahmins accordingly used religion for purposes of control, thereby inventing a religion ex post facto to justify their behaviors (according to materialist thinking). Religion was not an independent cause of said behavior, they say. Such explanations unfortunately do not go back far enough, indeed they cannot go back far enough in history to explain why religious practices originated before the Brahmins achieved their material hegemony. The argument is somewhat akin to 20th century explanations of racism, which claimed that racist ideology is a tactic to maintain white power. Targets of such ideology (or other noxious forms of beliefs such as anti-Semitism, xenophobia, supremacism, *et al*) thus cannot be racists—yet the Nazis in Germany were anti-Semites long before they came to power. The Ku Klux Klan practiced racism while enjoying power in the southern United States; after the Klan lost power, the Klan was still racist. Most such materialist claims are suspicious, the exalted stature of Karl Marx in the West notwithstanding.

Figure 5.2.   Conjectural depiction of Sanskrit performance space.

Karma

The argument that ideas such as justice, love, power, beauty, or purity are immanent and independent of material concerns is more convincing, Plato clearly believed. One such idea closely related to Plato's thinking was the Brahmin concept called *karma*. In Indian religious practice *karma* it means "action" or "deed," though it can also mean "destiny" or even "fate." It essentially means "whatsoever a man soweth, that shall he also reap" (from Galatians 6:7 in the New Testament). Though some Westerners such as Boy George and his band Culture Club had a hit with "Karma Chameleon" in 1982, there was little *karma* nor an understanding of it in that delightful song.

There is also little understanding in the West of how the concept of *karma* contributed to the evolution of the caste system in India. *Karma* is intrinsic to all human endeavor and indeed to all of life, the Brahmins believed, because it is deeply imbedded in Brahminic conceptions of purity. *Karma* is present in all human activities, usually manifested in human occupations. According to the doctrine of *karma*, caste is determined by proximity to or distance from sources of pollution. "Pollution" is a Brahminic concept closely knit to physical existence. Occupations or individuals who must encounter blood, filth, dirt, decay, or death have been hopelessly polluted. Butchers, barbers, grave diggers, morticians, hide tanners, or anyone engaged in the disposal of waste products are impure. Brahmins, on the other hand, are the most pure because they have servants to perform services for them, allowing distance from pollution to be maintained. Individuals most interested in purity are usually vegetarians, since meat is basically the remains of the dead.

There are hundreds of interpretations of this and other Brahminic doctrines; for our purposes in theatre history, it suffices to explore the monopoly Brahmins exercised on learning and literacy. The Brahmins had achieved their status through an oral tradition. They passed on prayers, rituals, histories, epics sagas, chants, etc. by word of mouth to the next generation of Brahmins. Most secular rulers in the Indian subcontinent remained illiterate, as did nearly everyone else in India. Literacy was the privilege of the Brahmin caste alone. In China, as noted above, normalizing an alphabet and learning to write with it became state policy. Rulers, military leaders, and governmental administrators in India, on the other hand, found themselves completely at the mercy of the literate Brahmin caste. A set of religious beliefs and the social practices associated with it thus established the distinctiveness of Indian civilization long before the first well-known Sanskrit ruler emerged.

The Science of Theatre and Sanskrit Drama

Ashoka the Great (ca. 304–232 BC) emerged as the first Sanskrit-speaking ruler of note. He held much of the Indian subcontinent under his sway for about 35 years, from about 269 BC until his death. His realm spread from Afghanistan and the Indus Valley in the west to Assam in the east, then south all the way to Kerala. He was reputed to have ordered the deaths of his 99 brothers in the process of achieving power, and once in power he is said to have enjoyed nearly 400 wives and concubines in his harem. When some of them displeased him with their gossip, he had his entire harem murdered. A Bollywood film about Ashoka was completed in 2001, with a cast literally of thousands. It depicts him giving up war and violence when he converted to Buddhism, but evidence indicates he never relinquished the joy of rule by brute force, attempting mostly to maintain the status quo as much as he could.

During Ashoka's reign, a significant Sanskrit treatise on drama and dance is thought to have emerged, titled *Natya Shastra*, often translated as *The Science of Theatre*. The appearance of this treatise is fairly good evidence that performances in Sanskrit were already taking place, and in some venues (probably temples and/or shrines) theatre had become well established. Not only does the treatise contain substantial discussion of stagecraft, it provides abundant material on the content of Sanskrit drama at the time, little of which is extant. *The Science of Theatre* favorably compares in some ways with

Aristotle's *Poetics* because it discusses imitations of emotions (called *bhavas*) within actors, and the moods (called *rasas*) which actors are to engender among audiences. *The Science of Theatre* differs from Aristotle because there is scant mention in it of *mimesis*, the pivotal concept on which Aristotle bases his argument in *Poetics*. *The Science of Theatre* instead emphasizes the performers' attempts to evoke eight specific sentiments: erotic, comic, pathetic, furious, heroic, terrible, odious, and marvelous. Audiences in turn were expected to respond vociferously and loudly to praise the actors for their work. Brahmins and aristocratic nobility took pride of place within the audience, while other castes represented were financiers, the military, physicians, astrologers, or perhaps educators. There were others, of course, to whom theatres were forbidden territory. Among those refused admission (in addition to those aforementioned castes whose occupations caused profound pollution) were individuals involved in the growing, cultivating, and harvesting of crops, weaving of cloth, washing of any kind, or cooking. Purpose-built theatre structures were to maintain audience seating areas similar to those in temples and provide strict audience segregation. Colored pillars, usually painted white, red, yellow, or blue were to delineate the appropriate locations for different castes. Audiences at Sanskrit theatre performances were generally of the higher, more educated castes—educated enough, at least, to appreciate the performers' attempts to evoke the eight specific sentiments mentioned above.

A curtain usually divided a raised, platformed stage area in half, with the front half used exclusively for performance, the rear for costuming, make-up, entrances, and exits. The platforms are thought to have measured about 24 feet by 40 feet, with the floor kept smooth and clean by constant washing to maintain spiritual purity. Its center was raised slightly to allow for drainage after washing. The proceedings were highly stylized and presentational, as few props were used and no scenery represented specific locations. Costumes and makeup were important for identifying characters, of which there were numerous types: heroes, villains, low-caste (usually in blue) and high-caste (usually in yellow), teachers, cooks, petty criminals, etc. In most cases, professional or semi-professional troupes performed plays in Sanskrit. Each company was self-contained, featuring actors, musicians, and technicians required for the "proper" production values. Some companies featured all-male performers, while others were all-female. Most were mixed, usually headed by a male director who was also the leading actor. Some companies were well known and even renowned for the talent they possessed, usually having won a number of theatrical competitions, usually on a smaller scale but not too dissimilar from the competitions in ancient Greece.

The aforementioned eight basic sentiments were, according to *The Science of Theatre*, expected to dominate the experience of Sanskrit theatre performance: These sentiments were analogous to Aristotle's six "killer apps" in Western theatre, yet they depended upon the actor for the "proper" response to them among audience members. Actors were thought to have mastered a wide range of gestures for the purpose, among them 13 distinct gestures for the head, 36 for the eyes, seven for each eyebrow, six for each cheek, six for the nose for nose, nine for the neck, 24 for each hand, and 32 for each foot. There was extraordinary emphasis on "decorum" in performance. No play was to end unhappily, nor could characters fight with one another, fondle each other, kiss each other, nor even eat with one another.

Unlike the Chinese, the peoples of the Indian subcontinent were not susceptible to dynastic rule. Religious practices and prejudices oddly united the Indian people culturally but served to prevent rulers from uniting them effectively or for lengthy periods of time. Not until five centuries after Ashoka did the Guptas establish another Sanskrit dynasty large enough to rule most of the subcontinent parts of India, from about 320 to 550 AD. During their reign, according to the Sanskrit poet and playwright Kalidasa, the Guptas conquered about 21 kingdoms. The Gupta period meantime saw the creation of great epic poetry, including early versions of both *The Mahabhrata* and *The Ramayana*.

These two masterpieces of Sanskrit narrative provided a wealth of characters for Sanskrit dramatic presentation. Most theatre audiences during the Gupta period were likely familiar with those characters and their deeds, and Kalidasa was one of the most accomplished dramatists in Sanskrit. He is thought to have been born and to have lived in the 4th century AD; many of his plays incorporate episodes from the *Mahabharata*, such as *The Recognition of Shakuntala*. Other significant playwrights besides Kalidasa figure prominently during the Gupta reign; they include Sudraka, Bhasa, and Asvaghosa—though there is little specifically known about them.

Many scholars posit Sanskrit drama's apex sometime during the 4th and 7th centuries AD. There were presumably thousands of scripts written in Sanskrit, but few have survived to the present day. We do not really know for sure when such dramas premiered, nor is there a firm idea of their authors' identities. Kalidasa is most often associated with *The Recognition of Shakuntala*, a romantic drama in verse about the love of a great king for the beautiful wood nymph of the title, and her love for him. *Sakuntala* is based on an episode in the *Mahabharata*, though the play features complications absent in the original. Shakuntala is destined to become the mother of Bharata, considered the founding poet and progenitor of the Indian peoples. Various and sundry curses thwart her union with King Dushanta, but ultimately she and the king overcome obstacles and are blessed with the birth of a son. The play has a huge cast of diverse characters, including a charioteer who flies over the stage and a chorus of warrior women. Sanskrit scholars consider the play's language deeply sensuous, with scenes evocative of natural splendor alternating with sumptuous courts and palaces.

The Little Clay Cart by King Sudraka is thought to predate Kalidasa's *Shakuntala*, but it remains unclear by how much. *The Little Clay Cart* likewise differs from *Shakuntala* by virtue of its middle class characters and its numerous urban scenes. Like *Shakuntala* it also features a large cast, including merchants, weavers, prostitutes, priests, drivers, and even monkeys. A bankrupt merchant woos a prostitute with lines such as "Come, my dear one, to the banks of the Ganges; there I know the most beautiful prospect" and "the lovely deer there await their beautiful sister." These are good examples of King Sudraka's gift for poetic expression, which always remains within circumspect bounds when erotic sentiments arise. The bankrupt merchant is married, but his patient and loving wife accepts her husband's longing for the prostitute. The prostitute agrees to become the merchant's slave, but a base and degenerate courtier wants her for himself. Denied his pleasure, the courtier strangles her. When faced with charges of murder in court, the courtier claims the merchant killed the girl. The merchant is then tried, convicted, and nearly executed—but saved at the last minute when the prostitute is led into the courtroom, still alive, having been revived by a compassionate monk. The lovers are then reunited and all ends happily.

Classical Sanskrit plays have some general characteristics in common. Usually the protagonist declares his desire to achieve a certain objective, and he then makes a distinct effort to achieve his goal. He encounters substantial difficulty, but he eventually surmounts it. The hero and/or heroine in the process must demonstrate virtue or constancy throughout. More than one hurdle appears in their path towards achievement of their goal, but ultimately all difficulties are resolved to their benefit.

The use of gesture became crucially important in Sanskrit theatre, largely because most audiences spoke a vernacular tongue and could not for the most part understand the Sanskrit used in performance. Today there are over 200 recognized languages in India (though only 22 are permitted for official business). The number of languages in use two millennia ago was in all likelihood even greater. The languages in India are furthermore complicated and structurally different from each other (especially those derived from the indigenous Dravidian idiom). Gesture, as a result, often comprised a sign language almost as complicated as spoken speech, yet comprehensible to many in the audience. Sanskrit was a language regulated by pitch, so the stage idiom tended to be highly musical. There was an emphasis on voice in performance in an effort to maintain a lilting quality in poetic expression. The actor's control over numerous pitch levels and dexterity in volume usually accompanied the movement of other actors moving or dancing in complicated ways. The performance spaces as a result tended to be small so that audiences could see the gestures and experience the lyricism of the text (even while they could not fully comprehend the words).

Weather in the Indian subcontinent is often unbearably hot and humid, making it imperative that theatres were open to breezes. Yet the roof was of crucial importance, not only to protect actors and audiences the natural elements, but also to shade them from supernatural demons. The proximity of the audience to the weather allowed audiences a higher consciousness of natural forces, some observers have noted. The close proximity of weather variations helped to create a sense of varying moods that in the play were prone to change quickly. These moods reflected Nature's whims, manifested in rain, wind, storms, breezes, cloudiness, sunshine, etc.). Nature is rarely neutral in Sanskrit drama: rain can signal sorrow about events, wind can augur fury, while lightning foretells impending disaster.

There is a distinct "story telling" aspect to Sanskrit performance, de-emphasizing character or plot, often abandoning causality completely. One major reason for the preeminence of narrative in Sanskrit performance was the initial presentation of it in palaces and temples, when a local ruler sponsored religious ceremonies or seasonal observations that stipulated recitation. As we have seen, religion played a significant role in all aspects of Indian life during the classical Sanskrit period. "Hinduism" is a word Arabs used when they began their invasions of the Indus Valley in about 730 AD, describing the religious practices of people they encountered and ultimately vanquished. To this day, Hinduism embraces a broad array of devotional practices, philosophical concepts, innumerable sects, and over 350,000 deities. Most practitioners of Hindu, however, pay homage to three principal gods: Brahma the creator, Shiva the destroyer, and Vishnu the preserver. In the 1830s, the term "Hindustan" ("nation of Hindus") emerged to describe all of India, though that term rarely appears in regular use today. Most Sanskrit drama included Hindu deities or spiritual values in one way or another, fixated on internalized emotions rather than external particulars. Realism was not conceived of; the ceremonial nature of a presentational-style performance was paramount. Ceremonies offering sacrifices to various gods were however often part of most pre-performance activities.

Muslim invasions of the 10th century onwards were different from earlier incursions that had taken place in northern India during centuries previous. Those invasions had assimilated the prevalent social system. The Muslim conquests during and after the 10th century retained Islamic theology and created new legal and administrative systems that often replaced existing institutions. The Muslim legal system and its Sharia courts began to impose a commercial and legal system in northern and western India. This system was familiar in most parts of the Muslim Empire, which extended from Morocco in the West to Mongolia in the North, to Indonesia in the East. While southern India was already engaged with Arab Muslims, northern India often experienced wholesale conversions and declarations of allegiance to Allah, the only deity permitted in Islam.

The impact of Islam on Indian culture has been inestimable. It permanently influenced the development of all areas of human endeavor—language, dress, cuisine, architecture, urban design, social customs and values, and all forms of the performing arts. Conversely, the languages of the Muslim invaders were modified by contact with local languages, particularly Urdu, which derived originally from Sanskrit. Urdu is today one of the two official languages (the other is English) of Pakistan, which was formed from the predominantly Muslim areas of India.

In many areas of human activity, the followers of Mohammed brought innovations and made contributions to the fields of medicine, mathematics, the manufacture of paper, and the use of the compass. Yet Islam's stance towards theatre has historically been antipathetic, perhaps even more negative in attitude than that of early Christianity. Islam exercises a strict and inflexible ban against depictions of Mohammed, whom Muslims revere as Allah's principal prophet. Any image of a human Muslims considered a creation that usurped Allah's role as prime mover in the universe. If Allah is the sole creator of life, to create characters for a stage presentation runs the risk of competition with Allah. Such competition is heresy which must be avoided and, if possible, prohibited. Some crude forms of story-telling survived in the Muslim-occupied areas of India, but such is the fear of representation among Muslims only two dimensional puppet shows were allowed public performance, and even then only as shadows cast against a white screen. With the Muslim invasions of the Indian sub-continent by the end of the 10th century, the era of Sanskrit theatre and drama effectively came to an end.

JAPAN

Just as Brahminic religious practices influenced the classical Sanskrit theatre of India, and as Confucian and Taoist belief systems left their mark on ancient Chinese theatre, so Zen Buddhism and traditional shintoist practices had a strong impact on Japanese culture and theatre practice. Shinto is the ancient form of ritual worship, tracing its beginnings to reverence for various deities, forces of Nature, creation myths, and ancestors. Buddhism arrived in Japan sometime during the 7th century AD and is thought to have transformed Japanese aesthetic sensibilities by about the 11th century. Buddhism and Shintoism are not opposed to each other. Many Japanese scholars believe they shared a mutually "syncretic" influence over the years, their concepts on dance combining particularly at shrines and temples. Dance included acrobatics, tumbling, and movement to music at temples. By the beginning of the 12th century Buddhists are thought to have adopted many of the conventions of temple dance, including some narrative elements, to help them demonstrate Buddhist observances and teachings. Whether or not these dances were theatrical in the sense of mimesis is doubtful, but numerous professional performance troupes began to emerge by the 13th century in any case, competing with each other for audiences at festivals and ceremonies taking place throughout much of feudal Japan.

Noh and Zeami

During the 14th century, a significant change in both Japanese governmental structure and cultural taste emerged when the emperor turned over day-to-day operations of government in his realm to military men, called *shogun*. The Shogunate of the Ashikaga clan who took power in 1338 promoted and patronized a form of dance called *sarugaku-no*. From this form, most observers believe, emerged what is today called Noh theatre, a form which manifests the Japanese fascination with the ephemeral quality of existence. This fascination was characteristic of Kyotsugo Kanami (1333–1384), the leader of a *sarugaku-no* troupe. Kanami incorporated several Zen ("meditative") Buddhist ideas into his work, while his son and fellow performer Motokiyo Zeami (1363–1444) brought the Noh form to what many consider its zenith of development. Zeami wrote over 100 Noh plays, along with numerous treatises on the aesthetics of Noh.

Zeami's thought is inseparable from Zen Buddhism, especially his concept of *monomane* (usually translated as "technique of imitation") as manifested in the actor's work. According to Zeami, the actor has a "hand-in-glove relationship" with the role he is playing, something he calls *yugen*, a complex term variously translated as "what lies beneath the surface," or "mysterious beauty of impermanence" or "transcendental phantasm." Essentially it is a concept which must become the aesthetic force behind *monomane* on stage, something which the artistry of Noh seeks to summon and momentarily to apprehend. For example, Zeami called for the portrayal of an old man or old woman "to bring forth the flower." He often uses the term "flower" (*hana*) as an image of beauty with deep roots, such as a blossom that springs from an old tree. It is an inherent connection of beauty that extends all the way to the roots, not stopping at the beautiful petals. Such a conception is related to Zeami's interpretation of the Zen Buddhist belief in *mu*, i.e., "nothing." It is a kind of nothing that is always prepared to take shape, color, and form because it is in the hands of a master. Mere words or gestures alone cannot express beauty, according to Zeami; neither can mere imitation of an object (e.g. an old man), because they are of themselves "masterless." *Yugen* is thus also a sense of "contemplative prowess" over one's work, due to the Zen emphasis on physical and mental discipline.

Many of Zeami's plays feature ghosts, lost souls, supernatural personages, or profoundly sorrowful individuals—for all of whom existence is a

Figure 5.3.   Noh Stage.

torment, because in this life and the next they are preoccupied with some
worldly attachment, from which they cannot free themselves. That torment or
preoccupation lies at the Buddhist core of the nearly all Zeami's plays, as his
characters wrestle within themselves to learn three basic assumptions of Zen
Buddhism: existence is sorrow; the origin of sorrow is desire or attachment;
sorrow ceases when attachment ceases.

In a play attributed to Zeami titled *The Shrine in the Fields*, attachment is
the central premise. A girl in the central, or *shite,* role enters with a branch of
evergreen, the symbol of timelessness. She laments the fate of flowers after
autumn passes and continues a lament about the tear-soaked sleeves on her
costume. Her heart is taking on the fading colors of a thousand flowers,
withering as all things do when they are neglected. "I go back and forth/
Again and again on my journey/Through this meaningless, fugitive world."
A priest appears and notes the "sudden appearance" of "a charming young
lady" and asks her who she is. She launches into the history of the Shrine of
Ise, where on the seventh day of the ninth month, the past is recalled. She has
come to tidy up the place and tells the priest that he should leave. The priest
replies that no one will take offense at his presence—but "what is this business of recalling the past?"

She tells the story of when Prince Genji passed by the shrine years ago on
the seventh day of the ninth month. She dances and sings her sad tale of

attachment and the longing within her breast. She tells of a woman named Miyasudokuro, who became Prince Genji's lover. The chorus sings of how Genji and Miyasudokuro used to meet at this shrine. The Priest asks, "Who are you? Certainly no ordinary girl!" She admits that she is the ghost of Miyasudokuro. She disappears through the "hurry-door" upstage left, used for fast exits. The Priest says he will pray all night long for the girl's repose, as Miyasudokuro re-appears as herself. She tells of the catastrophic episode in which she violated court protocol, taking the parking space of the Princess Aoi's carriage. Princess Aoi's retainers pushed Miyasudokuro's carriage into the street, "among the ranks of the servants." The incident rendered Miyasu-dokuro's life purposeless, and she saw her life spinning round aimlessly like the wheels of her carriage. That is why she returns again and again to the shrine in the fields, still in love with Genji, who dumped her for another woman. She remembers those nights with him in the shrine, as she passes "to and fro through this world, I seem to wander on the path of delusion/Wavering between life and death."

Though some scholars have recently disputed Zeami's authorship of *The Shrine in the Fields*, the play remains a good example of Noh drama because of its adherence to the numerous principles Zeami outlined in his treatises. Its beauty derives from its restraint and power of suggestion, since the acting required in Noh (a word which in Japanese literally means "skill") carries most of the burden for its effectiveness in performance. The text itself is extremely short, and the principal performer, the aforementioned *shite*, is required to master dance, singing, and poetic utterance. An immobile chorus sings rhythmically during the *shite* actor's dance, and the secondary character, or *waki*, leads the *shite* character to the climactic point of the drama. The *shite* almost invariably wears a traditional Noh mask, which is usually smaller than the performer's face and whose expression changes with the tilting of the head. Costumes for the principal characters are elaborate, but those of the chorus and small orchestra are predominantly black. Hand properties are few, though a fan is used to symbolize a wide range of objects. The fan assumes symbolic value, depending on the actor's movement and his use of it to signify blowing breezes, a sword, the falling of flower petals, a lantern, or even an emotional state.

The Noh stage is likewise highly conventional, consisting of two separate platforms connected by a flat gangway or bridge. It leads from the small stage in the upper stage right area of the performance space (from which characters make their entrances) to the central roofed platform which serves as the principal performance space, or main stage. At the rear of this main stage sit members of the orchestra, who never feature more than four instrumentalists, but always a minimum of one flutist and one percussionist. At extreme stage left of the main stage sit members of the chorus, eight men in two rows. The wall upstage of the main stage depicts a pine tree, carefully painted in restrained, organic colors to remind audiences perhaps of the natural surroundings in which most of the plays are set. The most unusual structural aspect of the main stage is its floor, made of highly polished wood that enables actors to slide from position to position according to the demands of both the script and the movements of conventional Noh dance. Under the floor are placed sounding planks or terra cotta pots to create resonance, as the actors periodically stamp on the floor for emphasis.

The audience members at Noh performances sit close to the performance spaces, their seats facing the main stage on three sides. Noh places enormous demands on the audience (usually numbering between 300 and 500 patrons), who must, like the actors, exert severe mental discipline during the proceedings. Audiences in most cases understand only a fraction of the poetic dialogue, since nearly all Noh dramas were completed by about the mid-17th century. Very few plays written since then are in evidence, so the language is antiquated and often unintelligible to modern Japanese audiences, who must remain open to suggestion. All stage apparatus remains in full view; there is no wing space, no scenery, no literal representation. A stagehand may set a pole to suggest a tree, a chair to suggest a house, or he may carry onto the stage a miniature construction to represent a palace or a mountain. The stagehands, dressed in black, interact with and assist performers in full view of the audience, handing them props, helping them to sit on the floor, or to rearrange their costumes.

Bunraku and Chikamatsu

Bunraku is the name for a uniquely Japanese form of puppet theatre, one that features puppets one-quarter life size, requiring three operators to manipulate not only the puppet's body movements but also its fingers, mouth, eyes, and eyebrows. But puppet shows in Japan did not always feature such manipulable figures; evidence as early as the 12th century indicates the existence of wandering troupes performing with simple hand puppets. By the late 16th century, puppet performances began to use a separate narration that accompanied the action, creating the sensation that puppets were actually involved in events the audience was witnessing. By mid-17th century, a puppet theatre company opened in Tokyo, and in 1685 another one opened in Osaka. There, a playwright named Chikamatsu Monzaemon (1653–1724) began writing for the theatre. The result was some of the best plays ever written in Japanese. Chikamatsu became best known for the creation of what seem to be three-dimensional, fully human characters speaking dialogue which many Japanese to this day find beautiful and evocative. The lines are uttered by one chanter, accompanied by a lute-like instrument called a *samisen*. The puppets at the Osaka and Tokyo puppet theatres originally had only a movable head and one operator. In the 18th century they developed the aforementioned movable body parts and their present size, requiring three men to operate them.

The 18th century also witnessed some remarkable developments in stage-craft for the puppet theatre, beginning with movable scenery. Rivers were depicted on stage, houses rose above through the floors and disappeared below through traps, rain clouds appeared in the heavens, while the illusion of puppets walking along a narrow road was executed by a painted backdrop that unrolled behind the moving puppets. Conventions of the stage space itself developed, including its division into three levels to accommodate the puppet operators. To stage left of the main level sat the narrator and the samisen player; they both are dressed in black and wear hoods. These conventions persisted into the 19th century, when the puppet operator and theatre manager Uemura Bunrakuken (1737–1810) became active in Osaka. His family remained in Osaka for three generations and their name became the source of a new label for the puppet theatre, namely *bunraku*.

Kabuki

The city of Osaka also saw the beginnings of a new, entertainment-oriented form of Japanese theatre, called *kabuki*. Most historians place its beginnings sometime around 1603, when a woman dancer began public performances on the banks of the Yamato River. Her entertainments were a combination of dances and improvised playlets, and she soon began attracting audiences and other female dancers, many of them prostitutes from nearby brothels. When she was invited to perform before the emperor, several more kabuki troupes formed in imitation of her "bizarre performance" (the literal translation of *kabuki*). Most of these troupes consisted of prostitutes, and around 1630 the local Osaka authorities banned women from performing the increasingly popular kabuki shows; male troupes sprang up in their forced absence, many of them featuring attractive boys. They too were eventually banned and ultimately kabuki troupes consisted of all-male adults, many of whom, however, specialized in transvestite roles.

The tradition of all-male kabuki troupes persists to this day, though by the latter part of the 17th and early 18th centuries the genre had begun to expand its repertory to include plays by the aforementioned Chikamatsu Monazae-mon, along with adaptations of plays he had written for the puppet theatre. His success with "love suicide" plays held substantial appeal among kabuki audiences, and his work spawned several playwriting imitators. Such writers did not concentrate, however, on the tragic aspects of unrequited love but included comic scenes that alternated with serious ones. Many of these plays came to be known as "domestic dramas" since they featured the foibles of family life, both in its humorous and sometimes tragic manifestations. In most cases, kabuki "programs" included plays, dance programs, and what we in the West might term interludes, usually of a comic or musical variety. Since dance had been the original basis of kabuki, the rhythmic movement, stylized posture, special effects, and ornate gesture of kabuki became important features of kabuki aesthetics. Such features had to follow the script, however, even if stylization accentuated a particular moment. A change in a character's emotional state could, for example, require a spectacular change of costume. The costume change was quickly executed in front of the audience with the help of a well trained stagehand, whereupon the performance would resume. Singing is an important part in kabuki performance, though rarely do the actors themselves sing. A chorus instead intones the lines which explain the actor's motivation or state of mind, a convention borrowed from the puppet theatre. The actors meanwhile speak their lines of dialogue.

Acting for the kabuki theatre requires diligent training, and in most cases an actor is rarely considered accomplished until he is well into his 40s—even though his training began in early childhood. Most actors are descendants of acting families and are allowed to use their family names only after a long apprenticeship with a kabuki company. Actors study and are expected to master one of several character types, which include villains, heroes, comics, and females. These groups are subdivided into servants, soldiers, prostitutes, cooks, princesses, merchants, elegant ladies, and tradesmen, which are then subdivided further into several more types. Actors do not wear masks but paint their faces according to character type. Most characters require a white base with deeply saturated colors to indicate villainy, heroism, servitude, etc. The female role, called *onagata* in Japanese, wears little color makeup except a touch of rouge at the corner of the eyes and mouth. Each character type requires a distinct costume, usually based on historical precedent. Audiences seem unaware of such precedents, however, since costumes from various historical periods mingle among each other in most kabuki productions. One of the most fascinating features of kabuki costume design is the aforementioned necessity at times for rapid costume change onstage in full view of the audience. Many costumes, despite their great weight (some weigh over 40 pounds), fall from the actor at what seems a slight tug on a single thread, and in a matter of seconds the actor simply steps out of the old costume, revealing another one more suitable to the emotional state a text requires. Stage properties, as in Noh theatre, serve a variety of functions. That is particularly true of the fan, which can function as a bow and arrow, an ocean breeze, or a raging fire. Other props, however, serve realistically in ways familiar to Western audiences.

The kabuki stage floor is highly mechanized, with numerous traps, elevators, and revolves. The kabuki theatre in the 18th century indeed invented the stage revolve, which was introduced in the West in the late 19th century. Most characteristic of kabuki stagecraft are the dual *hanamichi*, gangways which proceed through the audience from back of the house to the stage apron.

Actors make elaborate entrances on these *hanamichi*, much to the delight of audiences. Other noteworthy aspects of kabuki stagecraft include the use of painted flats at the rear of the stage, which usually depict a realistic image of some kind—but the flats are separated to break up the unity of the stage picture. Other devices include sliding flats in the wings, sliding doors, and large traps that seem to enfold entire scenic structures and swallow them whole into the floor. Rarely, however, is anything "flown in" from above as is often customary in Western theatres. The emphasis in kabuki is the floor itself and the actor's relationship to it—an emphasis borrowed from Noh. In Japanese culture, man is regarded more "earthbound" than in the West, and soaring above buildings or among the clouds is a usurpation at best, seeking to become godlike at worst.

CONCLUSIONS

Overextended generalizations are probably unavoidable when discussing a topic so broad as "the theatre of Asia." Generalizations and vague speculations can lead to further misconceptions about Asian theatre traditions, which many observers regard as utterly foreign anyway. A good way to get beyond the superficialities of difference is to discover similarities and cross-cultural influences. In recent decades the economic influences of Japan and China in particular have made themselves felt in the West; it is difficult nowadays to find any manufactured product in the West not "Made in Japan" or "Made in China." The enormous growth in the Japanese and Chinese economies have led to increased awareness of the cultural assets present in the East, from many of which the West has benefited. The example above of the stage revolve, invented for the Kabuki theatre, made its Western debut in 1896 at the Deutsches Theater in Berlin. Since then, stage revolves have become standard equipment in many theatres throughout the West. Director Max Reinhardt (1873–1943) was especially fond of them, using revolves in repeated productions of Shakespeare's *A Midsummer Night's Dream* and in many other productions as well. The presentational conventions intrinsic to most Asian theatre traditions have had an even greater impact on Western theatre practice, fostering a readiness to depart from predominant representational styles in the West. Among the most well-known of advocates for Asian-style performance conventions were the aforementioned Bertolt Brecht and Antonin Artaud (1896–1948). The latter wrote rhapsodically about the Balinese Dance, and the former praised the Beijing Opera star Mei Lanfang (1894–1961) as an ideal precedent for Western actors to follow. Meantime the work and theories of Japanese director Tadashi Suzuki (1939–) have found an appreciative audience in the United States among actors desirous of incorporating the techniques of Noh, Western ballet, and the "power of silence" in performance.

Chapter Six

The Theatre of France to 1658

The beginnings of Italian Renaissance influence made their way to France in the reign of François I by about 1515, the year his reign as King of France began. François recognized that Italy by then had become the source of new styles in literature, fashion, architecture, painting, sculpture, learning, culture, and much more. Italian ideas represented an altogether new orientation of cultural consciousness for France, and that kind of culture the "bold, unscrupulous, talented, and dissolute" François desired for his kingdom. He set about "Italianizing" Paris by offering court positions to artists Leonardo da Vinci (1452–1519), Benvenuto Cellini (1500–1571), and most importantly for French theatre to the designer and architect Sebastiano Serlio (1475–1554). François was so devoted to "his" Italians that several later paintings fictionally depicted the king with Leonardo at the moment of the artist's death. Leonardo's most famous painting, the Mona Lisa, hangs to this day at Louvre Museum in Paris. François subsidized numerous stagings of Roman and Greek plays translated into French and presented them "in the Italian style" in his court ballroom, the Salle du Petit-Bourbon. There Serlio had transformed the ballroom into an Italianate theatre, with settings in perspective. François also saw to it that Italian plays were translated and staged, while subsequently ordering the translation and publication of Italian neoclassical treatises on Aristotle and Horace. François was intent on proclaiming his status as a "with-it" sovereign by embracing Italianate ideals, much as contemporary financiers and industrialists today display their wealth with art collections and build splendid residences for themselves. François' own residence, the Palace of Fontainebleau, he had renovated from 1522 to 1540 into an elaborate Italianate showplace, the largest in France at the time.

During François I's reign, the curriculum in Latin drama at the University of Paris began to incorporate works by Roman playwrights, many of which are thought to have been performed by students in the original Latin. By about 1540, classical plays by the Greeks and Romans began to appear in French translation, and soon thereafter Italian plays "composed in the classical style" began to appear. No one really knows how many such plays in French or Italian were performed in the 16th century, but treatises by Aristotle and Horace (along with critical commentaries on both) were in evidence, lending credence to the notion that by the time of his death in 1547, François I had indeed been the first Renaissance monarch in France.

François' son Henri succeeded him and reigned as Henri II until his death at a jousting tournament in 1559. He had married Catherine de Medici (1519–1589) when both bride and groom were fourteen years of age. Catherine was a daughter of Lorenzo de Medici in Florence, and she used what little influence she had during her marriage to Henri II to continue cultivating the Italianate neo-classical ideals of theatre and drama in France. When Henri II died, Catherine's influence expanded considerably because she became regent for her 15-year old son, the king in waiting. But the son died only a year later and was succeeded by his 10-year old brother. At that point Catherine became the principal ruler of France, a post at which she remained even while the second son occupied the throne as Charles IX. She dominated him completely until his death in 1574, and when her third son became King Henri III, she dominated him, too. Catherine de Medici became most famous (or rather, infamous) for inviting thousands of Huguenots (French Protestants) to the 1572 marriage of her daughter Margot and the Huguenot Henri of Navarre. Six days after the wedding ceremony (on St. Bartholomew's Day, 27 August), Catherine is reputed to have orchestrated the murders of nearly all of the Huguenot guests. Their number was thought to have approached 10,000, based on body counts in the Seine River. Catherine de Medici thus became the embodiment of the Chinese aphorism, "If you sit by the river long enough, you will see the bodies of your enemies floating by." The great American filmmaker David Wark Griffith (1875–1948) included in his 1916 epic-length film *Intolerance* a startling scene of the slaughter that took place on St. Bartholomew's Day. The horrific events of that day are perhaps best viewed in the excellent 1994 film *La reine Margot* (Queen Margot) starring Virna Lisi as Catherine. Lisi received the Best Actress Award at the Cannes Film Festival for her work in this movie, and rarely since has any actress achieved Lisi's malevolence and murderous intensity.

ITALIANATE IDEALS AND THE GROWTH OF FRENCH TOURING TROUPES

Prior to ordering, or at least planning those murders, Catherine de Medici is thought to have been instrumental in fostering several French playwrights who were interested in imitating Italian styles. Chief among them was Etienne Jodelle (1532-1573), whose *Cleopatra captive* met with widespread official approval in 1552—though little is known about response to the play's premiere, in which Jodelle himself played Cleopatra. Jodelle had many imitators, and like Jodelle their plays are noteworthy only from the standpoint of their ability to replicate declamatory verse and a commensurate inability to invest dramatic action in the proceedings. Most of the characters in these dramas recite their misfortunes and decry the fickleness of fate—all the while maintaining a stoic calm which many in the audiences at the time associated with classical forbears.

Such plays were largely court entertainments, and though they adhered to many neo-classical conventions, their staging was for the most part in the old-fashioned style of "scenic plantation" that featured structures pictorially identifying locations referred to in the script. Sebastiano Serlio, as noted earlier, had been present in the court of François I and had published his 1545 treatise of perspective (*Tutte l'opere d'architettura et prospetiva*, All Works on Architecture and Perspective) in Paris. But old staging habits die hard. Theatre for public performance in Paris did not begin to accept Italian scenic practices until after the 1570s, and by that time France was embroiled in a series of destructive religious and civil wars. The St. Bartholomew's Day Massacre in 1572 is thought to have instigated those conflicts, though there had been bloody engagements between French Catholics and Huguenots in the 1560s.

The conflicts which followed the St. Bartholomew's Day Massacre historians have termed the "Fourth French Civil War" of the 16th century. The Edict of Boulogne, which ended this war, provided peace that remained in force for only about six months. Protestants and Catholics thereafter again engaged each other in battle, resulting in more destruction and even more edicts that called temporary halts to hostilities. Assassinations, intrigues, ambushes, and other attacks led to battles throughout France until at last the Protestants held the western and southern parts of France, while the so-called "Catholic League" held the rest. The stalemate was broken when the Protestant leader (and son-in-law of Catherine de Medici) Henri of Navarre converted to Catholicism and agreed to appoint only Catholics to his new kingdom-wide government in 1594. Military encounters continued to take place thereafter, but Henri IV (as he now styled himself) was able partly to unite the country in 1597 by declaring war on Spain. The resolution of that conflict ended in Henri's favor, and in 1598 he was able to engineer the Edict of Nantes, which gave crown guarantees to Protestants, effectively ending the numerous civil wars.

The civil wars had wrought substantial havoc on theatre practice in France during the latter third of the 16th century, since nearly all theatre took place "on the road" and little in Paris, where the biggest and most affluent audiences were to be found. Paris could boast the best theatre building in France at the time with the Hôtel de Bourgogne. Note that "hôtel" in French did not mean a business or building which accommodated guests overnight or for longer stays if the guests preferred; it connoted instead a kind of stately residence. In this case it referred to the aristocratic Burgundy family (the Bourgogne), on whose property the structure was situated. An organization known as the "Confrarie de la Passion" had the structure built in 1548. Such organizations were common in many continental cities; their original purpose was to produce medieval cycle plays. In Paris, the organization's influence grew in power, wealth, and influence to the point where it had veto power over any theatrical performance anywhere in the city. In 1548 the Confrarie had obtained property from the Burgundy family, and the building they erected on the property was named in the family's honor.

That building, the Hôtel de Bourgogne, became the first permanent structure in Europe dedicated to theatre performances since the Roman Empire. The investment of the Confrarie in this building, however, confirmed in the minds of Parisian municipal authorities that the organization should retain its monopoly on all performances in the city. That monopoly assured the Confrarie a cut of all box-office proceeds from any troupe that rented the ve-

Figure 6.1.   Conjectural depiction of stage space in Hôtel de Bourgogne.

nue—or indeed any other venue in Paris. Few troupes, however, could afford the cost of both rent and payoff. The result was a remarkable paucity of theatre in Paris, but by the 1570s a network of venues around the country had emerged, and most of them were far more reasonable in their financial demands from touring troupes. In the bigger towns and cities (e.g., Bordeaux, Lyon, Marseille, Montpellier, Rouen, Toulouse, *et al*) there were furthermore no monopolies in effect as was the case in Paris. The aforementioned civil and religious wars, however, had a devastating effect on touring troupes, because the conflicts frequently destroyed roads, bridges, canals, ferry docks, performance venues, and often whole portions of cities.

Cardinal Richelieu and the Reform of French Theatre

The return of stability under the Edict of Nantes in 1598 coincided with the retreat of the Confrarie de la Passion from active involvement in Parisian theatrical affairs. It is not clear whether or not the Confrarie reduced its rents or relented in its somewhat restrictive rental policies; it is believed, however, that the Hôtel de Bourgogne began to allow the sojourns of non-French companies from Italy and England in Paris, with the result that far more numerous French troupes began to perform in Paris than was previously customary. The most noteworthy of the French troupes was that of Valleran LeComte and Marie Vernier, who grandiloquently billed their troupe *Les Comédiens du Roi*, though they enjoyed neither connection with nor patronage from the French king. They did, however, benefit from the work of Alexandre Hardy (1572–1632), whom many consider the most accomplished playwright of his time. Hardy was probably the first professional playwright in France; he claimed to have written over 500 plays, though that is a distinctly liberal estimate. About 30 of his plays remain extant, and they reveal a writer in touch with the popular audience, one who in all likelihood concocted dramas with members of the Valleran LeComte troupe in mind. He had accompanied the LeComte troupe on numerous tours, and his quasi-tragedies had pleased audiences seeking an alternative to the prevailing repertoire of farcical entertainments most troupes were in the habit of providing. Hardy based most of his dramas on classical precedents, such as episodes from Homer's *Iliad*, Vergil's *Aeneas*, Plutarch's *Lives*, Ovid's *Metamorphoses*, Boccaccio's *Decameron*, or legends about classical figures such as Alexander the Great or the Persian King Darius. By no means, however, was Hardy a neo-classicist, though he attempted to structure his plays in five acts and used confidants and messengers as plot devices. He paid little attention to the unities of time, place, and action, while presenting brutal deaths onstage in full view of the audience. Valleran LeComte produced Hardy's work at the Hôtel de Bourgogne until about 1612; by that time the assassination of

King Henri IV and again stirred up religious enmity and theatre troupes found renewed civil strife an impediment to business.

The general trend among theatre troupes after the restoration of order was a renewed emphasis on farce, and almost always among French troupes that meant an attempt to imitate Italian models of *commedia dell'arte*. The most well-known of such performers were three men who specialized in improvisational vulgarity and obscenity. They were known primarily by the types they played: Turlupin (Henri LeGrand, 1587–1637), a comic servant type; Gros-Guillaume (Robert Guerin, 1554–1634), an obese and lecherous clown; and Gaultier-Garguille (Hugues Gueru, 1573–1633), a contortionist. These performers had at one time performed with the LeComte troupe, but when LeComte departed permanently from Paris in 1612, the trio remained at the Hôtel de Bourgogne and presented themselves in performances of their own devising.

Other troupes played, when they could afford to pay off the Confrarie de la Passion, in Paris at renovated indoor tennis courts. Indoor tennis courts provided troupes in France with performance spaces that were remarkably versatile. They provided ready-made seating for audiences, usually in galleries along both sides of a lengthy rectangular court, while the court itself served as standing room. At one end of the court, troupes usually placed a platform approximately six feet high, on which they conducted most of their performances. Any settings with which they toured were also on that platform, unless the set piece was too large; in that case they installed it on the floor. Perhaps the most significant advantage a French tennis court provided was lighting; above the seating area most courts had rows of windows set immediately below the roof. The result was a well-lit (in the afternoons, at any rate) theatre space that geometrically approximated the Hôtel de Bourgogne's dimensions (thought to be about 100 feet long by about 35 feet in width). The Hôtel de Bourgogne meanwhile depended on artificial lighting. The Bourgogne remained the venue of choice for touring companies, however, due to the familiarity of its location among audiences. No company was permitted permanent residence in Paris until 1629, regardless of the venue in which they played. In that year the Parisian government finally abrogated the Confrarie de la Passion's monopoly, and troupes found themselves free to make their own deals with individuals or organizations desirous of renting venues to troupes.

The personality behind this kind of "theatre reform" in Paris was Armand Jean du Plessis (1585–1642), best known to history as Cardinal Richelieu. Richelieu had become influential in French government circles in 1606 by virtue of his close association with the Queen Regent Marie de Medici (distant cousin of the aforementioned Catherine de Medici), and in 1624 he was named "chief minister" of King Louis XIII. As such he is thought to have become the first known Prime Minister in European history. He solidified his hold on power in 1630, when he renewed his policy of using theatre in an effort to spread French culture and influence throughout Europe. There have been many stage and film incarnations of Richelieu, including dozens of actors who played him in the widely popular 19th-century drama by Edward Bulwer-Lytton (1803–1873) titled *Richelieu*. The most well known actor to play Richelieu in the 20th century was probably Charlton Heston (1923–2008), playing the Cardinal in two movies, *The Three Musketeers* (1973) and *The Four Musketeers* (1974). Heston captured the unbridled ambition of Richelieu, and fortunately for French culture, Richelieu himself directed a generous portion of that ambition towards "re-inventing" the French theatre.

Cardinal Richelieu, like some of his aforementioned predecessors in the French court, recognized that neo-classicism (as defined in 16th century Italy) was a powerful tool to renew and shape French cultural life. There had already been numerous Italianate processions, court extravaganzas, water fêtes, elaborate ceremonies, ballets de cour, and divertissements in the Italianate style at court by the beginning of the 17th century. Richelieu doubtless realized that such displays of pomp and circumstance had little influence over public taste, but he was eager to solidify his power at large within the French state and beyond its borders. He had brought Italian stage designers to Paris, whose installations included a raked stage and perspective scenery, along with moveable wings and drops. Few dramas of the first two decades of the 17th century, however, included the Italianate "unities" (of time, place, and action), nor did they incorporate the neo-classical emphases of "verisimilitude" (generality, morality, and reality). Richelieu let it be known among educated gentlemen that he sought such dramas for public presentation, and the response was gratifying (to the cardinal, at least). Among the learned gentlemen who responded with dramas in the neo-classical style were Pierre du Ryer (1600–1658), Jean de Mariet (1604–1686), Jean de Rotru (1609–1650), and the most significant of them all, Pierre Corneille (1606–1684).

The Triumph of Neo-Classicism in French Theatre and Drama

Corneille joined a group Richelieu had organized called *Les cinq auteurs* (The Five Poets) and instructed them in the kind of literature he thought best for France. Richelieu had seen Corneille's comedy *Mélite* in 1629 and requested more such work for the French public stage. The Montdory troupe had presented the play in Paris after its world premiere in Corneille's native Rouen; the result was widespread approval from both critics and audiences. It was a clear departure from the improvised and inelegant buffoonery which had begun to weary audiences at the Hôtel de Bourgogne. *Mélite* instead focused on the frustrations of two lovers misled by forged letters, written by amorous rivals. There was little in the way of sexual innuendo or vulgar boorishness in this comedy; both Mélite and her lover Éraste are sincere, though Mélite is easily duped and Éraste initiated the confusion by forging the letters. Éraste at one point loses his mind and imagines himself in hell, so profound is his remorse from writing forgeries. But all ends happily as confusions are clarified and the "true lovers," not Éraste and Mélite, are married. Corneille continued to write comedies, but they did not enjoy the success of *Mélite*. In 1635 he tried his hand at serious drama and premiered an adaptation of Euripides' *Medea*; response to it was lukewarm at best, but the results of his next effort were far noteworthy than he, or Richelieu, could have anticipated.

Corneille adapted a lengthy Spanish play called *Las Mocedades del Cid* (*The Adventures of the Cid*) by Guillen de Castro, based on the life of the 11th-century Spanish nobleman best known for his defeat of Muslim armies in several encounters. He severely edited the Castro script, transforming it from a six-act epic taking place over a decade into a model of neo-classical style, observing all the required unities and conventions which the Italianate ideal demanded. The play was wildly popular with audiences, but many of Richelieu's learned authorities found *Le Cid* overwrought.

The problem, the learned believed, was credulity. In Act I, for example, Chimene confesses to her governess that her father has consented to a marriage between her and her boyfriend Roderick. In the next scene, the Infanta, or Princess Royal, confesses to her governess that she too is in love Roderick. The next scene depicts an argument between two older knights, Diegue and the Count of Gormaz. They trade insults until finally Gormaz slaps Diegue across the face; they agree to a settle their dispute in an honorable, gentlemanly fashion. But Diegue feels his advanced age will handicap him, and orders his son Roderick to defend the family honor against Gormaz. But Gormaz is Chimene's father, and Roderick finds himself duty-bound to fight his future father-in-law. In Act II, Roderick defeats and kills Chimene's father. Then comes word that ten Muslim ships have been spotted off the coast of Castile and are about to sail up the river and attack. Roderick offers to lead a force of Spaniards against them. Chimene is confused. Her admiration for Roderick remains, but he did, after all, kill her father. In Act III, Roderick has defeated the Muslim forces after three hours' combat. The Infanta tells Chimene she should not demand Roderick's death for killing her father, but rather his exile. That way, the Infanta herself may have access to Roderick. In Act IV, Roderick returns, a national hero. He tells the king of his exploits and honors, which include the name "al said," which in Arabic means "the master." The King thanks Roderick and asks him to step into another room. The King then summons Chimene to inform her that Roderick has fallen in battle and enjoys a hero's death. She faints, assuring the King that she is still in love with Roderick. In Act V the Infanta pines for Roderick, especially in view of the fact that he is now The Cid. Chimene mean-time is suffering mightily, wishing Roderick were still alive. The King then tells her that Roderick yet lives; Roderick enters with the Infanta, who urges Chimene to marry Roderick. Roderick sinks to his knees before Chimene and asks forgiveness for killing her father. She tells him to rise, but still wonders how it will be possible for her to accept him in marriage. The King says time will change her mind, since Roderick will be off to battle again soon, to "plunder all the Muslim lands." Such exploits will convince her to accept him, and he gives the couple his blessing.

Le Cid violated the neo-classical demand for decorum, claimed one of its severest critics, the influential professor of drama Georges Scudery (1601–1667). "Within the space of twenty-four hours a father is murdered, the murderer (also the hero of the play) goes off to defeat the Muslims in a huge battle, the daughter marries the murderer, and other violations of common sense take place." It was almost, he concluded, as if the playwright were writing a parody of a neo-classical tragedy. Such criticism inaugurated what became known as "the Cid Controversy," a vigorous debate within intellectu-al and government circles about the direction French theatre culture should now take. In an effort to resolve what had become a serious dilemma, Riche-lieu in 1637 granted the Academie-Française (which had been informally organized in 1629 merely to discuss matters of literature and culture) a state charter to resolve the Cid Controversy. The Academie-Française published its "Judgment on *Le Cid*" in 1638, in which it condemned the play for its multiple departures from good taste, decorum, verisimilitude, and Nature itself. This play, they wrote, "squeezes several years into one day." Moreover "the marriage, the capture of the Muslim kings, and other events take place so quickly, one atop the other, [that] they violate Nature." The Cid Contro-versy marked a turning point in French theatre culture, one which set its direction for the next 150 years.

French Neo-classical Acting

French playwrights and theatre companies made prodigious efforts to con-form to the norms established under Richelieu, maintaining neo-classical constraints long after his death in 1642. He was succeeded by Cardinal Mazarin (Giulio Raimondo Mazzarino, 1602–1661), an Italian native whom Richelieu had tutored in the art of cultural statecraft. As Chief Minister of France he worked closely, as had Richelieu, with the Queen Regent of France (in this case Anne of Austria). Mazarin oversaw an expansion of theatre life in Paris, continuing and expanding Richelieu's policy of provid-ing generous subsidies to troupes whose work found favor among govern-ment officialdom. The first troupe of note to present neo-classical drama was the aforementioned Montdory company. The troupe took its name from Guillaume des Gilberts (1594–1654), who styled himself "Montdory" beginning in 1612 as a member of Valleran LeComte company. He joined the Prince of Orange troupe in 1622 and later established himself in Richelieu's cultural consciousness with the *Mélite* production in 1629. Richelieu awarded him a subsidy in 1634, allowing him and his company to settle permanently in the Theatre du Marais, a renovated tennis court and the first theatre to challenge the Hôtel de Bourgogne's pride of place in Paris. Montdory continued to present neo-classical tragedies until a stroke felled him in 1637; his successor was Josias de Soulas (1608–1672), who styled himself "Floridor." Floridor continued the Montdory precedent of emphasizing a neo-classical style in tragic performance, which in most cases meant grandiose declamation and elaborate gesture. This baroque style called attention to the actor's voice, especially as he swooped from high to low pitches, underscoring a desired intensity of the "tragic mood." At the Hôtel de Bourgogne, the actor Zacharie Jacob (1600–1667), known as "Montfleury," equaled Floridor in vocal dexterity and baroque pomposity. You may catch a delightful parody of such pomposity in the performance of Gabriel Monnet (1921–2010) as Montfleury in the 1990 film *Cyrano de Bergerac*, starring Gerard Depardieu.

Montfleury joined the Hôtel de Bourgogne company in 1639 where he starred in a number of Corneille tragedies, including *Horace* and *Cinna* (both in 1640), *Polyeucte* in 1642, and *The Death of Pompey* in 1643. Ten years earlier, the Bourgogne company had secured a royal subsidy from King Louis XIII through the efforts of actor Pierre Le Messier (1592–1670), who styled himself "Bellerose." Bellerose, like Montdory, had worked for Valleran LeComte and enjoyed considerable sympathy at court—even though his artistic goals were somewhat at odds with those of Richelieu. Bellerose was adept at both farce and tragedy, and perhaps as a result played tragic heroes with less bombast than did his colleagues Montfleury or Floridor. Some observers even termed Bellerose's style a "natural" one, which probably means it somehow contained more subtlety than that of his rivals. In any case, the Bourgogne company could boast of two substantial tragedians in Bellerose and Montfleury, though Bellerose retired in 1647. In that year Floridor transferred to the Bourgogne, bringing with him an important new playwright named Jean Racine (1639–1699).

Floridor turned the Marais company over to his friend Jehan Mathee, who styled himself "Filandre." Yet the Marais company never fully recovered its eminence. Meantime Cardinal Mazarin attempted to present opera at the renovated Palais Royal, the former Palais Cardinal (and residence of Richelieu). Mazarin had used government funds to install Torelli's chariot-and-pole system of scene shifting, which was used initially for the Luigi Rossi opera *Orphée*. Since Mazarin, Torelli, and Rossi were all Italians, members of the royal court expressed outrage that French governmental funds had financed the project. In response, Mazarin commissioned Corneille to write

Figure 6.2.   French tennis court.

the libretto for *Androméde*, one of the most spectacular productions ever staged in France. The Theatre du Marais then attempted to win favor by staging several productions boasting similar extravagance, but the cost of mounting them was so enormous that the theatre was forced, on the verge of bankruptcy, to abandon them. Yet the staging techniques of Torelli found favor among theatre audiences, and subsequent decades saw wide use of changeable scenery for spoken drama.

The coming decades were also to witness some of the most significant and subsequently most well known premieres of all French drama. They included the works of Corneille's younger brother Thomas Corneille (1625–1709), the aforementioned Jean Racine, and the greatest playwright of them all, Jean-Baptiste Poquelin, an actor who styled himself as "Moliére." Moliére received a royal audience before the new King Louis XIV in 1658 at the Louvre, then gained a generous subsidy and the use of the Salle du Petit-Bourbon near the Louvre for his company. Lucky for him and his company (known then as the Théâtre Illustre), their theatre venue far exceeded in luxury the confines of both the Bourgogne and the Marais. But greater things awaited them: the title "Troupe du Roi" (The King's Troupe), and for Mo-liére himself the appointment as "official" author of court entertainments, along with a royal pension for himself, his actresses, and his actors.

CONCLUSIONS

The works of Moliére represent the culmination of various developments in 17th-century French theatre, most notably the triumph of the neo-classical ideal. Moliére had begun his career as a playwright composing comedies based on commedia scenarios, but by the time he completed numerous mas-terpieces such as *The School for Wives* (1662), *Tartuffe* (1664), *The Misan-thrope* (1666), *The Miser* (1668), and *The Imaginary Invalid* (1673), he was acknowledged (in France, at least) as the greatest dramatic poet in the French language, one whom who many today consider the greatest comic playwright since Aristophanes.

What often goes unacknowledged is the role that powerful women played in the ascent of French theatre, from inelegant vulgarity and semi-literate touring troupes performing quasi-tragedies to the remarkable, much-emulat-ed Racine in tragedy and the majestic accomplishments of Moliére. France had welcomed "the first professional actress in Western civilization" when Isabella Andreini and her troupe of commedia performers played Paris dur-ing the reign of Louis XIII. As we have seen, the formidable Marie de Medici (1575–1642) was instrumental in fostering Italianate ideals in the theatres of France. Anne of Austria (1601–1666) was the mother of Louis XIV, using her influence with Cardinal Mazarin during her regency to subsidize numer-ous troupes in Paris.

Chapter Seven

The Theatre of Spain in the *Siglo de oro*

The Iberian peninsula, consisting of today's Spain and Portugal, was a fully incorporated province of the Roman Empire: the Emperors Trajan, Hadrian, and Marcus Aurelius were born there, in what the Romans then called "Hispania." The Roman playwright Seneca was born in Hispania, too. If you have seen the film *Gladiator* (2000), directed by Ridley Scott and starring Russell Crowe as "the Spaniard," you are familiar with brief episodes which depict the Spanish landscape in the film and the intense desire of "the Spaniard" always to return there. Hispania was important to the Romans as a source of cereal grains, wool, olive oil, wine, and fish. Hispania's silver mines were also significant, because Roman coinage consisted almost exclusively of Spanish silver until the 1st century BC. The Romans cultivated land and developed Hispania's agricultural productivity to a substantial extent, introducing both field drainage and irrigation projects, many of which one may see to this day. With the decline of Roman authority and occupation in the 5th century, Germanic Visigoths ruled Hispania from their capital Toledo, and by 585 AD the Visigoths controlled almost all of the Iberian peninsula.

In 711, Muslim armies from North Africa, a mix of Berbers and Arabs (generally referred to as Moors), conquered most of Hispania. They called it Al-Andalus and made present-day Cordoba its capital. The northern Christian realms in Spain periodically went to war with the occupying Muslims, whose wars the Frankish king Charlemagne most conspicuously assisted in 777. Charlemagne and his invasion with the Frankish army under his command marked the beginning of a centuries-long campaign by European armies of Spanish *reconquista* (re-conquest). The campaign at times achieved stunning victories, e.g., the one at Valencia in 1094 under the leadership of Rodrigo Díaz de Vivar (1043–1099) known as "El Cid." In the 13th century, other campaigns drove the Muslims into the southernmost regions of Spain, while in 1479 the kingdoms of Aragon and Castile united the Christian parts of the country. In January of 1492 the armies of those kingdoms defeated the last remnants of Muslim forces at the Battle of Granada, and Spain was for practical purposes united. The year 1492 also marks the Spanish sponsorship of the first voyage by Christopher Columbus (1451–1506) to the Western Hemisphere. His discoveries there were to alter European history completely.

The Moorish occupation of Spain (which lasted more than 750 years) and the re-conquest of the peninsula, along with the wealth extracted from the Americas, made Spain the most powerful country in Europe for about two centuries. The defeat of the Moors gave the Spaniards a sense of enormous confidence, while the gold and silver expropriated from the aboriginal natives in Mexico, Peru, and other territories established Spain as the foremost colonial power among the Europeans. In 1519 the Spanish King Carlos I was elected Holy Roman Emperor Charles V, and large parts of Europe came under his control from the Spanish capital, Madrid. Carlos' son, the Spanish King Felipe II (1527–1598) became the most powerful ruler in Europe when he ascended the Spanish throne in 1556. Spain in the 16th and 17th century became a powerful cultural influence as well, boasting numerous achievements in literature, theatre, architecture, scholarship, music, and philosophy. Its navy spread Spanish influence throughout many parts of the globe during the 16th century, and the Battle of Lepanto in 1571 decisively defeated a Muslim navy sent by the Ottoman Empire. The Battle of Lepanto, in which the writers Miguel de Cervantes and Lope de Vega actively participated, featured Spanish leadership and the presence of naval forces from Spain's Italian territories. The Spanish army established beachheads of commerce and Roman Catholicism in many parts of Asia. The Spanish Empire in the Americas, called "New Spain," extended from Patagonia in the southeast of South America to California in the northwest of North America. The riches this empire earned allowed Felipe II to engage in all kinds of intrigues, wars, and dynastic maneuverings through the remainder of the 16th century. Spanish possessions and dominions in Europe itself included the Netherlands and parts of Italy, France, Germany, and along the Mediterranean coasts of eastern Europe and northern Africa. Spanish military decline began with defeat at the Battle of the Spanish Armada in 1588, when Felipe attempted the overthrow of the English Queen Elizabeth I. Spanish dominion reached its nadir with the War of Spanish Succession (1701–1714), which reduced Spain to second-rate status among European powers.

Between about 1580 and 1680, however, there evolved what many historians consider a *Siglo de oro* (Golden Age), marking the zenith of Spanish cultural accomplishments, particularly in theatre and drama. Those accomplishments had their beginnings, many believe, in the wake of the re-conquest; many of the Spaniards in re-conquered territories knew little of Roman Catholic doctrine, so religious dramas played an important part in re-educating the populace in those territories. Many such dramas came to be called *autos sacramentales* because they emphasized the importance of Church sacraments. Trade guilds, as elsewhere in Europe, presented *autos sacramentales* usually during the festivals of Corpus Christi, which unlike the rest of Europe took place three times a year in many parts of Spain. *Autos sacramentales* were also a significant part of Lenten observances in Spain, which traditionally took place 40 days prior to Easter. Professional troupes began presenting *autos* by the mid-16th century, and Spain is one of the few European countries in which religious drama continued to be presented well into the 18th century. The troupes performing them maintained a medieval method of performance, featuring pageant wagons, sometimes as many as four for the presentation of one play. They were ultimately discontinued in 1765.

HUMANISM AND SECULARISM IN SPAIN

Spain had closer ties to Italy than did other European states, largely because of Spain's occupation of southern Italy and Sicily, beginning in 1442. Spanish schools began teaching Greek and Latin texts thereafter, and in the 16th century many schools encouraged pupils to perform plays in Latin. The majority of such schools were "Jesuit" schools, administered and staffed by the powerful Roman Catholic order of priests formally known as the "Society of Jesus," founded by the Spaniard Ignacio de Loyola in 1539. Meantime a number of professional touring troupes appeared in Spain during the 16th century, the most significant of which was probably the one organized by Lope de Rueda (1510–1565) sometime in the 1540s. In the early 1550s his troupe was noteworthy enough to be summoned for a command performance before Felipe II, who then hired Lope's troupe to perform at Corpus Christi festivals throughout Spain. Lope and his troupe toured many cities and towns in Spain, presenting plays most notably in Cordoba, Madrid, Segovia, Seville, Toledo, and Valencia, for which they earned generous commissions. It was the kind of regular employment of which few actors could boast in Spain, but it allowed Lope time to write secular plays adapted from Italian precedents in a vernacular Spanish that later attracted a popular and sizable audience. With plays such as a farce titled *The Incident of the Olives* Lope de Rueda became known as the first professional playwright in Spain.

The professional theatre of Spain, however, did not initially have playhouses in which to perform. They staged their plays outdoors on boards set up for the purpose against painted backgrounds of some kind. Scholars believe that by the 1570s there were several other troupes in competition with the one Lope de Rueda had led, and in many Spanish cities permanent theatrical structures began to appear. The first of them was built in Seville, though most of what evidence remains about Spanish playhouses in the 16th century dates from Madrid. Regardless of the venue, these theatres became known as *coralles*, which in Spanish literally means "enclosed space." The first of the *coralles* in Madrid were probably unroofed courtyards within hospitals, which featured three or four balconies surrounding a courtyard on three sides where patrons could be seated. In the courtyard itself was the main seating area, called the *patio*. Against the permanent façade of the courtyard was placed a raised platform of boards, with no proscenium arch nor front house curtain. Actors probably often made their entrances and exits from behind a traveler (a transverse curtain which actors manually pulled across the stage) creating a backstage area, enabling exits and entrances, while also masking costume changes. Some historians believe the stage platform abutted a façade that had doors in it, much as the English playhouses did; if that is true, there would have been no need of a traveler. Others have conjectured that the platform itself, also similar to the English model, measured about 20 feet deep by 30 feet wide at the Corral de la Cruz in Madrid; it was slightly smaller, many believe, than the city's Corral del Principe. The acting platforms in both venues were stationed about five feet above the *patio* surface. There was no scenery as such, though there seems to have been a curtained "discovery space" upstage center that could reveal a painted vista or city square. In most cases, audiences were requested to imagine the details of a locale where the action was taking place.

The fraternal organizations who owned or administered the hospitals whose courtyards became theatrical spaces were essentially the "producers" of theatre in Spain. These organizations (e.g. La Cofradia de la Pasion y Sangre de Jesucristo, the Brotherhood of the Passion and Blood of Jesus Christ and La Cofradia de la Soledad de Nuestra Señora, the Confraternity of the Loneliness of Our Lady) were analogous to the Confrarie de la Passion in Paris. They received a share of the box office take which the actors had earned. The acting troupes never owned the theatre structures in which they performed; as a result, theatre in Spain became identified with charitable activity, a coincidental and beneficial effect which in subsequent years prevented some political interference. That included outright bans of theatre performances, as happened in some cities other than Madrid. The city's Corral de la Cruz was completed in 1579, making it the first permanent theatre building in the Spanish capital. It proved to be so popular that four years later another was built, the Corral del Principe. Both of these structures borrowed architectural features from hospital courtyards, though they added side seating adjacent to both sides of the *patio* which was graded upwards to improve sight lines. The upper balconies were roofed, as was the platform used for acting. Spain's weather is rarely inclement, but the sun can create unbearable heat for both actors and audiences at mid-day. As a result, awn-

Figure 7.1.   Stage structure for use in Spain.

ings sometimes were spread over the central patio to deflect direct sunlight, and performances usually began around 4:00 PM in the fall and winter. In the spring season prior to Lent they began around 2:00 PM. Spanish theatre troupes rarely toured during the summer months of July and August, and theatre activity in the permanent theatre buildings ceased operations during those months as well. During the Lenten season (from Ash Wednesday to Easter Sunday) only religious drama was allowed performance.

Seating capacity for the *corrales* is unknown, but some students of the subject have conjectured that both the Corral de la Cruz and the Corral del Principe accommodated about 1,000 patrons at the time of their construction in Madrid; Madrid itself had at the time a population of about 150,000. By the 17th century, seating is thought to have been expanded to about 2,000—though no one knows for sure. Among the more peculiar characteristics of the Spanish theatre in the *corrales* was the strict segregation of audiences by sex. Men were allowed in the *patio* and the seating adjacent to it; unaccompanied women or women in groups were allowed admission only to the *cazuela*, a gallery far to the back of the patio. Government officials attended every performance to make sure segregation took place. Sometimes women were allowed to sit in box seats located in side galleries, but only if they were accompanied by members of their family—and only if the officials granted them that privilege.

In 1640, the first Italianate theatre was constructed at the new royal residence in Madrid, called *El Buen Retiro*. The theatre was called the Coliseo and was considered the height of humanist and Renaissance theatre architecture present anywhere in Spain. It boasted not only a proscenium arch but a mechanism for changing scenery through a system of grooves in the stage floor. True to the elitist expectations of humanism generally, audiences for performances at this theatre were much different from those at the public theatres. At the Coliseo a more formal degree of dress and behavioral decorum was observed, unlike the noisy crowds in the *corrales*. In the latter, audiences were known to call out insults to actors and on occasion pelt them with rotten fruit and vegetables. The courtly audiences always comported themselves with civility. Wives were permitted to sit with their husbands, while single women could be escorted by courtiers.

Spanish Professional Acting Troupes

There were thought to have been about 2,000 actors and actresses in Spain by around 1600, who toured throughout the Iberian Peninsula by virtue of Spain's political and economic hegemony over Portugal. For the most part these performers presented plays in the Castilian dialect of Spanish, the official court language of the houses of Aragon and Castile, which had united the country. Acting companies were organized either on a shareholder or contractual basis, usually with an actor manager (and his wife) in positions of artistic leadership. In most cases, troupes had between 15 and 20 performers, which included both men and women. It was not always so: in the 15th and early 16th centuries, the troupes tended to be all male, but actresses began to be appear more frequently by about 1587, when women were first licensed to appear onstage. At that time the acting profession languished to some degree under a reputation of low status, even though troupes performed occasionally before the King of Spain himself.

At no time, however, did the troupes seek protection nor sponsorship from aristocratic families, which to some extent explains the presence of women as performers. The Church, however, frequently voiced its opposition to the presence of actresses, and Church officials obtained a royal decree in 1596 that banned women from the stage. Yet that decree was observed primarily in the breach, and women continued to perform with most troupes. In 1600 the crown privy council decreed that no actresses could perform with any troupe unless their husbands or father were also in the troupe. This decree was also largely ignored, for reasons not entirely clear. It was well known at the time that Queen Margareta of Spain, consort to Felipe III, greatly enjoyed theatre, attended it frequently, and supported it generously.

Whether she used her influence to assure the presence of women on the Spanish stage is not well known. It is well known, however, that official Church interference in theatre production continued well into the 17th century, banning the presence of priests at theatre performances and forbidding anyone but actors to go backstage at a *corral*. Church officials probably felt entitled to such exercises of control over theatre artists, for unlike other countries, Spain continued to sponsor the production and performance of religious drama well into the 18th century.

Censorship was in any case widespread, because troupes were obliged to submit scripts to local officials before any license was issued for performance. Since the troupes depended on touring for a good portion of their income, the troupe managers made sure the plays performed would give little or no offense. The plays were called *comedias* in Spanish, though they were not always comedies. In many cases touring troupes commissioned plays from playwrights, though prior to 1590 it appears that many playwrights toured with the troupes and at times even performed with them. Playwrights were well paid for their efforts, and many of them wrote hundreds of scripts. As in all of Europe at the time, no copyright laws protected a playwright's intellectual property, so his only source of income was the initial commission he received.

Among actors, two possessions were most prized: voice and costumes. Both attributes helped the actor find work, although in some sharing companies the cost of costumes was borne among the membership. Actors in outdoor theatres have always needed a strong voice to hold a sometimes rowdy audience's attention; Spanish actors were no exception. Most Spanish actors and actresses were required to dance and sing, since many of the plays, both secular and sacred, required such talent. Church officials often objected to dancing in *autos sacramentales*. One particular form of dance came in for harshest criticism, called the sarabande. It was thought to have originated in the New World among natives there as part of their fertility rituals, and some Churchmen found the dance sexually suggestive. They banned it from performances in 1583, but as was common in other Spanish theatre regulations, the ban was often ignored. Performers in the Spanish theatre they also needed to possess the kind of stamina that can pace itself, because the heat on many days could become burdensome. There were few siestas for actors in Spain, according to one contemporary record. They usually did some rehearsals during the cooler morning hours, then helped to prepare the performance space before audiences began to arrive. In most cases, box office receipts were shared among the performers immediately after the performance concluded; that was an unfortunate practice, since the amount of receipts could vary widely from day to day and performance to performance. The result was debt to meet unexpected expenses, and it was not always easy for actors to find loans at reasonable rates of interest.

Spanish drama of the *Siglo de oro*

Among the more well known of the early playwrights in Spanish was Miguel de Cervantes (1547–1616), though he is now principally remembered for his novel *Don Quixote*. He wrote several plays in the 1580s that were often in the repertoires of professional troupes, most of them now lost. Of the two that remain, *The Siege of Numancia* and *The Baths of Algiers*, the latter is more interesting: it treats Cervantes' experiences as a slave of Barbary pirates. He returned to playwriting in the early 17th century after *Don Quixote* had established his reputation as a writer of some import. Of those dozen or so later plays, *The Fortunate Ruffian* is perhaps the most characteristic.

Of all the playwrights during the Spanish Golden Age, Lope de Vega Carpio (1562–1635) remains the most well known, perhaps because over 1800 plays are attributed to his authorship. It is doubtful that he wrote that many plays, but it is a tribute to his reputation that so many authors used his name in an effort to get their plays produced. Like many of his contemporaries, Lope wrote in a variety of *comedias*: the *capa y espada* (often translated as "cloak and dagger") plays, which feature the adventures of a minor nobleman in the pursuit of justice. The character of Zorro in both movies and television is a good example of this type. The *cuerpo*, or "corpse" plays, features the ghost of someone whose honor needs repair. The *ruido* ("noise") plays are essentially situation comedies featuring numerous farce-like confusions. There were also numerous character *comedias*, featuring the misadventures of comic types, gentlemen, ladies, young gallants, or servants. Like Cervantes, Lope was often preoccupied with the Spanish nobility and its obsessions with itself and its status. The *pundonor* ("point of honor") became a hallmark in many of his plays, since it usually provided a ready-made conflict with romantic passion, around which he could structure a play. Many of his plays question outdated moral codes to which Spanish aristocrats subscribed; he also questioned the privileges that aristocrats enjoyed, though he did so with humor and irony. Almost none of his plays end unhappily, since his principal goal was to please his audience. His casts of characters nevertheless feature men and women from all strata of Spanish society, and he somehow is able to endow interest in each of them. Lope is infrequently, however, taken seriously as a playwright of universal renown largely because, according to several scholars, he avoided probing too deeply into the darker side of the human condition. His goal in most instances was to resolve conflict and provide a conclusion with which most members of his audience would express satisfaction. He also sought to flatter kings, as one may note in the following examples.

In *Peribañez* (1614), the eponymous hero is a peasant betrothed to the beautiful Casilda. The *commandante* of the local garrison finds Casilda to his liking and unsuccessfully attempts to seduce her. Frustrated, he makes

Peribañez a count, then assigns him a regiment to command and sends him off to battle. But Peribañez is wise to the *commandante*'s machinations and returns to rescue Casilda; in the process he kills the *commandante*. Shortly before Peribañez' planned execution for murder, the king becomes aware of the case and pardons Peribañez. *The King, the Greatest Alcade* (1635) like-wise features a peasant (this time named Sancho) who seeks justice from a dictatorial aristocrat. Said aristocrat prevents Sancho's marriage to the beau-tiful Elvira and then abducts her. Sancho appeals to the king, who orders the aristocrat to surrender the girl. He refuses, saying that only when the king in person orders him to release her will he do so. The king then disguises himself as an *alcalde* of the title, a kind of justice of the peace. He arrives however too late: the aristocrat has had his way with Elvira. The king then orders the aristocrat to marry Elvira before he is beheaded. Elvira then be-comes a widow and regains her lost honor by marrying Sancho. In what many consider Lope's greatest play, *The Sheep Well* (1614), the play's pro-tagonist is not one peasant but an entire village of them. They rebel against a tyrannical *commandante* and kill him. The king sends a judge to the village to investigate the murder and bring the perpetrators to justice. The judge puts all the village residents on trial and tortures many of them. But he gets no confession, only the repeated admission, "The sheep well did it." The king is deeply impressed by the villagers' solidarity with one another prompted by their sense of honor, and he takes them under his personal protection.

Lope de Vega was certainly not the only accomplished playwright in the Spanish Golden Age. His contemporaries Guillen de Castro (1569–1631), Juan Ruiz de Alarcon (1581–1639), and particularly Tirso de Molina (1584–1648) were his rivals, though none could match Lope's profuse out-put. Tirso, like Lope, subsequently became a Roman Catholic priest; as a dramatist he wrote "only" about 400 plays, of which about 80 remain extant. He is perhaps best known as the originator of the Don Juan character in a play titled *The Seducer of Seville* (1616); this character was already known in stories and popular legend, but Tirso gave him the outlines which show up later in numerous literary and musical treatments. The final scene in which Don Juan confronts the statue of a man he has killed, whereupon the statue comes to life and leads him to hell, is thought to be original with Tirso.

The most philosophical of Golden Age playwrights was Pedro Calderon de la Barca (1600–1681), whose career ultimately eclipsed that of Lope and his contemporaries. Calderon, however, wrote for a different audience than they did. His was the courtly audience, and many of his plays he wrote under royal command. His most well known is *Life is a Dream*, in which a prince is reared in anonymity at a rural mansion. Upon the death of the king he is taken to court unconscious, but his brief rule provides convincing evidence that he is unworthy of kingship. He is returned to the mansion of his birth, and when he awakes believes he has dreamed the entire episode. He subsequently discovers, in extremely long conversations with the court jester, that life itself is a dream, from which one awakens only in death. Like Lope, Calderon was also concerned with *pundonor*, particularly in relationships between men and women. In *The Physician to His Own Honor*, a man sus-pects his wife of adultery. In an effort to preserve his honor, he disguises himself as his wife's suspected suitor (the king's brother). He kills her—but is pardoned in an act of generosity by the king himself. Calderon is thought most accomplished in the creation of effective *autos sacramentales*, of which he wrote dozens and whose lyricism was unmatched by his contemporaries. They included Francisco de Rojas Zorilla (1607–1648) and Augustin Moreto (1618–1669). Like Calderon, both Zorilla and Moreto wrote primarily for the court theatre. There has been some debate as to whether the court had a debilitating effect on playwriting in Spain; in any case, the Golden Age came to an effective end with the death of Calderon, though the sheer number of plays written between about 1580 and 1680 was astounding. Some observers believe the number exceeds 30,000, while the number is conservatively esti-mated at 10,000. Even if the number is less than the latter figure, the quantity is extraordinary. By virtue of his own enormous output and the variety of styles he attempted, Lope de Vega is often compared to Shakespeare, who was roughly his contemporary. But Lope, like other playwrights of the Gold-en Age, differed markedly from Shakespeare in quality and profundity; scholarly and critical interest in the Elizabethan Period has historically far exceeded that of its Spanish counterpart.

CONCLUSIONS

That Spain was Europe's only "superpower" in the 16th and 17th centuries, only to fall into second-rate status by the 18th century and remain there to this day has intrigued historians for years. Since the Spanish crown had posses-sion of nearly all the "New World" and benefited enormously from the gold and silver it plundered there, one is shocked to learn that the Spanish govern-ment went bankrupt ten times between the years of 1557 and 1662. The reason, most economic historians agree, was utterly incompetent fiscal man-agement on the part of the Spanish government. Since the government en-joyed windfall after windfall of 22-carat gold and pure silver from its empire in the Americas, there was little incentive to impose a taxation system that met the vast expense required to maintain that empire. Some economists have estimated that the interest alone on government indebtedness alone exceeded tax revenues for over a century—hence the numerous declarations of default. In the numerous instances of those bankruptcies, it was customary for the Spanish crown to accuse lenders of deceit and fraud, which served only to increase skepticism about the government's real intentions to repay its debts, in turn causing higher interest rates when "debt renegotiations" began in the wake of every bankruptcy. In the midst of such fiscal chaos there was a similar lack of control over the Spanish empire. Once most of the gold and silver readily available had arrived in Spain (some historians conservatively estimate the total of gold and silver taken from Peru, for example, totaled 13,000 pounds and 26,000 pounds respectively), the Spaniards failed to invest in the economic development of their colonies and allowed them to deteriorate into unproductive demesnes of misery for the many and privilege for the few. It was similar, one scholar has noted, to countries in the 20th century who "enjoyed" vast resources of oil; those resources voided the motivation to seek productive economic endeavors elsewhere. Not only that, but the enormous of amount of gold and silver the Spaniards brought back to Spain caused the worth of those metals to decline precipitously in value.

The result, by the end of the "Age of Gold" (a term that appears ironic in retrospect) there was a profound loss of confidence among many Spaniards. Economic turmoil had little immediate effect on theatre production in Spain, but as the costs for lost wars in Europe and administration in far-flung territories continued to mount, the inevitability of degeneration began to have an impact. The plays of Calderon, some have observed, bear witness to a sense of national decline; some have asserted that Calderon's dramas are attempts to counteract or at least stem the decline, depicting kings in many of his plays as pillars of hoped-for justice and exemplars of longed-for virtue.

Chapter Eight

The Theatre of Elizabethan England

The Elizabethan period in English theatre history (dating from the ascension of Elizabeth I to the throne of England in 1558 to her death in 1603) is most renowned for the playwriting career of one man, namely William Shakespeare (1564–1616). But Shakespeare was an actor as well as a playwright (albeit the author of the some of the greatest plays ever written). Along with other actors and writers for the English theatre, Shakespeare was part of a "golden age" whose accomplishments many believe matched those of Aeschylus, Sophocles, and Euripides in ancient Greece. Shakespeare had little knowledge of ancient Greece except through some secondary sources translated into English. He and his contemporaries were not exactly humanists nor were they completely men of the Renaissance; they were, however, aware of Plautus, Terence, and Seneca. Adaptations and translations of those Roman playwrights became available in English during the early 16th century. The Elizabethan playwrights who used classical Roman precedents, many scholars believe, laid the foundation for English theatre culture as a whole.

English theatre and drama comprises a remarkable contribution to European culture in general, and yet England was a country conquered and occupied for much of its history. Its part in the annals of European history is a story worth repeating, for it has bequeathed a generous legacy to the growth of freedom around the world. Some historians mark the Norman invasion and the subsequent Battle of Hastings in 1066 as a critical juncture in English history, largely because it installed a European ruler (named William the Conqueror, later known as William I) on the English throne. William's conquest upended the English language, introducing an entirely new, Latin-based vocabulary to English natives. The conquering Normans actually did more than introduce their French language to the English; they forced them to speak it, since it became the official language of the new realm, which included large parts of Normandy in France. One can readily conceive of a writer like Shakespeare using French as his language of choice, but the English adapted to French by accretion; by the 14th century, English had become the dominant idiom, which most linguists identify as "Middle English." What Shakespeare learned as a child was "Modern English," which had experienced a number of changes since the 14th century. It had become a modern idiom that lent itself superbly to poetic utterance in public. Shakespeare was himself largely uneducated, having attended only grammar school in his native Stratford-on- Avon. Thereafter he presumably taught himself, according to many who study the language of Elizabethan tragedy, comedy, and history plays. What an intuitive student he must have been! Linguists have estimated that he used about 17,000 different English words to write his plays and sonnets—and 7,000 of those words he used only once. By comparison, the entire King James Bible uses just over 12,000 different English words.

ENGLISH ACTING

According to the scant evidence available, Shakespeare may have become an actor sometime in the early 1590s, for he appears to have been a member of a troupe called the Lord Chamberlain's Men by 1594. The Lord Chamberlain's Men took that name because their sponsor was Henry Carey, who in that year was Lord Chamberlain. Other troupes received sponsorships from powerful patrons, such as the Lord Strange's Men, whose patron was Ferdinando Stanley, Lord Strange. They later became the Earl of Derby's Men, joining the Earl of Pembroke's Men, the Admiral's Men, the Earl of Worcester's Men, and several other troupes who took the name of their sponsor to avoid arrest on charges of vagabondage. Such "Men" were technically servants in the household of the patron who offered them his protection; in reality they were performers almost identical to those medieval sojourners (sometimes called "strolling players") whom they had replaced by the 16th century. The major difference for performers in the latter third of the 16th century was the city of London, which by the 1570s had a population of about 50,000, a bustling port economy thanks to international trade, and audiences who wanted to see plays.

By 1572, actors were granted immunity from the law against vagabondage, and in 1574 the Master of Revels accepted licensing responsibility for and authority over all plays which troupes wanted to present. Theatre must have emerged as a worthy investment by the mid-1570s, for the first theatre structures were erected in 1576, first the Red Lion in Whitechapel (north of the River Thames), just outside the city's official borders. The Theatre was the second such structure, likewise constructed outside city precincts and on the north bank of the Thames. Building theatres outside the jurisdiction of London's Lord Mayor was a result of the 1572 mayoral ban against theatre, which the Lord Mayor's office considered a vector of bubonic plague. Three years later, the Mayor ordered the removal of all actors from the city. Thus James Burbage, manager of the Lord Chamberlain's Men, thought it best to erect his theatre (the aforementioned The Theatre) outside the city limits. Shakespeare is thought to have worked and premiered some of his plays with Burbage, though the company dismantled their theatre in 1598. They ultimately used the pieces of that dismembered building to build another structure, which they erected on the south side of the Thames in 1599 and christened it The Globe. That is the theatre with which Shakespeare is most closely associated, since it saw the premieres of his most famous tragedies.

The Globe was less a venue for viewing stagings of plays than a stationary machine for acting like its predecessor The Theatre and its architectural equivalents The Swan, The Red Bull, and the indoor theatres in London such as Blackfriars. In nearly all cases, Elizabethan playhouses featured a platform stage on which neither scenery nor settings were present. The platform was thought to be about 43 feet wide and 27 feet deep; over the platform was a roof-like structure to protect the actors from rain and other natural elements. If you are familiar with normal English climatic conditions, you know that the weather is frequently inclement; rainy days outnumber days without rain by more than 2 to 1 in England. Rain did not stop the actors from performing, however. The troupes could not afford to provide audiences with rain checks, so the show literally had to go on. The actors were in any case protected from the elements; so were most audience members. Some aristocrats or rich merchants bought the most expensive seats, located on the acting platform in full view of the audience. Sometimes these on-stage audience members interfered with actors in the middle of a performance; they felt entitled to do so, as they had paid the highest admission price. The "groundlings," those audience members who stood in front of and around the acting platform, were not so fortunate. But they had paid the lowest admission price and had no protection against rain, sleet, hail, or anything else falling from the sky during a performance.

The acting platform in most Elizabethan theatres stood about five feet above ground level. Under the platform were passageways which actors could use to enter from below or even speak from under the platform. This was a presentational style of theatre, in which the actors openly and often acknowledged the presence of the audience in the form of soliloquies and asides. There was no illusion as to the location of the action, either. Instead of visual scenery, the Elizabethan theatre employed "spoken" scenery, by which characters in the play usually described the location in which they found themselves. The most obvious entrances and exits onto and from the acting platform were two upstage doors, located on the back stage wall and separat-

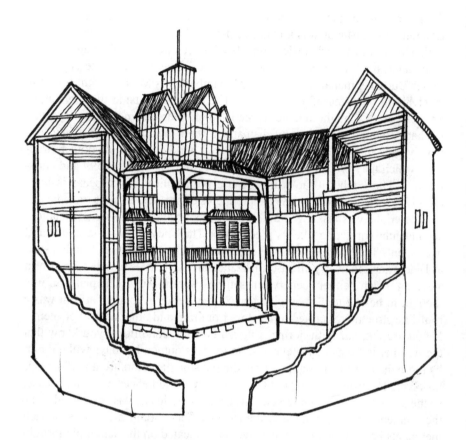

Figure 8.1.   Globe Theatre, London.

ed by what Shakespeare and others called the "within." The "within" was actually a small secondary stage located directly "within" the upstage wall at the center of the platform between the aforementioned two doors. A curtain concealed all manner of devices and stage properties on the "within," such as beds (in *Othello*), pillories (in *King Lear*), altars (in *Cymbeline*), and other contrivances. Directly above the "within" was the "above," which was essentially a balcony. From this balcony numerous scenes took place, most famously the encounter between Romeo and Juliet. Above that balcony was another balcony, where the musicians were seated. The musicians in Elizabethan theatres were crucially important because their efforts (and sounds) maintained the performance's pacing. Often in Elizabethan plays the stage directions call for "alarums within," which was a signal for musicians to create a kind of fanfare announcing the end of one scene and the beginning of another. Playwrights usually announced the end of one scene and the beginning of another by having a character speak a couplet, such as Hamlet's

> I'll have grounds
> More relative than this—the play's the thing
> Wherein I'll catch the conscience of the King.

Such poetic usage likewise signaled to the audience an exit of one group of characters and the entrance of another group. Since the Elizabethan playhouse had no house curtain, no lighting, and no sound equipment, it depended entirely on the actors' use of the theatre's architecture and the playwright's words to move the play from one scene to another. One can readily see the efficacy of such architecture and spoken scenery in a 1944 film of Shakespeare's *Henry V*, directed by Laurence Olivier in 1944 and starring himself in the title role.

Some observers have noted the complete absence of women as performers in these theatres (contrary to the plot of *Shakespeare in Love*, a 1998 Oscar-winning film). *Shakespeare in Love* features a short-lived performance at the Globe by a woman posing as a boy performer, who in turn plays a female role (by Gwyneth Paltrow; Joseph Fiennes plays Shakespeare). The absence of women on the English stage is best explained by the high status theatre troupes enjoyed by virtue of their aforementioned association with aristocratic households. There were no similar restrictions placed on female performers elsewhere in Europe at the time, with the possible exception of Spain. But even in Spain, the imagined association between a woman acting on the stage and a woman prostituting herself was a close one. The numerous published restrictions, decrees, and laws against women on the stage is a good indication as to how ineffective those measures must have been.

Boy Actors

We do well, then, to remember that all the roles in Elizabethan theatre were written for men or boys. Boys whose voices had not yet changed played fascinating female roles such as Rosalind, Ophelia, Beatrice, Cordelia, Cymbeline, Queen Anne, and others—a practice that seems culturally archaic by today's standards. Judging yesterday's performance practices by today's standards, however, is akin to judging yesterday's eating habits, sanitary standards, the institution of slavery, or the ownership of property by today's standards. Such judgments are best described as "intertemporal abstractions," according to one economist-historian who has studied such historical phenomena at length. That females were barred from performing onstage was similar to barring a female the command of an Elizabethan military regiment; some women could certainly perform or fight as well as any man. But Elizabethan society, like nearly all hierarchical societies, awarded positions of high status to men. Why?

When certain endeavors such as theatre become institutionalized, some philosophers have observed, hierarchical societies invest those endeavors with "transcendent meaning," which makes them objects in the primordial struggle for status. A struggle for status is not the same as the struggle for wealth, land, or possessions. Status cannot be consumed. Yet people strive nevertheless for status by competing for prizes, such as the prize of a goat in ancient Athens or for the prestige of being numbered among an aristocratic household in Elizabethan England. Status furthermore status has relative, rather than absolute value. When actors compete for juicy roles in movies or prizes such as the Oscar, the competition is different from their struggle for money or a fancy house in Hollywood or Bel-Air, California. In those struggles, somebody can achieve an economically valuable possession. But the struggle for status comes at the expense of someone else. For an actor to win an Oscar in Hollywood or a Tony on Broadway—or to have won a similar prize in 4th-century BC Athens—some other actor must lose the competition and go home empty handed. There are no "win-win" results in the contest for status. The struggle is a "zero-sum" game with distinct winners and losers, and the game can be indeed both brutal and bloody.

Males struggle viciously with each other for status, and hierarchical societies do not want men and women competing with each other for the same high-status positions. Why not? Such societies want their members (women, children, and men) to survive. The result, using the Academy Awards as an example, is a system of separate categories for "outstanding performance" by actors and actresses. The American Academy of Motion Picture Arts and Sciences makes a clear distinction between male and female performers. So did the Elizabethans, which demonstrates the importance of cultural activity in a hierarchical society. Like the Greeks, the Elizabethans viewed theatre as a kind of institution. Both developed values and institutions based on biological certainties, and those values were communicated to children in preparation for adulthood. As in all human societies, pre-adolescent girls and boys have roughly proportional levels of strength, talent, endurance, intelligence, and other characteristics. For every intelligent boy there was no doubt an equally intelligent girl, and for every girl talented in acting there was surely an equally talented boy. The same proportion holds for unintelligent or untalented children.

Yet all societies have recognized, in one way or another, the fact that boys possess greater tendencies towards aggression than do girls—especially as boys grow to manhood. That is because, according to several evolutionary biologists, the brain of the male is sensitized to the aggression-related properties of testosterone present during fetal development. The female brain *in utero* does not develop in a similar way. Feminists have argued that boys are more aggressive because society allows them to be, and many scholars agree with that assessment. Societies must accommodate male aggression and conform to biological fact if they want to survive. Societies thus socialize girls away from direct, aggressive competition with boys for positions of high status. By the time boys and girls reach adulthood, male aggression in most cases far outstrips its female counterpart. Because males compete for status and recognition so aggressively, some assume that males turn their aggressive energies toward females and "oppressed them out" of high-status positions. In reality, men have turned their aggressive energies towards attaining those positions against *all* competitors for high status. The fact that women lose out in the competition is a by-product of male aggression advantage. The establishment of an all-male hierarchy has neither purpose nor goal of excluding females. Whether the losers in the competition for status are females or males is important only insofar as society attaches different expectations to men and women. Such was the dynamic at work during every civilization we have undertaken to examine, and it was certainly at work during the Elizabethan period among actors, playwrights, and the aristocrats who endowed them with the status of the social positions. The "Lord Admiral's Men," the "Earl of Derby's Men," the "Earl of Pembroke's Men, the "Duke of York's Men," and ultimately the "King's Men" are all manifestations of such dynamics at work.

Elizabethan Acting Companies

Most Elizabethan acting companies consisted of ten to twenty members, all of whom toured with the company and many of whom sought to work in London. Half the men were "share holders" in the company, which means they were partners who divided among themselves company profits and expenses. Among the most significant of company expenses were the salaries of the "hired men," who played adult roles throughout the season and on tour, though strictly as employees, not as sharers. Hired men thus had little influence in the choice of plays for presentation, before a paying public or at court performances. Apprentices were boys who in nearly all instances played female roles. Boys received their training in "lines of business" (the character type they were assigned) by studying with and assisting share holders, many of whom had likewise begun their careers as boys in a theatre troupe.

Lines of business (sometimes called "type casting") were well known in Shakespeare's day, and perhaps the most well known among all the actors in Shakespeare's company was the leading man and hero-type Richard Burbage (1567–1619), the son of James Burbage and a leading share holder in the company. Shakespeare probably wrote roles like Hamlet, Othello, Richard III, Macbeth, Marc Antony, and Coriolanus for Burbage, and indeed he may have been the inspiration for Shakespeare in the creation of those great roles. Other share holders in the company included John Heminges, Augustine Phillips, Thomas Pope, William Kempe, and William Shakespeare himself. The comic actor Will Kempe was a skilled acrobat, juggler, and clown-type who is thought to have played the numerous comic roles in both tragedies and comedies. Tradition has it that Shakespeare played "character roles" (those parts which are essentially "supporting roles" that help move the plot forward or provide insights into the leading characters). The most noteworthy non-actor among the share holders in the Lord Chamberlain's and later the King's Men was Cuthbert Burbage (1566–1636), who was James Burbage's elder brother. Cuthbert's financial and managerial skills were thought to have equaled his brother's as an actor.

Before rehearsals began, each actor received as "side" of the play, never a whole script. Such practices protected the company from plagiarized performance by another troupe, since there were no copyright laws in effect during the Elizabethan period. Every play, however, required the permission of the Master of Revels for public performance, and every company had to pay the Master of Revels a substantial fee before such permission was granted. The opportunities for graft and corruption were abundant in such an arrangement, so there is small wonder that the Master of Revels was a much sought-after position at the English court.

Audiences for public performance were heterogeneous, consisting of aristocrats, merchants, families, tradesman, and the "general," largely illiterate, scum of the earth. Yet this heterogeneous audience had by the 1570s developed a taste for poetic expression, perhaps the way American pop music audiences had developed a taste for street poetry in 1980s. Such poetry came to be known as "rap music" or "hip hop" in the United States, but the emphasis was, as in Elizabethan England, on rhythm. Some cultural historians have insisted that human beings need and seek out poetic expression. In our world, as in the Elizabethan world, most language is mundane, functional, and prosaic. Compared to the rhetorical content of even the average letter in Elizabethan times, our contemporary speech is mediocre indeed; but what seems to be a need for rhythmic utterance is the same. Rhythmic, often lyrical delivery by actors has the potential to capture the imagination, hold our attention, and provoke deep emotions—at least, that is what experts such as Aristotle say. What many fail to mention, however, is the practical application of poetic utterance in performance. That application was probably discovered thousands of years ago among ancient bards, fabulists, grios, raconteurs, balladeers, and rhapsodists who nightly gathered informal audiences by the campfire and retold tales of gods and tribal enmity, suffering and heroics. That is essentially what Homer did when he is thought to have recited his tales and sung his songs in mid-9th century BC Greece. Homer's innovation was to recite in Greek hexameters; hexameters in Greek, like pentameters in English, force hearers initially to concentrate on what the bard is saying. Why? Due to the many distractions around a campfire, a bard's encantatory utterance had to attract and then hold his audience's complete attention. That encantation was initially difficult to understand, but subsequently the audience became "enchanted," which caused them (or at least most of them) to pay closer attention. Remember also that Homer and other rhapsodists needed to make a living. That was especially true of Homer, who was not only homeless but blind. Thus if he did not capture the audience with his tale, he was likely to remain hungry as well.

Elizabethan Drama

The same encantatory dynamic that profited Homer was at work in the creation of Elizabethan drama. There were myriad sounds outside the theatre structures to distract Elizabethan audiences. Pedestrian tumult in the street, the sound of barge traffic on the River Thames, fishmongers hawking their wares—these and many other noises combined to form a clamor not easily overcome during the performance of a play. There were no microphones, no megaphones, no means of amplification, just the actor and the words he had memorized. Those words the playwright had carefully selected on the basis of their rhythmic potential, their rhyme scheme, and their intestinal impact (sometimes called the "gut response") to capture the audience's attention and then hold their attention for up to three hours—and in some plays, even longer.

Elizabethan playwrights are thought to have begun writing in blank verse during the 1560s, but the one most often credited with creating the kind of language most applicable to the Elizabethan stage was Christopher Marlowe (1564–1593), who is thought to have begun his playwriting career around 1586. Marlowe's extraordinary innovation was the "mighty line," according to playwright Ben Jonson. Jonson was referring of course more than just one line; it was Marlowe's use of unrhymed blank verse that seemed rhythmically to push a line of iambic pentameter into the following line, giving the aural impression of a mighty current. Or perhaps it was like a mighty wind in the sails of a ship, pushing it through the waves. A good example of Marlowe's use of iambic pentameter comes at a play's beginning (where the Elizabethan playwright had to establish rhythmic patterns to capture the audience's attention). *Tamburlaine the Great*, Part I, written in 1587, is thought to have been Marlowe's first big hit play:

> From jigging veins of rhyming mother-wits,
> And such conceits as clownage keeps in pay,
> We'll lead you to the stately tent of war,
> Where you shall hear the Scythian Tamburlaine
> Threatening the world with high astounding terms,
> And scourging kingdoms with his conquering sword.
> View but his picture in this tragic glass,
> And then applaud his fortunes as you please.

Such opening speeches appeared in many plays (including those of Shakespeare), "setting the stage" for the full-length drama to come, while also setting the tone of the proceedings and allowing the audience members to settle in their places, usually within a rounded arena meant to display blood sports such as dog fights and bear baiting. Blood sports were a long way from drama's beginnings in the Elizabethan period; drama had been taught in school for at least a century before plays began to be performed. Most schools' curricula used plays by Plautus, Terence, and Seneca as devices for teaching Latin to pupils. Those pupils presumably began to imitate Roman playwrights, but also to write in English and give the plays English settings and characters. Nicholas Udall (1505–1556), for example, wrote *Ralph Roister Doister* in the late 1530s as an imitation of Plautus's *Miles Gloriosus* (The Braggart Warrior). Thomas Norton (1532–1584) and Thomas Sackville 1536–1608) wrote *Gorboduc* in 1561, based on Seneca and is thought to be the first English tragedy to employ blank verse. *Gorboduc* is more importantly a forerunner to Shakespeare's *King Lear*, since its plot involves an old king who divides his realm among his two sons; they then quarrel over their legacy and the younger kills the elder. Thomas Preston (1537–1598) was a schoolmaster whose *Cambyses, King of Persia* (1561) was among the first "chronicle" plays. It set forth a figure from history as a kind of object lesson, much as Marlowe later with *Edward II* (1593) and Shakespeare with *Richard III* (1594) were to do. The chronicle play employed a compressed episodic structure of historical events into about two and one half hours of performance, often with a strong secular ruler at the center of the action.

Other important Elizabethan dramatists were Thomas Kyd (1558–1594), whose *The Spanish Tragedy, or Hieronymo Is Mad Again* (1587) was among the first "revenge" tragedies of the 16th century. This form was so popular that many scholars believe *The Spanish Tragedy* to be the most frequently performed tragedy of any in that century. Kyd was influenced in large measure by Seneca's use of the revenge motif, as Shakespeare later was most famously to do in *Hamlet* (1602). Still later we see revenge as a central motivation in *The Maid's Tragedy* (1619) by Francis Beaumont (1584–1616), completed by John Fletcher (1579–1625). John Lyly (1554–1606) was best known for "pastoral comedies" such as *Campaspe* (1584), *Endimion, The Man in the Moon* (1588), and *Love's Metamorphosis* (1590). His were considered delicate plays with sylvan settings, where shepherds and shepherdesses tended their flocks while speaking refined, artificial prose. We find similar characters in some of the pastoral comedies of Shakespeare, just as there are precedents for Shakespeare in the works of Robert Greene (1558–1592). The most noteworthy of Greene's precedents is the charming and resourceful heroine, who appears later as Shakespeare's Beatrice in *Much Ado About Nothing* (1598), Rosalind in *As You Like It* (1599), and Viola in *Twelfth Night* (1600).

Who was William Shakespeare?

We perhaps know more about Jesus of Nazareth than we do about William Shakespeare of Stratford upon Avon. We know that Stratford was his birthplace, and there is evidence that he attended school there until he was about 14 years old. At age 18 he married a woman named Anne Hathaway in Stratford. She was about seven years his senior. Pregnant at the time of their marriage, she bore him twins six months after their marriage. He was a share holder in the Lord Chamberlain's Men, and they esteemed him. He died in Stratford in 1616. Other than that, there is little else concrete to report. There have long been rumors that he did not write the plays attributed to him, largely because his lack of a formal education would have prevented his knowledge of courtly language and made the sheer sophistication of his work impossible. Yet he was a *bona fide* share holder in the Lord Chamberlain's Men and its successor company the King's Men. His college-educated contemporaries, such as the aforementioned Richard Greene and later Ben Jonson (1572–1637), mildly mocked him as a plagiarist and unlettered primitive. No one has any idea where Shakespeare, whoever he was, actually learned the difficult skills required of playwriting and poetic composition, though many have surmised that he was a keen observer of mores and manners as a member of the Elizabethan theatre word. Some have maintained, as noted earlier, that he was an outstanding actor in the company, but little evidence supporting such claims exists. A writer named Nicholas Rowe (1674–1718) attempted to write the first biography of Shakespeare, and from it have sprung many assumptions which later proved apocryphal. A 2011 film titled *Anonymous* (directed by Roland Emmerich and starring Rhys Ifans as Edward de Vere, Vanessa Redgrave as Queen Elizabeth I, Sebastian Armesto as Ben Jonson, and Rafe Spall as Shakespeare) insists, as do many serious scholars, that Shakespeare's plays were actually the product of the 11th Earl of Oxford (the aforementioned Edward de Vere). Subsequent efforts to discover more evidence of Shakespeare's identity have resulted in even further guesswork. Shakespeare died a relatively affluent landowner, which some believe is testimony to his value as the premiere writer associated with the King's Men. Members of the company published his work in 1623 (called the "First Folio"), probably because they wanted to capitalize on his name before the plays (which were, as were all plays at the time, in the public domain) became a highly profitable source of income for various other theatre troupes. Shakespeare is thought personally to have overseen the publication of his poetry in the 1590s and of his sonnets in 1609, which were purely profit-making ventures. His earnings as a member of the Lord Chamberlain's and the King's Men were based, however, on his status as a company share holder, not as a writer.

But Shakespeare the playwright remains the most well-known, widely studied, and most frequently performed individual Elizabethan—perhaps indeed the most frequently performed playwright in history. Few argue with his "rank" as an equal to the ancient Greeks. His colleagues, when they published his plays in 1623, regarded him so. While "ranking" playwrights, poets, composers, painters, or artists of any kind, is often a foolhardy task, it is clear that William Shakespeare occupies an exalted place in the annals of literature for the stage. But Shakespeare is more than just an author for the stage, or a "dramatic poet," as he is sometimes described. He was a complete man of the theatre with a total comprehension of acting, staging, and design who attempted all the popular dramatic modes and subjects of his day and gave each their most accomplished—and at times, their most profound—form and expression.

Shakespeare was most accomplished in speech and character. His plots are largely forgettable—or at least unmemorable. It is true that Romeo and Juliet die, but who remembers their sad end before they remember lines like, "Romeo, Romeo, wherefore art thou Romeo?" The same is true of masterpieces like *Hamlet*. It is never completely clear, for example, what Hamlet does or does not do, nor why he hesitates in doing. And what does Hamlet do, anyway? He is lured into a sword fight at the end of the play and a series of accidental deaths ensue—but is that important? No. What makes the play memorable are Hamlet's lengthy speeches about himself and why he can't seem to make up his mind about killing his father's murderer. In well-acted and superbly staged productions of *Hamlet, Macbeth, Othello*, or any of the other masterpieces Shakespeare wrote, most audiences do not care so much about the play's plot so much as they care about what happens to the characters. Audiences are fascinated by the way Iago takes advantage of Othello's natural tendency towards jealousy, or the way Lady Macbeth can manipulate her husband. Richard Plantagenet, the Duke of Gloucester (later King Richard III) is among the most manipulative and nefarious of all Shakespeare's characters, yet audiences consistently find him fascinating—as well as profoundly evil. *Richard III* was probably Shakespeare's first hit play (it is generally assumed that it premiered in 1594) and in it, Shakespeare manifests a number of skills that reappear in his later plays and mark him as a masterful dramatist.

Shakespeare was a poet able to create dialogue that was riveting and able to hold an audience's attention simply from the standpoint of sound and melody; today most people study Shakespeare as a poet before they realize that most of his poetry was intended to be spoken before a paying audience. Shakespeare was furthermore capable of creating aphorisms that remain current to this very day, an indication of his ability to embed himself in the human subconscious. "All at one fell swoop," "The play's the thing," "Sweets to the sweet," "All the world's a stage," "Out, damned spot!,"

"Pomp and circumstance," "It was all Greek to me," "A man more sinned against than sinning," "He wears his heart upon his sleeve," "A tale told by an idiot," "Neither a borrower nor a lender be," "Something wicked this way comes," "Farwell the tranquil mind!," and dozens of other aphorisms have incalculably enriched the English language. Many of them have been transferred into other languages, where they enjoy a similar level of familiarity. Shakespeare was also adept at inventing words. There are, linguists estimate, about 1700 words in his plays which were not in use in use before his lifetime. As noted earlier, Shakespeare's characters are often so three-dimensional that they transcend the normal barrier of "stage figure" and to many observers become individual personalities in their own right. The numerous and diverse types he created make up large casts composed of various individuals, from inept to heroic, the stupid to brilliant, the young and innocent to the old and corrupt—yet he was able to invest sympathy and interest in all of them.

How did Shakespeare create such compelling figures for the stage? For one, he benefited from a system where plays could be re-worked, re-written, and fine-tuned over and over again for years. Remember that the Lord Chamberlain's Men, like all acting troupes in the Elizabethan era, did their plays in rotating repertoire so as to attract the largest number of paying customers repeatedly. Their performances were by no means set in stone; that is, a mistake by an actor in one performance might prove beneficial to the play as whole and become incorporated into subsequent performances. In like manner, the company would cut from the play a speech or section of dialogue that was not working. This process of "organic editing" by the entire cast of actors served to sharpen, define, and make the playwright's work more effective. As a result, Shakespeare's colleagues in the plays were likely as responsible for the characters' magnetism as was the playwright himself. Among the greatest of the characters Shakespeare created are found in the following plays (by title), listed alphabetically: *A Midsummer Night's Dream, As You Like It, Hamlet, Henry IV* Part 1, *Julius Caesar, King Lear, Macbeth, Measure for Measure, Merchant of Venice, Much Ado About Nothing, Othello, Richard III, The Taming of the Shrew,* and *The Tempest*. Remember, however, that Shakespeare wrote 37 plays. What about the plays which feature somewhat tedious characters and are less frequently performed? To some, for example, *All's Well That Ends Well, Love's Labours Lost,* or *Richard II* are remarkable works, and indeed they may be. But among Shakespeare's truly bad plays are *Titus Andronicus, King John, Henry IV* Part 2, *Troilus and Cressida, Timon of Athens, Cymbeline, Pericles,* and probably worst of all, *The Winter's Tale*. But what makes them bad? Probably the same things that make the great plays good: character and speech.

Shakespeare's plays feature a dramatic structure similar to nearly all Elizabethan plays: short scenes, most of them lasting between five and 15 minutes. Most the plays have about 35 scenes, with no divisions into acts. Such a structure forces the audience to pay closer attention. The plays then cleverly manipulate the architecture the playhouse for which the playwright specifically wrote, using the various entrances, exits, balconies, and platforms available. He employed sub-plots, contrivances, and intrigues which he in most cases was able to unite by play's conclusion. Shakespeare's plays are episodic, as opposed to the climactic structure of Greek tragedies. Many of his plays take place over years and vast geographical areas. A complex network of associations often links the immediate dramatic situation with audience preoccupations, regardless of what language in which the play is performed, irrespective of audience expectations of the play, despite the economic, political, or social situations of audience members. Scholars and critics thus often refer to Shakespeare as a "universal" playwright. Some scholars also refer to him as a "Renaissance" playwright, though the viewpoint in nearly all his plays is medieval, at times Biblical.

In Shakespeare's plays, for example, there are frequent discussions and even instances of the negative response of Nature to any departure from God's plan for mankind. Such responses are most frequent whenever the topic of royal usurpation (the violent overthrow of a king) arises, as it often does in the "history plays." These plays (usually with "Henry" or Richard" in the title) focus on the "Wars of the Roses." Those conflicts were civil combats involving the houses of Lancaster and York in the aftermath of the Lancastrian Henry Bolingbroke's 1399 usurpation of Richard II, the last Norman king. Shakespeare took as his New Testament text in this and other history plays the admonition of St. Paul in his Epistle to the Romans (13: 1-7): "Let every person be subject to the governing authorities. For there is no authority except from God, and those that exist have been instituted by God. Therefore he who resists what God has appointed will incur judgment. For rulers are not a terror to good conduct but to bad. Would you have no fear of him who is in authority? Then do what is good and you will receive his approval, for he is God's servant for your good . . . ." Usurpation is present in Shakespeare's tragedies as well, as storms arise, rains fall, and winds howl in response to the treatment King Lear endures. Hamlet likewise suffers psychological storms and disturbances when he is unable to act in accordance with God's plan to "set right" the time in which he lives, his uncle having thrown it "out of joint" by pouring poison into the rightful king's ear, thus killing him.

Perhaps the best example of Shakespeare's medieval, non-Renaissance dramatic viewpoint is from a famous passage from one of his worst plays, titled *Troilus and Cressida*. In this passage, the Greek warrior Ulysses tells King Agamemnon that he is getting bad advice from his underlings, and Nature abhors such activity. Since the gods have placed Agamemnon in the position of king, he should therefore act like a king, telling him

"The heavens themselves, the planets and this center
Observe degree, priority, and place,
Insisture, course, proportion, season, form,
Office, and custom, all in line of order.
And therefore is the glorious planet Sol
In noble eminence enthroned and sphered
Amidst the others, whose medicinable eye
Corrects the ill aspécts of planets evil
And posts like a commandment of a king,
Sans check to good and bad. But when the planets
In evil mixture to disorder wander,
What plagues and what portents, what mutiny,
What raging of the sea, shaking of earth,
Commotion in the winds, frights, changes, horrors,
Divert and crack, rend and deracinate,
The unity and married calm of states
Quite from their fixure! Oh, when degree is shaked
Which is the ladder to all high designs,
The enterprise is sick! How could communities,
Degrees in schools and brotherhoods in cities,
Peaceful commerce from dividable shores,
The primogenitive and due of birth,
Prerogative of age, crowns, scepters, laurels,
But by degree, stand in authentic place?
Take but degree away, untune that string,
And hark, what discord follows! Each thing meets
in mere oppugnancy. The bounded waters
Should lift their bosoms higher than the shores
And make a sop of all this solid globe.
Strength should be lord of imbecility,
And the rude son should strike his father dead.
Force should be right, or rather, right and wrong,
Between whose endless jar justice resides,
Should lose their names, and so should justice too.
Then everything includes itself in power,
Power into will, will into appetite,
And appetite, a universal wolf,
So doubly seconded with will and power
Must make perforce a universal prey
And last eat up himself. Great Agamemnon,
This chaos, when degree is suffocate,
Follows the choking.
And this neglection of degree it is
That by a pace goes backward, and with a purpose
It hath to climb. The general's disdained
By him one step below, he by the next,
That next by him beneath. So every step,
Exampled by the first pace that is sick
Of his superior, grows to an envious fever

Of pale and bloodless emulation.

The Elizabethan world was full of ambitious courtiers seeking favors from the Queen, her advisors, or others in power. Shakespeare often made use of a visual metaphor called the "Wheel of Fortune" to describe the intricacies of power relations at court. Man disrupts the divine plan for victory, peace, or prosperity through ambition. It is a medieval concept, many scholars agree, to describe the fickle arbitrariness of human fate. Shakespeare makes mention of Fortune's wheel in *Henry V, King Lear, Hamlet*, and it shows up in numerous other Elizabethan dramas. The medieval world, certainly in the Elizabethan period, cherished domestic tranquility because there was so much evidence of its opposite everywhere they looked. Yet no one could reasonably claim all the privileges and protections of society and then refuse its duties. Man was bound up in the unity of life, as part of the body of the Church and also part of the body of the nation. There was no such thing as an isolated individual. A man has a duty to the state, and he must discharge that duty, as one theologian has put it, "even if a Nero is on the throne."

Shakespeare benefited nevertheless from Renaissance winds and the increasing flow of knowledge coming up from Italy, along with ideas and conventions that influenced several other of his contemporaries. As noted earlier, the sources for his plays were sometimes English translations of classics by Ovid, Plutarch, and Pliny. Among the most well known of classical sources was Plautus, whose *The Menaechmus Twins* Shakespeare transformed into *The Comedy of Errors*. He was also aware of Italian neo-classical writers who pre-dated him, such Ludovico Ariosto (1474–1533), Giovanni Fiorentino (1418–1506), and Giovanni Battista Giraldi Cinthio (1504–1573), often borrowing from their works when writing plays set in Italy. The writer most predominant in the works of Shakespeare, Marlowe, John Webster and other contemporaries was Seneca, as noted earlier. The use of extreme violence such as the on-stage blinding of Gloucester in *King Lear*, the mutilations and tortures of *Titus Andonicus*, the dismemberments in *The Duchess of Malfi*, and the impalement of Marlowe's Edward II with a red hot iron poker up his anus ("a willing sodomite in life, hence a hell-bound sodomite in death," according to one critic) are examples of the "Senecan" fascination with cruelty that was popular among the English.

Shakespeare Subsequent to the Elizabethan Period

Shakespeare lived and thrived after Queen Elizabeth's death, both literally and figuratively. In 1603, King James VI of Scotland became King James I of England, ushering in the so-called "Jacobean" period of theatre and drama; during this period Shakespeare wrote some of his most well known and skillfully written works, including *Measure for Measure* and *Othello* (1604), *Macbeth* and *King Lear* (1605). *Antony and Cleopatra* (1606) and *The Tem-*

pest (1612). After his former colleagues published his plays in 1623, any troupe could perform, edit, abridge, or alter them any way they saw fit. The immediate result is not clearly known, but the easy accessibility to and wide popularity of his work leads most observers to believe that it remained in the repertoires of English playhouses until the "Puritan Termination" closed all theatres in London and curtailed touring troupes throughout England in September of 1642. The Puritans had gained martial control of London in 1645, and in that year they ordered the cessation of all theatre activity in the realm. The theatres remained closed until 1660, when the monarchy was restored.

With the Restoration came numerous Renaissance ideas, such as neo-classicism. As we have already seen, neo-classicism consisted for the most part of theories attempting to recapitulate the theatrical concepts of theorists such as Aristotle and Horace. Neo-classicism demanded the clear separation of tragic and comic genres; Shakespeare's tragedies almost always included comic scenes. Neo-classicism also demanded that the action of plays take place in one day—and Shakespeare's plays often cover lengthy periods of time, while also taking place in a variety of venues. Such conventions stood in clear violation of the neo-classical demand for the setting to be in one specific locale. Since Shakespeare was in many instances a playwright whose assumptions bore a distinctly medieval stamp, his reputation went into a kind of eclipse in the later 17th century; those decades embraced a rationalism which rejected most of the Middle Ages as superstitious and crudely old-fashioned. Critics and commentators in the later 17th and early 18th centuries admired the poetry in his plays, but the plays themselves they considered clumsy and "unrealistic." Theatre managers often abridged comic passages from his plays and used them for laughs between acts of other plays. Actors such as Thomas Betterton (1635–1710), however, continued to use Shakespeare's most famous plays as vehicles for themselves in star productions. You may see a superb rendition of Betterton in the 2004 film *Stage Beauty*, with Tom Wilkinson as Betterton playing a rather overwrought Othello. By the mid-1700s Shakespeare's plays found a more welcoming audience, as actors like David Garrick (1717–1779) in England and Friedrich Ludwig Schroeder (1744–1816) in Germany found in Shakespearean heroes the kind of vehicle nearly every actor needs to advance his career. The fact that women were allowed on English stages beginning in 1660 is also significant, since their performances of Shakespearean heroines were altogether novel when compared with the original performances of boys in such roles. Maria Hughes (played by Claire Danes in the aforementioned *Stage Beauty*) and Anne Bracegirdle (1671–1748) were early successes as Desdemona in *Othello,* while Peg Woffington (1720–1760) and Sarah Siddons (1755–1831) were often Garrick's colleagues as Lady Macbeth, Rosalind, Ophelia, and Volumnia (in *Coriolanus*). As a result of the successful productions of Shakespeare both in England and in continental Europe, critics such as Samuel Johnson

(1709–1784) and Edmond Malone (1741–1812) in England, along with Johann Wolfgang von Goethe (1749–1832) in Germany extolled Shakespeare as an exemplary playwright, even if he was a primitive and largely ignorant of neo-classical rules of playwriting.

The "Storm and Stress" movement in Germany re-discovered in Shakespeare a kind of authenticity which was lacking in neo-classical tragedies. Numerous playwrights attempted to imitate Shakespeare by creating plays employing large casts, violent imagery, lyrical dialogue, and arresting characters. The German theatre did more than simply imitate. Several gifted writers created numerous prose translations in German by the end of the 18th century. By the early 19th century translations into verse were published, and they proved to be so popular that many Germans began to assume that Shakespeare was actually a German playwright. In England, Shakespeare's medieval characteristics found new appreciation, largely for the same reasons the Germans found in him a singular authenticity. The fact that so many characters in Shakespeare have such intense feelings pleased critics and audiences who believed that the emotions were closer to the force of truth in human existence than was reason. Romanticism completely discredited neo-classicism with its restraints and ushered in a new era of acting that privileged oration and declamation, and actors won the most praise for something called "poetic fire" in performance. Scholars began to rediscover the Elizabethan stage space by the mid-19th century, substituting unit stages for changeable scenery and allowing the stage to function as a bare set, permitting the primordial cinematic structure of the plays to prevail.

In the 20th century Shakespeare became emblematic of that century's obsession with cultural decay, fragmentation, distortion, and atrocious violence. Thousands of productions attempted to "contemporize" Shakespeare in ways he himself of course could never have imagined. But the rise of the modern director in the early 20th century allowed individuals to make "statements" about the contemporary world, about the relations among ethnic groups, between the sexes, about homosexuality, colonialism, and myriad other identity-based compulsions. Most significant of all treatments were those found in film, which became the 20th century's predominant and most popular form of performance. In 1908 versions of *Antony and Cleopatra* and *Romeo and Juliet* appeared, and one observer has estimated that over 400 creditable feature-length films with Shakespeare's plays as their basis were made after them through the 1900s. It is beginning to look as though the 21st century will witness the continuation of such film making. Among the first in the 21st century was a British production of *Othello* in 2001), set in the police force of contemporary London. *Kannaki*, an Indian film in the Malayalam language based on *Antony and Cleopatra*, appeared in 2002. In 2010 Julie Taymor directed a version of *The Tempest* with Helen Mirren as "Prospera" as a sorceress, normally played by a male performer as Prospero. Reviews of that film were generally negative, though it was nominated for an Academy Award in costuming. Few movies based on Shakespeare do well with critics or audiences, largely because the plays remain blueprints for live performance. Some, however have won numerous accolades: the 1948 Laurence Olivier production of *Hamlet* won the Academy Award for Best Picture. Akira Kurosawa's 1961 film version of *Hamlet*, titled *Warui yatsu hodo yoku nemuru* (*The Bad Sleep Well*) likewise won numerous awards a decade later. Kurosawa's other adaptations of Shakespeare, such as his 1957 *Throne of Blood* (*Macbeth*) and his 1985 *Ran* (*King Lear*) are as different from each other as are the Ukrainian versions of *King Lear* (1971) and *Hamlet* (1964), both adapted and directed by Gregori Kozintsev.

CONCLUSIONS

The few film examples cited above serve to demonstrate how Shakespeare will likely remain important in both theatre and film history. His plays will no doubt continue to manifest a unique, character-based intensity in both live and recorded performance for a succession of generations, well into the future. Because Shakespeare historically has been so popular and has also won so many admirers who neither speak nor understand English, his work has served as a common denominator among numerous cultures. One may see what constituted "neurotic," for example, when one sees the Olivier 1948 film of *Hamlet*. The 1936 film production of *As You Like It* with Olivier seems hopelessly romanticized now, just as his 1955 portrayal of Gloucester in Richard III seems now so hopelessly idiosyncratic. One may experience what was considered "realistic" when one studies the 1920 stage version of *Hamlet* starring John Barrymore. One can discover what audiences considered "heroic" in Edmund Kean's 1814 performance of *Hamlet*, what was "American" in Edwin Forrest's 1837 performance of *Macbeth*, or "noble suffering" in Tommaso Salvini's *Othello* in 1886. Similar discoveries can occur when studying Shakespeare's characters when Germans, Russians, or Swedes play them. The same may be said of acting performances that took place centuries ago when David Garrick created a sensation as Coriolanus in 1754, as did Thomas Betterton in 1681 as King Lear, despite—or because— Betterton played Lear in a bizarre adaptation of the play. One might list hundreds of actors and actresses who have played Shakespeare over the centuries, and in almost every instance there is ample evidence of both unique individuality and a concomitant universality present.

By contemporary standards of Shakespearean performance, very few productions from history would seem realistic, heroic, noble, idiosyncratic, or even convincing. Yet in a world like ours, dominated by mass media, devoid of poetic expression, speaking for the most part in language that is mundane, functional, and prosaic, audiences continue to crave a spoken idiom capable of capturing the imagination, holding our attention, and provoking intense feelings. Many of Shakespeare's characters bear startling resemblance to contemporary characters. Richard III, for example, is a possible prototype for Saddam Hussein, Fidel Castro, Robert Mugabe, or Nancy Pelosi. *Much Ado About Nothing* is about accepting gossip as truth, much as the press and mass media nowadays spread rumors and gossip in supermarket tabloids. *Richard II* is about the role of personality in government leadership, a problem similar to "cults of personality" in North Korea, Russia, Iran, or under Cold War regimes in the persons of Stalin, Mao Zedong, Pol Pot, or Ho Chi Minh. We remain fascinated by such people—perhaps because they remind us of others we know—or perhaps because they provide us with engrossing depictions of ourselves.

Chapter Nine

The German Theatre to 1700

The German-language theatre in Europe had several promising starts, despite the fact that "Germany" as a unified state never formally existed until the 19th century. There were scores of small German-speaking courts and numerous wealthy cities in which theatre could have developed supportive audiences, as had been the case with the English in London, the French in Paris, and the Spaniards in Madrid. German-speaking touring troupes had performed throughout the Middle Ages, and German bishoprics often supported performances of ecclesiastical drama such as morality plays, saints' plays, and passion plays. Only after the Protestant Reformation, however, did a secular tradition of dramatic performance become firmly established. That tradition developed mostly in towns along the Baltic coast, in present-day Hessia, Swabia, Tyrol (the German-speaking part of northern Italy), Eger (the German-speaking part of the present-day Czech Republic), and most significantly in parts of Franconia. Secular play production became singularly established in Franconia's largest city, Nuremberg. Festivals celebrating Shrovetide (Carnival Season) there had begun to feature the performances of anonymous farces by about 1400. By mid-century at least one author of some of those farces became known in scripts that listed his pen name, Hans Rosenplüt (Hans Schnepper, ca. 1400–ca. 1450). Rosenplüt was by profession an iron monger, whose specialty was making chain-mail. He is thought to have written about 25 Shrovetide farces, while his "successor" in Nuremberg was a barber named Hans Folz, thought to have been the first Nuremberg author to have printed his plays.

Chapter 9

GERMAN HUMANISM

The inception of German Humanism began to take shape in emulation of northern Italian cities by 1350, as interest in ancient classical values began in southern German-speaking territories bordering the Alps. The reign of Karl IV as Holy Roman Emperor from 1346 to 1378 is noteworthy for the spread of humanism, since two years into his reign he founded a university Prague, a university that still bears his name. It was the first German-speaking university anywhere, and Karl appointed to its faculty men who had studied in Italy and whose fluency in academic Latin was accomplished. The result, according to several historians, was a newly polished form of German usage appearing alongside Latin equivalents; Karl's civil servants were likewise expected to employ the new usage in official imperial business.

Humanism in German experienced additional support during the reign of Holy Roman Emperor Friedrich III, who appointed Enea Silvio Piccolomini (1405–1464) as his chancellor. Piccolomini wrote several treatises flattering the German character, German geography, and many of the Germans' practices, usages, and customs. His work endeared him to many in the Empire, and his translation into German of Tacitus' *Germania* was a revelation to many Germans. Most of them had no previous idea that the Romans possessed any knowledge about Germans (Roman settlements in Vienna, Cologne, Aachen, Trier, and elsewhere notwithstanding), much less that Tacitus bestowed the Germans with generous praise. Emperor Friedrich crowned Piccolomini poet laureate of the Empire in 1442, allowing Piccolomini to bring other Italian intellectuals, writers, and translators to Vienna (the emperor's official residential seat of government), where at the University of Vienna their lectures on the ancient world had a lasting and positive effect. Many Italian scholars, critics, and intellectuals found employment at the Universities of Heidelberg, Cologne, Erfurt, Leipzig, and Rostock, where their influence grew substantially until Piccolomini was elected Pope Pius II in 1458. By that time, German universities had begun cultivating humanists of their own, eventually the most notable of whom was Conrad Celtis (1459–1508). Celtis was a widely published poet when he turned 25 years of age, and in 1487 Emperor Friedrich named Celtis (as he had done with Piccolomini nearly a half century earlier) poet laureate of the Empire. Celtis capitalized on the German fascination with Tacitus and produced an annotated version of *Germania*.

Celtis remains most significant, at least in theatre history, for a discovery he made in 1492. In the library at the local monastery in Regensburg, Celtis found a 500-year old manuscript containing the plays of a 10th-century Saxon nun named Roswitha, who had been canoness of a Benedictine abbey near Gandersheim in Saxony. Her aristocratic ancestry granted her an education in Latin, while her position in Gandersheim allowed her time to write. She wrote legends of saints and other ecclesiastical figures, but most noteworthy were her dramas in Latin. Those dramas were adaptations of comedies by the Roman playwright Terence. Roswitha's works were utterly ignored for five centuries until their discovery, but Celtis managed in 1501 to publish an elaborate edition of them with illustrations by Albrecht Dürer (1471–1528). As he had done with his publication of *Germania*, Celtis used the publication of Roswitha's plays to promote the idea that Germans were indeed partici- pants in the renewal of classical learning that began in Italy. He even boasted that German efforts equaled those of the Italians. Such claims found wide acceptance among the Germans, and they helped win for Celtis an imperial professorship at the University of Vienna.

The 15th century witnessed not only the efforts of Celtis and others in the promotion of German humanism, but also in technological and military events which were to have direct consequences on German culture as a whole. The first was the invention of movable type in around 1450 (some believe the year was 1455, but no one knows precisely) by Johannes Guten- berg (Johannes Gansfleisch, 1398–1468). The printing press had immediate implications for humanism, as readers began to benefit from the rapid dis- semination of knowledge that printing made possible. The fall of Constantin- ople in 1453 vastly increased the flow of documents attesting to the intellec- tual heritage of the West, which mechanical book printing operations all over Germany (there were about 250 presses in Germany by 1500) made readily accessible. Finally, the advances taking place in the science of lens grinding and polishing in the 15th century allowed for the creation of eyeglasses worn on the nose, allowing many scholars, scribes, poets, playwrights, critics, and even actors to prolong considerably their active working years.

The beginning of the 16th century witnessed an explosion of available information, not only in Germany but elsewhere in Europe; humanists had translated a wide array of works from Latin and Greek into vernacular lan- guages, and one of the most significant for 16th century studies in history was Ulrich von Hutten's translation of Lorenzo Valla's treatise on the "Donation of Constantine." The original treatise supposedly came directly from Roman Emperor Constantine the Great in the 4th century AD, granting the Roman popes subsequent dominion over the entire Western Roman Empire. The "Donation," however, proved to be a forgery dating to about 750 AD. Valla and other humanists detected a number of philological inconsistencies in the document and his argument insisting on the fraudulence of "Donation" was so convincing that it gained wide acceptance by the time it was officially published in 1517.

The German Reformation

The year 1517 was important in Germany for another reason: in that year an obscure Roman Catholic priest named Martin Luther initiated the Protestant Reformation by nailing his enumerated objections to the sale of indulgences on the cathedral door in Wittenberg. Luther was interested at first only in reforming a Church practice which he and many other good Catholics found corrupt. He had received a humanist education at the University of Erfurt and like most humanists he was a devout Christian—yet keenly aware of questionable practices within the Roman Church. Like many other humanists, he thought it possible to find points of agreement between Christianity and the classical tradition. But Luther's proposition that the New Testament (first in Greek, which he translated into German in 1522) was alone the basis of Christianity proved to be too much for traditionalists. Many humanists believed the Church could voluntarily cleanse itself of the evils it had created, but Luther called for an end to religious orders and their monasteries, the abolition of saints' days and pilgrimages to saints' shrines, the termination of all inquisitions, and the expulsion of Italians meddling in German affairs.

Luther became a best-selling author as early as 1520, when he published three popular treatises that sold out by the thousands within days of their printing. When his aforementioned translation of the New Testament appeared two years later (with illustrations by Lukas Cranach) the initial run of 3,000 copies sold out within eight weeks and over 300 editions were published during the next quarter century. In 1530 Luther published the work for which he is perhaps best known: the Augsburg Confession, which became (and largely remains) the primary document of the Lutheran profession of faith. His publication of the Old Testament from the original Hebrew, combined with his translation of the New Testament from the original Greek had a widespread impact on German usage and the transformation of written German into an idiom that allowed Germans to look each other (as Luther said) "in the mouth." Luther's use of German was based on the idiom of the Saxon court at the time, which he believed to be the usage most comprehensible to the most Germans. Its use as the "official" vernacular proliferated as the century progressed.

Hans Sachs

Luther encouraged the creation of drama as a means of evangelizing the Protestant cause, and among 16th century playwrights who sought to deploy drama for the purpose of winning support for the Reformation were Georg Wickram (1505–1562), Paul Rebhun (1505–1546), Sixtus Birck (1501–1554), Nicodemus Frischlin (1547–1590), and Thiebolt Gart, whose 1546 *Joseph* became the most popular of Protestant comedies during the

period. Hans Sachs (1494–1576) was the most prolific of Reformation playwrights. He was, in fact, among the most recognized, published, and celebrated writers of vernacular literature during the entire 16th century. His 1523
poem in praise of Luther titled "Die Wittenbergisch Nachtigall" (The Wittenberg Nightingale) proved to be popular among early Protestants—yet it was
so controversial among Catholics that he decided to cease such overt advoca-
cy if he valued his life. He thereafter turned to writing songs, short fiction,
and drama for the remainder of his life. He ultimately composed over 4,000
songs and hundreds of *Schwänke* (humorous anecdotes with moral endings),
while also writing over 200 plays, the best known of which are Shrovetide
comedies.

Sachs he began his apprenticeship as a cobbler in his native Nuremberg in
1508; the following years as a journeyman brought him to Lübeck, Vienna,
Frankfurt, and other prosperous locales that offered him opportunities to
witness a wide variety of 16th-century plays in performance. He attained the
title of master cobbler in 1520, about the same year he began intensive
activity with the Meistersingers, a lay brotherhood descended (according to
some authorities) from singers of ecclesiastical music in the Rhineland. Richard Wagner's 1868 opera *Die Meistersinger von Nürnberg* features Sachs as
a major character, and that opera remains the most well known manifestation
of the group in the public mind to this day. The secretive nature of the
organization, however, precludes any connection between it and Sachs' work
as a playwright. Sachs' work with journeymen and apprentices during the
Shrovetide season is, however, well documented. Sachs had a less than merry
attitude towards Shrovetide celebrations than did many of his contemporaries; he saw the days leading up to Lent as a time to employ theater performance for a moral purpose. To that end he wrote and adapted material familiar to his audience, usually structuring it in ways that were at once humorous
and didactic. Many of his short farces are small masterpieces.

Two good examples of Sachs' once-act Shrovetide farces are *The Play of
Sir Neidhardt* and *The Wandering Scholar from Paradise*. The former was a
short farce dating from the mid-14th century; in it, the knight Sir Neidhardt
and a noblewoman wager that if he can find the season's first violets, she will
accept his poem. He proceeds to find said flowers, place his cap over them,
and returns to her with the news. Meantime peasants find the cap, uproot the
flowers, and leave a "repulsive substance," i.e., fecal matter, under the cap.
Neidhart returns with the lady to present her with his discovery; she is justifi-
ably outraged, Sir Neidhardt is perplexed and aggravated, and the peasants
enjoy the whole spectacle. *The Wandering Scholar from Paradise*, written
and premiered in Nuremberg around 1550, is less scatological and more
didactic. A peasant wife laments the passing of her late husband, singing a
pathetic song in the doorway of her cottage. A "scholar," that is, a student on
semester break, appears at her doorway and asks for money. He claims to

have left Paris not three days ago—but the woman misunderstands him and thinks he said "Paradise" and not "Paris" (in German pronunciation the two are easily confused). She asks if he saw her late husband there, and the student claims he did, though the man was in need of boots, a sturdy pair of pair of trousers, and money. The woman begs the student to return to Paradise and give her late husband a bundle of clothing and a wallet filled with twelve gold guldens. The student accepts the bundle and the money, promising to deliver both to her late husband. She gives him a thaler for his trouble and he then hastily departs.

Soon her present husband appears and asks her why she's so happy. She tells him of her chance meeting with a scholar from Paradise and how she gave him money as a comfort to her late husband. Her husband tells her "Thou gav'st him far too little money/For thy dead husband's alimony!" and prepares to set off in search of the scholar before he makes his getaway to "Paradise." He orders his wife to saddle his horse, and as he pulls on his riding boots spurs, he looks forward to retrieving the money and beating the student senseless. After he beats him, he says, he will return and beat the wife as well: "With two fists in her face, I'll blacken her eyes,/'Til to her folly she testifies!" He departs the stage, and a traverse curtain is pulled across it to reveal the student standing near a tree. He notices a rider coming towards him at great speed. The peasant appears and asks the student if he has seen a young man burdened down with pack and guilt. The student says he has indeed seen such a man, but he ran directly into yonder bog. The credulous peasant gives the student a kreutzer and tells him to watch his horse. As the peasant proceeds into the bog, the student offers Fortune his thanks, and prepares to ride off on the peasant's horse. The traverse curtain then reveals the peasant woman worrying about her husband, who has not returned for some time. The peasant then enters from side, claiming that his horse did not return, which means the young man he met stole it. His wife asks if he found the Scholar from Paradise. He says he did, and to speed him on his journey, gave him his horse. The wife hugs her husband and praises him for his generosity and kindness.

Sachs wrote his plays in Knittelverse couplets, a popular form of doggerel that featured rhyming pairs of lines with irregular numbers of stressed and unstressed syllables, often with an over-emphasis on rhyme. The couplets were an effective medium for embellishing details in a humorous and performable style. The accessibility of Sachs' writing also enhanced his appeal among audiences, who in Nuremberg for the most part had little appreciation for finely tuned versification. In any case, the performers were amateurs with day jobs that allowed them little time to polish their performance skills. "Professional" players were a rare sight in German-language territories during most of the 16th century in any case, unlike the situation among actors in contemporaneous England, France, Italy or Spain. But that situation was about to change, as the English theatre by the late 1580s began to make its prodigious influence felt among German-speaking audiences.

The English Comedians

In about 1586 (the year is inexact) a troupe of English actors arrived in Germany and are thought to have approached the palace of Wolfenbüttel, residence to the Duke of Brunswick. Previous to their arrival, an English troupe said to have been led by the aforementioned English comic actor Will Kempe had toured Denmark and Holland. The troupe which arrived in Wolfenbüttel were thought to perform under the leadership of Robert Browne (1563–1622) and a comic actor named Thomas Sackville (not to be confused with Thomas Sackville, the Earl of Dorset, whose plays had premiered during the 1560s in England). Browne and his troupe found favor with the Duke of Brunswick. Their number included musicians and acrobats, and it is not clear if they departed Brunswick for points east, but English troupes began showing up in several German towns and cities during the 1590s, often to the delight of German audiences who welcomed them in venues as disparate as Münster, Graz, Danzig, Tübingen, Frankfurt am Main, Strassburg, Cologne, Augsburg, and Nuremberg. Records indicate that ticket sales to their performances were substantial indeed, and additional English troupes arrived in their wake. The successes enjoyed among English troupes is nothing short of remarkable in view of the fact that all performances were in English, and few Germans could understand much of what the actors were saying.

The popularity of the English troupes led to three important developments for German theatre practice. First was the acceptance of German-speaking actors as members of the troupes, beginning in sometime in the late 1590s. Second, the presence of a clown in every troupe led to additional imitations of English theatre practice, resulting ultimately in German-language plays of a stock clownish figure, sometimes called named "John Posset," "Hanswurst," and at other times called "Pickelherring." The last name may have come from Shakespeare's comedy *Twelfth Night*, when in Act I Scene 5 Sir Toby Belch refers to a visitor with "'Tis a gentleman here—a plague o' these pickle-herring!" The figure of Sir John Falstaff is also thought to have contributed to the creation of the stock clown in German, since Falstaff also attained substantial popularity among audiences. The most singular aspect of the German enthusiasm for the English troupes, however, was the immediate acclaim German audiences felt for the playwright William Shakespeare. As Shakespeare's career progressed through the beginning of the 17th century, so his appeal in Germany seemed likewise to increase. When his *Hamlet* proved to be a hit in London (probably between 1601 and 1607) the play began to show up in Germany thereafter—albeit in abridged versions and often with a

German title, *Der bestrafte Brudermord* (The Punishment of Fratricide). An-other staple in many a German troupe's repertoire was a saint's play based on *The Virgin Martyr* (1620) by the English playwrights Thomas Dekker (c. 1572–1632) and Philip Massinger (1583–1640). A poster advertising the appearance of a troupe presenting the play proclaimed that the performance would include "the public decapitation of the Holy Martyr Dorothea, and how the Grand Chancellor Theophilus is torn apart by red-hot tongs, enliv-ened by Pickelherring's jests." By the 1620s, German-language troupes be-gan to perform in competition with each other, expanding their repertoires to include adaptations of French and Italian plays. Many therefore believe there is a direct connection between the English troupes and the beginnings of a German professional theater tradition.

Some historians believe the Nuremberg playwright Jakob Ayrer (ca. 1543–1605) may have seen the English troupes in the late 16th century, since in his plays he often featured a clown like Pickelherring who offered com-mentary on his fellow characters. One of Ayrer's tragedies seems to have been an adaptation of *The Spanish Tragedy* by the Elizabethan playwright Thomas Kyd (1558–1594). Many of his other plays, however (he is thought to have written over 100, of which 69 are extant) are in imitation of his fellow Nuremberg citizen Hans Sachs. Like Sachs, Ayrer wrote farces, Shrovetide comedies, tragedies, and historical dramas. Ayrer was a skillful imitator, though his knittelverse was not nearly so appealing to German audiences as Sachs' had been. Ayrer is nevertheless thought to have been the second-most prolific playwright of the century, exceeded only by Sachs.

Many students of German history believe that the German theatre was on the verge of developing great playwrights and acting troupes by the begin-ning of the 17th century. Several German principalities were among the wealthiest in Europe, as the presence of natural resources such as copper, tin, and other metal ores encouraged extensive mining operations. Banking in the southern districts of Germany and shipping along the North Sea coast like-wise produced unprecedented wealth. Cities positioned along established trade routes such as Strassburg, Leipzig, and Nuremberg grew wealthy enough to purchase their independence from the Holy Roman Empire and become "free imperial cities." Agricultural production in Saxony, Bavaria, and the Rhineland flourished. But the Thirty Years' War, which began in Bohemia during 1618, exacted a hideous toll on the Germans, largely be-cause for three decades German territory was a killing ground on which the most ferocious fighting among foreign troops took place. Armies from Swe-den, France, Ireland, Spain, Croatia, Denmark, and Hungary marched back and forth across German soil so often that the German states lost about 40 per cent of their population in the conflict. Many bridges, roads, dams, canals, ports, cities, towns, farms, estates, and settlements were obliterated. The Holy Roman Empire fractured into about 300 pieces, with tiny semi-sovereign dukedoms competing with each other, while petty princes tried to outdo each other in imitating French fashions in architecture, clothing, upholstery, and ballet. The chaos and turmoil that resulted were not overcome for decades after 1648, when the Peace of Westphalia signaled the end of hostilities. The Thirty Years' War had also damaged the German language, because stronger cultures led most of the incursions. Subsequent generations of critics have denounced the writing that developed during and after the war as excessively ornamental, bombastic, rhetorically mannered, and grotesque.

The Rise of Successful Touring Troupes

Many believe that the devastation of the Thirty Years' War left in its wake an obsession with order among the remaining German populace and their myriad domains. That obsession manifested itself in drama and its presentation among troupes forced to make their way through the wreckage of the war, burdened with a pervasive emphasis on caution. Linguists have asserted that the war damaged the German language to such an extent that it lagged behind French, English, and Italian throughout the 17th century—even though numerous writers of substantial talent were present and were often prolific. Other observers of the period agree that German lacked the potential for great literary attainment, largely because German had been cut off from the rest of Europe for three decades and new translations of other works in German were comparatively scarce. On the other hand, some linguistic historians surmise that an inappropriate insistence on neo-classical precedents, such as were present before the war, actually stunted the development of an adequate German idiom for both literature and the stage. As a result, much of the German drama that developed in the second half of the 17th century was adapted from other vernacular languages.

   Carl Andreas Paulsen (ca. 1620–ca.1685) was among the first theatre managers to emerge in the cataclysmic ravages of the Thirty Years' War. He did plays adapted from the English troupes but also from Molière in French and Tirso de Molina in Spanish. Of all the English-language plays to be "Germanized" in the 17th century, Marlowe's *Dr. Faustus* seems to have been the most popular. The original Dr. Faustus was indeed a German, and Paulsen's troupe performed a version of Marlowe's play throughout the 1660s. The account of a highly successful scholar, dissatisfied to the depths of his soul and willing to make deal with the Devil for a happier existence, held endless fascination for Germans. Plays, puppet theatre, and vulgar entertainments based on the legend of Faust were likewise popular throughout Germany in the 17th century. The first known printed version of the legend is a 1587 chapbook titled *Historia von D. Johann Fausten*. The real origin of the Faust character is unknown, though many believe there was a Johann Georg Faust (c.1480–1540) who worked as a magician, alchemist, or mountebank

Figure 9.1.   Conjectural depiction of stage structure used in Germany.

in southern German provinces and may have earned a divinity degree at Heidelberg University around 1509.

Johannes Velten (1640–1697) married Paulsen's daughter Catharina Elisabeth Paulsen sometime in the 1670s and he soon became the company's leading player. Velten was the first *Prinzipal* (actor/manager) of note among the German touring troupes after the Thirty Years' War. He had studied theology in Wittenberg and later received a master's degree from the University of Leipzig, though it is not entirely clear how or why a man with his education should have become an actor. Most actors in German touring troupes were social outcasts. Some, like Velten, actually had studied at universities—but most actors remained targets of ridicule and ostracism. Velten himself was not immune from attacks from clergy and other notables in many of the towns and cities his troupe visited. German public officials, like such officials in many parts of Europe, sought to keep alive in the public mind an association of actors with mountebanks, puppeteers, tooth pullers, prostitutes, acrobats, animal tamers, and other "disreputable" performers. Velten nevertheless translated several plays from the English, French, and Spanish repertoire long before any other troupe had done so, and with the Paulsen troupe he toured several northern German cities as well as some Scandinavian ones, particularly in Denmark. In 1678 Velten and his wife left the Paulsen troupe to reside at the Saxon Court in Dresden at the invitation of Johann Georg III, King of Saxony and Imperial Elector. The troupe Velten assembled in Dresden were known officially as the "Saxon Elector's Court Comedians." With Dresden as their base of operations, the troupe appeared in several venues. Most notable among them were Frankfurt am Main, Leipzig, Nuremberg, and eventually in the Imperial Court of Emperor Leopold I in Worms. Despite the burdensome economic and logistical obstacles he had to overcome as *Prinzipal*, his troupe survived and, at times, prospered. Among the many arduous tasks of a *Prinzipal* was to seek and receive a *Privileg*, or license, to perform in a court or city. The troupe then needed to remain in such a venue long enough to accumulate operating capital with which it could obtain a license for the next engagement. It is no exaggeration to say that troupes lived from engagement to engagement, and in some cases from hand to mouth.

Velten's company not only performed his translations, but also the original works of Andreas Gryphius, whom many scholars consider the most accomplished of German dramatists during the latter part of the 17th century. Gryphius learned playwriting while a university student at Leyden in the Netherlands. There Gryphius had occasion to read and see many of the works by Dutch dramatists Joost van den Vondel (1587–1679) and Pieter Corneliszoon Hooft (1581–1647). Their work comprised the "Dutch Golden Age" of dramatic writing, featuring abundant classical references with an emphasis on "loftiness" in language. Gryphius is known for the same characteristics, along with several "Senecan" tendencies such as a preoccupation with blood, torture, suffering, and martyrdom. Similarities to Seneca, however, found favor among many influential readers and theatre-goers, who encouraged emulation of the classics in German. One of Gryphius' most admired plays was *Catharina von Georgien* (Catherine of Georgia), whose eponymous heroine suffered hideous martyrdom at the hands of the Persian shah. Gryphius has the distinction of being the first German dramatist to put successfully into practice many of the neo-classical strictures the learned of Italy and France had propagated, though he also employed the non-neo-classical convention of supernatural intervention to remarkable effect. Such intervention is especially obvious in his tragedy *Carolus Stuardus* (Charles Stuart, 1657). At one point in the play, the ghosts of murdered English kings make their entrance as a tragic chorus. In many of his plays Gryphius also evinced a concern for anachronistic Biblical references and allusions, especially those passages of the Old and New Testaments that feature a reward to the right-

eous and a severe punishment to the wicked. Much of the dialogue is taken
up with ponderous stichomythia, containing alternating sententious declama-
tions in neo-classical Alexandrine verse form. Gryphius was also accomplished at writing comedy, exemplified in *Herr Peter Squentz* (derived from
Peter Quince in Shakespeare's *Midsummer Night's Dream*) and *Horribili-
cribifax*, featuring seven pairs of lovers.

The plays of Gryphius, perhaps because of the neo-classical aspects of
some and the Biblical references in others, found a welcome in German
school theatres, where in almost all cases clergymen held strategic positions.
One area where Roman Catholic priests and Lutheran pastors agreed was a
belief that the boys and young men in their charge benefitted from theatre
education. By acting in plays, their pupils were thought to acquire skills in
both Latin and German that would later "encourage them in brave and confident speech," and endow them with a spirit enabling them to declaim "forth-
rightly on religious as well as secular affairs." Luther himself encouraged his
followers to build theatres in their schools, so that the pupils might be "kept
from sin and vice" and exposed to "decent conduct as well as useful virtues."
Such demands, however, predisposed school administrators to literary drama, the kind that required of both student actors and their audiences an
ability to understand allegory and be familiar with classical allusion. Such
audiences had long attended court performances of opera and French tragedy
by Racine, on the assumption among many educated Germans that the common man could not follow polished verse. The average German theatregoer
could, it was thought, judge good poetry the way a blind man judges color.
Tooth-pullers, conjurors, and/or jugglers in the typical touring troupe had
furthermore rarely been educated in the art of poetic expression. Given such
assumptions and prejudices, the achievements of Johannes Velten loom even
larger. His troupe in Dresden prospered until the death of their patron Johann
Georg III in 1691; the troupe was then forced out of Dresden and its attempts
to tour or to find another home court were unsuccessful.

CONCLUSIONS

The history of German theatre provides an intriguing set of "what if" dilemmas. What if, for example, playwrights in other German towns and cities
besides Nuremberg had followed the Hans Sachs precedent in Knittelverse
comedy ? After the precedents of the English Comedians, what if native
German troupes had pursued performance venues and court appointments in
the tradition of Johannes Velten? The loudest "what if," of course, is "What
if the Thirty Years' War had never happened?" That question, like the others,
is impossible to answer. It stands to reason nonetheless that the German
theatre would sooner have equaled its English, French, Spanish, and even

Dutch counterparts had not the Thirty Years' War visited such unprecedented ruination on the German countryside and inflicted wholesale slaughter upon its population. Foreign troops remained on German soil long after the Peace of Westphalia concluded official hostilities in 1648. Theatre troupes, if there were any left, could hardly expect to mount productions of much quality anywhere, much less find regular paying audiences for any of them.

Most German troupes, if and when they were able to get back on the road in the later 17th century, managed to travel, walk, or often limp from one engagement to the next with about a dozen performers. Their number included female performers; Velten always cast women in female parts, and his widow continued the tradition after his death in 1697. Women in trouser roles were especially praised in the records left by some observers who saw them. Most of those records also emphasized the poor quality of the troupes. In the words of one observer, costumes were ragged and filthy, actors expectorated onstage, they unceremoniously scratched themselves, the platform stage floor wobbled under the actors' steps, the audience chattered constantly during the performance, and in most cases "theatre performance" was more akin to a novelty entertainment at a third-rate county fair than to an artistic enterprise.

Yet the German theatre ultimately overcame such poverty and degradation. While touring conditions remained primitive into the 18th century, some troupes were able to establish themselves as "moral reformers" and even "language cleansers" to broaden their audience base. Their success came in the form of court appointments and municipal residencies that convinced talented authors to become playwrights. Three of those playwrights were Gotthold Ephraim Lessing (1729–1781), Johann Wolfgang Goethe (1749–1832), and Johann Christoph Friedrich Schiller (1759–1805). Their plays were by the 1770s to establish the German theatre as one comparable with its European counterparts—and in some cases, to exceed them considerably. Goethe's novel *Wilhelm Meisters Lehrjahre* (Wilhelm Meister's Apprenticeship, 1795) provides a wealth of information about German touring companies and has provided generations of students a fascinating depiction of the German actor's brutal existence prior to the re-birth of German theatre in the 18th century.

Bibliography

GENERAL STUDIES

Bial, Henry. *The Performance Studies Reader.* New York: Routledge, 2004.

Brockett, Oscar G. *Making the Scene: a history of stage design and technology in Europe and the United States.* San Antonio, TX: Tobin, 2010.

———. *History of the Theatre*, 10th Ed. Boston: Pearson, 2010.

Brooke, Iris. *Western European Costume and its Relation to the Theatre.* New York: Theatre Arts, 1963.

Cahill, Thomas. *Desire of the Everlasting Hills: the world before and after Jesus.* New York: Talese, 1999.

———. *The Gifts of the Jews.* New York: Talese, 1998.

———. *How the Irish Saved Civilization.* New York: Talese, 1995.

———. *Sailing the Wine-dark Sea: why the Greeks matter.* New York: Talese, 2003.

Goldberg, Steven. *The Inevitability of Patriarchy.* New York: Morrow, 1974.

———. *Why Men Rule: a theory of male dominance.* Chicago: Open Court, 1993.

Gruen, Erich S. *Studies in Greek Culture and Roman Policy.* New York: Brill, 1990.

Hanson, Victor Davis. *Makers of Ancient Strategy: from the Persian wars to the fall of Rome.* New York: Princeton, 2010.

Harrington, Austin. *Art and Social Theory.* Malden, MA: Polity Press, 2004.

Harrison, Jane Ellen. *Prolegomena to the Study of Greek Religion.* New York: Meridian, 1955.

Low, Jennifer A. *Imagining the Audience in Early Modern Drama, 1558-1642.* New York: Palgrave Macmillan, 2011.

Nicoll, Allardyce. *The Development of the Theatre: a study of theatrical art from the beginnings to the present day.* New York: Harcourt 1969.

Paglia, Camille. *Sexual Personae.* New Haven, CT: Yale, 1990.

Riccoboni, Luigi. *A General History of the Stage, from its Origin.* New York: AMS, 1978, 1754.

Shelley, William Scott. *The Origins of the Europeans.* Lanham, MD: Rowman and Littlefield, 1998.

ANCIENT GREECE AND ROME

Allen, James Turney. *The Greek Theater of the Fifth Century before Christ.* New York: Haskell, 1966.

————. *Stage Antiquities of the Greeks and Romans and their Influence*. New York: Cooper Square, 1963.

Bain, David. *Actors and Audience in Greek drama*. New York: Oxford, 1977.

Baldry, H. C. *The Greek Tragic Theatre*. New York: Norton, 1972.

Benediktson, D. Thomas. *Literature and the Visual Arts in Ancient Greece and Rome*. Norman, OK: Univ. Oklahoma Press, 2000.

Bieber, Margarete. *The History of the Greek and Roman Theatre*. New York: Princeton, 1961.

Braund, David. *Athenaeus and his World: reading Greek culture in the Roman Empire*. Exeter UK: Univ. Exeter Press, 2000.

Butler, James Harmon. *The Theatre and Drama of Greece and Rome*. San Francisco: Chandler, 1972.

Carter, D. M. *Why Athens?: a reappraisal of tragic politics*. New York: Oxford, 2011.

Coolidge, Archibald Cary. *Beyond the Fatal Flaw*. Lake MacBride, IA: Maecenas, 1980.

Driver, Tom Faw. *The Sense of History in Greek and Shakespearean Drama*. New York: Columbia, 1960.

Easterling, P. E. *Greek Religion and Society*. New York: Cambridge, 1985.

Else, Gerald F. *The Origin and Early Form of Greek Tragedy*. Cambridge, MA: Harvard, 1965.

Erp Taalman Kip, A. Maria van. *Reader and Spectator : problems in the interpretation of Greek tragedy*. Amsterdam: Gieben, 1990.

Garton, Charles. *Personal Aspects of the Roman Theatre*. Toronto: Hakkert, 1972.

Gibbon, Edward. *The Decline and Fall of the Roman Empire*. New York: Harcourt Brace, 1960.

Goldberg, Sander M. *The Making of Menander's Comedy*. Berkeley: University of California Press, 1980.

Goldhill, Simon. *Performance Culture and Athenian Democracy*. New York: Cambridge, 1999.

Goodell, Thomas Dwight. *Athenian Tragedy: a study in popular art*. New Haven: Yale, 1920.

Goodman, Martin. *Jews in a Graeco-Roman World*. New York: Oxford, 1998.

Green, J. R. *Theatre in Ancient Greek Society*. New York: Routledge, 1994.

Lindsay, Jack. *The Clashing Rocks: a study of early Greek religion and culture and the origins of drama*. London: Chapman & Hall, 1965.

Norwood, Gilbert. *Greek comedy*. New York: Hill and Wang, 1963.

Parker, Robert. *Athenian religion: a history*. Oxford: Clarendon, 1996.

Pelikan, Jaroslav. *Christianity and Classical culture*. New Haven: Yale, 1993.

————.*The Excellent Empire: the fall of Rome and the triumph of the Church*. San Francisco: Harper and Row, 1987.

Pickard-Cambridge, Sir Arthur Wallace. *The Dramatic Festivals of Athens*. London: Oxford, 1968.

Preus, Anthony. *A to Z of Ancient Greek Philosophy*. Lanham: Scarecrow, 2010.

Rehm, Rush. *Greek Tragic Theatre*. New York: Routledge, 1994.

Rose, H. J. *Gods and Heroes of the Greeks*. New York: Meridian, 1958.

Sifakis, G. M. *Studies in the History of Hellenistic Drama*. London: Athlone, 1967.

Skinner, Marilyn B. *Sexuality in Greek and Roman culture*. Malden, MA: Blackwell, 2005.

Spence, I. G. *A to Z of Ancient Greek Warfare*. Lanham, MD: Scarecrow, 2010.

Stierlin, Henri. *The Cultural History of Rome*. London: Aurum, 1983.

Vince, Ronald W. *Ancient and Medieval Theatre: an historiographical handbook*. Westport, CT: Greenwood, 1984.

Walcot, Peter. *Greek Drama in its Theatrical and Social Context*. Cardiff: Wales, 1976.

Walton, J. Michael. *Menander and the Making of Comedy*. Westport, CT: Greenwood, 1996.

Webster, T. B. L. *Greek Theatre Production*. London: Methuen 1970.

Wiles, David. *The Masks of Menander : sign and meaning in Greek and Roman performance*. New York: Cambridge, 1991.

Yunis, Harvey. *Written Texts and the Rise of Literate Culture in Ancient Greece*. New York: Cambridge, 2003.

THEATRE OF THE MIDDLE AGES

Axton, Richard. *European Drama of the Early Middle Ages.* London: Hutchinson, 1974.
Beadle, Richard. *Cambridge Companion to Medieval English Theatre.* New York: Cambridge, 2008.
Bevington, David M. *Medieval Drama.* Boston: Houghton Mifflin, 1975.
Chambers, Edmund K. *The Mediaeval Stage.* Mineola, NY: Dover, 1996.
Collins, Fletcher. *The Production of Medieval Church Music-drama.* Charlottesville, VA: Univ. Virginia Press, 1972.
Corbett, Tony. *The Laity, the Church, and the Mystery Plays: a drama of belonging.* Dublin: Four Courts, 2009.
Edwards, Francis. *Ritual and Drama : the mediaeval theatre.* Guildford, UK: Lutterworth, 1976.
Ferguson, Everett. *Backgrounds of Early Christianity.* Grand Rapids, MI: Eerdmans, 1993.
Gertsman, Elina. *Visualizing Medieval Performance.* Burlington, VT: Ashgate, 2008.
Harris, Stephen J. *Misconceptions about the Middle Ages.* New York : Routledge, 2008.
Harris, John Wesley. *Medieval Theatre in Context: an introduction.* New York: Routledge, 1992.
Kipling, Gordon. *Enter the King: theatre, liturgy, and ritual.* Oxford: Clarendon, 1998.
Liebeschuetz, J. H. W. G. *The Decline and Fall of the Roman City.* New York: Oxford, 2001.
Ogden, Dunbar H. *The Staging of Drama in the Medieval Church.* Cranbury, NJ: Associated, 2002.
Ruggiers, Paul G. *Versions of Medieval Comedy.* Norman, OK: Univ. Oklahoma Press, 1977.
Simon, Eckehard. *The Theatre of Medieval Europe.* New York: Cambridge, 1991.
Southern, Richard. *The Staging of Plays before Shakespeare.* New York: Theatre Arts, 1973.
———. *The Medieval Theatre in the Round.* New York: Theatre Arts, 1975.
Tunison, Joseph S. *Dramatic Traditions of the Dark Ages.* New York: Franklin, 1970.
Tydeman, William. *English medieval theatre, 1400-1500.* Boston: Routledge, 1986.
Vince, Ronald W. *A Companion to the Medieval Theatre.* Westport, CT: Greenwood, 1989.
Wickham, Glynne. *The Medieval Theatre.* New York: Cambridge, 1987.
Young, Karl. *The Drama of the Medieval Church.* Oxford: Clarendon, 1933.

THE THEATRE OF THE ITALIAN RENAISSANCE

Beecher, Donald. *Renaissance Comedy: the Italian masters.* Toronto: University Press, 2008.
Braden, Gordon. *Renaissance Tragedy and the Senecan Tradition.* New Haven, CT: Yale, 1985.
Brubaker, David. *Court and Commedia: the Italian Renaissance stage.* New York: Rosen, 1975.
Cairns, Christopher. *Scenery, Set, and Staging in the Italian Renaissance.* Lewiston, ME: Mellen, 1996.
Clubb, Louise George. *Italian Drama in Shakespeare's Time.* New Haven, CT: Yale, 1989.
Günsberg, Maggie. *Gender and the Italian stage.* New York: Cambridge, 1997.
Herrick, Marvin T. *Italian Comedy in the Renaissance.* Urbana: Illinois, 1960.
———. *Italian Tragedy in the Renaissance.* Urbana: Illinois, 1965.
———. *Tragicomedy; its Origin and Development in Italy, France, and England.* Urbana: Illinois, 1955.
Kennard, Joseph Spencer. *The Italian Theatre.* New York: Blom 1964, 1932.
Lea, Kathleen Marguerite. *Italian Popular Comedy.* New York: Russell and Russell, 1962.
Luciani, Vincent. *A Concise History of the Italian Theatre.* New York: Vanni, 1961.
Marco Institute for Medieval and Renaissance Studies. *Spectacle and Public Performance in the late Middle Ages and the Renaissance.* Leiden: Brill, 2006.
Radcliff-Umstead, Douglas. *The Birth of Modern Comedy in Renaissance Italy.* Chicago: University Press, 1969.

Rowland, Ingrid D. *Vitruvius: Ten Books on Architecture.* New York: Cambridge, 1999.
Russo, Mauda Bregoli. *Renaissance Italian Theatre.* Florence: Olschki, 1984.
Sand, Maurice. *The History of the Harlequinade.* New York: Blom, 1968, 1915.
Smith, Winifred. *The Commedia Dell'arte.* New York: Blom, 1964.

THE THEATRE OF ASIA

Bhat, Govind Keshav. *Theatrical Aspects of Sanskrit Drama.* Poona, India: Bhandarkar, 1983.
Bowers, Faubion. *Japanese Theatre.* Rutland, VT: Tuttle, 1974.
Brown, John Russell. *New Sites for Shakespeare: theatre, the audience, and Asia.* New York: Routledge, 1999.
Ernst, Earle. *The Kabuki Theatre.* Honolulu: Univ. Hawaii Press, 1974.
Garagi, Balawanta. *Know India: Theatre.* Delhi: Tata, 1985.
———. *Theatre in India.* New York: Theatre Arts, 1962.
Horrwitz, E. P. *The Indian Theatre: a brief survey of the Sanskrit drama.* New York: Blom, 1967.
Hsü, Tao-ching. *The Chinese Conception of the Theatre.* Seattle, WA: Univ. Washington Press, 1985.
Kale, Pramod Keshav. *The Theatric Universe: a study of the Natyasastra.* Bombay: Prakashan, 1974.
Kawatake, Shigetoshi. *The Development of the Japanese Theatre Aart.* Tokyo: International Cultural Relations, 1935.
Keene, Donald. *Bunraku: the art of the Japanese puppet theatre.* Tokyo : Kodansha, 1965.
Kenny, Don. *On Stage in Japan: Kabuki, Bunraku, Noh, Gagaku.* Tokyo: Shufunotomo, 1974.
Kincaid, Zoë. *Kabuki: the popular stage of Japan.* New York: Blom, 1965.
Kominz, Laurence Richard. *The Stars who Created Kabuki.* New York: Kodansha, 1997.
Leiter, Samuel L. *The A to Z of Japanese Traditional Theatre.* Lanham, MD: Scarecrow Press, 2010.
Majumdar, Ramesh Chandra. *The History and Culture of the Indian People.* London: G. Allen & Unwin 1951-1969.
Miller, J. Scott. *The A to Z of Modern Japanese Literature and Theater.* Lanham: Scarecrow Press, 2010.
Muni, Bharata. *The Natyasastra: Treatise on Ancient Indiana drama and Performance.* New Delhi: Munshiram Manoharlal, 1996.
Olson, Carl. *The A to Z of Buddhism.* Lanham, MD: Scarecrow, 2009.
Ortolani, Benito. *The Japanese Theatre: from shamanistic ritual to contemporary pluralism.* New York: Princeton, 1995.
Panchal, Govardhan. *The Theatres of Bharata and Some Aspects of Sanskrit play-production.* New Delhi: Munshiram Manoharlal, 1996.
Rath, Eric C. *The Ethos of Noh: actors and their art.* Cambridge, MA: Harvard, 2004.
Raz, Jacob. *Audience and Actors: a study of their interaction in the Japanese traditional theatre.* Leiden: Brill, 1983.
Riley, Jo. *Chinese Theatre and the Actor in Performance.* New York: Cambridge,1997.
Scott, A. C. *The Kabuki Theatre of Japan.* New York: Collier Books, 1966.
Scott, A. C. *The Classical Theatre of China.* London: Allen & Unwin 1957.
Tarlekar, Ganesh Hari. *Studies in the Natyasastra.* Delhi: Banarsidass, 1975.
Vatsyayan, Kapila. *Bharata, the Natyasastra.* New Delhi: Sahitya, 1996.
Wichmann, Elizabeth. *Listening to Theatre: the aural dimension of Beijing Opera.* Honolulu: Hawaii, 1991.
Ye, Tan. *The A to Z of Chinese theater.* Lanham, MD: Scarecrow, 2010.

THE THEATRE OF FRANCE THROUGH 1658

Clarke, David. *Pierre Corneille: poetics and political drama.* New York: Cambridge, 1992.

Frank, Grace. *The Medieval French Drama.* Oxford: Clarendon, 1954.

Howarth, W. D. *French Theatre in the Neo-classical Era.* New York: Cambridge, 1997.

Jeffery, Brian. *French Renaissance Comedy, 1552-1630.* Oxford: Clarendon 1969.

Jondorf, Gillian. *French Renaissance Tragedy.* New York: Cambridge, 1990.

Knight, Alan E. *Aspects of Genre in Late Medieval French Drama.* Manchester, UK: University Press, 1983.

Lawrenson, T. E. *The French Stage and Playhouse in the XVIIth century.* New York: AMS, 1986.

Lockert, Lacy. *Studies in French Classical Tragedy.* Nashville: Vanderbilt University Press, 1958.

Lough, John. *Seventeenth-Century French Drama.* Oxford: Clarendon, 1979.

Lyons, John D. *A Theatre of Disguise: studies in French baroque drama, 1630-1660.* Columbia, SC: French Literature Publications, 1978.

———. *Kingdom of Disorder: the theory of tragedy in Classical France.* West Lafayette, IN: Purdue Univ. Press, 1999.

Mahelot, Laurent. *Le mémoire de Mahelot.* Trans. Henry Carrington Lancaster. Paris: Champion, 1920.

Maskell, David. *Racine: a theatrical reading.* New York: Oxford, 1995.

Maxwell, Ian Ramsay. *French Farce and John Heywood.* London: Oxford, 1946.

Murray, Timothy. *Theatrical Legitimation.* New York: Oxford, 1987.

Perret, Donald. *Old Comedy in the French Renaissance, 1576-1620.* Geneva: Droz, 1992.

Scott, Virginia. *The Commedia dell'arte in Paris, 1644-1697.* Charlottesville: Virginia, 1990.

———. *Women on the Stage in Early Modern France: 1540-1750.* New York: Cambridge, 2010.

Stone, Donald. *French Humanist Tragedy.* Totowa, NJ: Rowman and Littlefield, 1974.

Symes, Carol. *A Common Stage: theater and public life in medieval Arras.* Ithaca, NY: Cornell, 2007.

Waith, Eugene M. *French and English Drama of the Seventeenth Century.* Los Angeles: Univ. California Press, 1972.

Wiley, William L. *The Early Public Theatre in France.* Westport, CT: Greenwood, 1972.

———. *The Hôtel de Bourgogne.* Chapel Hill: Carolina, 1973.

THE THEATRE OF SPAIN IN THE SIGLO DE ORO

McKendrick, Melveena. *Theatre in Spain, 1490-1700.* New York: Cambridge, 1992.

Polito, Antonio R. *Spanish Theatre: a survey.* Salt Lake City: Utah, 1967.

Surtz, Ronald E. *The Birth of a Theater: dramatic convention in the Spanish theater.* Madrid: Castalia, 1979.

Rennert, Hugo Albert. *Spanish Stage in the Time of Lope de Vega.* Ithaca: Cornell, 2009, 1909.

Shergold, N. D. *History of the Spanish Stage.* Oxford: Clarendon, 1967.

Shoemaker, William Hutchinson. *Multiple Stage in Spain.* Princeton: University Press, 1935.

Williams, Ronald Boal. *Staging Plays on the Spanish Peninsula Prior to 1555.* Iowa City, IA: Univ. Iowa Press, 1935.

Lund, Harry. *Pedro Calderon de la Barca.* Edinburg, TX: Norriega, 1963.

Thompson, Peter E. *Triumphant Juan Rana: a gay actor of the Spanish Golden Age.* Toronto: Atticus, 2006.

THE ELIZABETHAN THEATRE

Adams, John Cranford. *The Globe Playhouse: its design and equipment.* New York: Barnes and Noble, 1961.

Barnet, Sylvan, ed. *The Genius of the Early English Theater.* New York: New American Library, 1962.

Beckerman, Bernard. *Shakespeare at the Globe, 1599-1609.* New York: Macmillan, 1962.

Bentley, Gerald Eades. *The Profession of Player in Shakespeare's Time, 1590-1642.* New York: Princeton, 1984.

Bridges-Adams, William. *The Irresistible Theatre: growth of the English stage.* New York: Collier, 1961.

Cohen, Walter. *Drama of a Nation: public theater in Renaissance England and Spain.* Ithaca, NY: Cornell, 1985.

Cook, Judith. *Roaring Boys: playwrights and players in Elizabethan and Jacobean England.* Stroud, UK: Sutton, 2004.

Cook, Judith. *At the Sign of the Swan.* London: Harrap, 1986.

Ellis-Fermor, Una Mary. *The Jacobean Drama: an interpretation.* New York: Vintage, 1964.

Farley-Hills, David. *Jacobean Drama: a critical study of the professional drama, 1600-25.* New York: St. Martin's, 1988.

Foakes, R. A. *Illustrations of the English Stage, 1580-1642.* Palo Alto, CA: Stanford, 1985.

Forse, James H. *Art Imitates Business.* Bowling Green, OH: Popular Press, 1993.

Gibson, Joy Leslie. *Squeaking Cleopatras: the Elizabethan boy player.* Stroud, UK: Sutton, 2000.

Grote, David. *The Best Actors in the World: Shakespeare and his acting company.* Westport, CT: Greenwood, 2002.

Gurr, Andrew. *Playgoing in Shakespeare's London.* New York: Cambridge, 1987.

———. *The Shakespearean Stage, 1574-1642.* New York: Cambridge, 1970.

Harrison, G. B. *Elizabethan Plays and Players.* Ann Arbor, MI: Michigan, 1956.

Hattaway, Michael. *Elizabethan Popular Theatre.* Boston: Routledge & Kegan Paul, 1982.

Hodgdon, Barbara, ed. *A Companion to Shakespeare and Performance.* Malden, MA: Blackwell, 2005.

Joseph, Bertram. *Elizabethan Acting.* London: Oxford, 1964.

Leggatt, Alexander. *Jacobean Public Theatre.* New York: Routledge, 1992.

Orgel, Stephen. *Shakespeare in the Theatre.* New York: Garland, 1999.

Orrell, John. *The Human Stage: English Theatre Design, 1567-1640.* New York: Cambridge, 1988.

Shepherd, Simon. *Marlowe and the Politics of Elizabethan theatre.* New York: St. Martin's, 1986.

Sprague, Arthur Colby. *Shakespearian Players and Performances.* Cambridge, MA: Harvard, 1953.

Tomlinson, Thomas Brian. *A Study of Elizabethan and Jacobean Tragedy.* New York: Cambridge, 1964.

Wilson, F. P. *The Elizabethan Theatre.* Groningen, NL: Wolters, 1955.

Woods, Leigh. *On Playing Shakespeare:* Westport, CT: Greenwood, 1991.

THE GERMAN THEATRE TO 1700

Aylett, Robert, ed. *Hans Sachs and Folk Theatre in the late Middle Ages.* Lewiston, ME: Mellen, 1995.

Brandt, George W. and Wiebe Hogendoorn. *German and Dutch Theatre, 1600-1848.* New York: Cambridge, 1993.

Cohn, Albert, ed. *Shakespeare in Germany in the 16 th and 17 th Centuries.* London: Asher, 1865.

Ehrstine, Glenn. *Theater, Culture, and Community in Reformation Bern, 1523-1555.* Boston: Brill, 2002.

French, Walter. *Mediaeval Civilization as Illustrated by the Fastnachtspiele of Hans Sachs.* Baltimore: Johns Hopkins, 1925.

Garland, Henry and Mary. *Oxford Companion to German Literature.* New York: Oxford, 1986.

Grange, William. *Historical Dictionary of the German Theatre.* Lanham, MD: Scarecrow, 2006.

Hayman, Ronald, ed. *The German Theatre: a Symposium.* London: Wolff, 1975.

Kurtz, John. "Studies in the Staging of German Religious Drama of the late Middle Ages." PhD diss., University of Illinois, 1932.

Limon. Jerzy. *Gentleman of a Company: English Players in Central and Eastern Europe, 1590-1660.* New York: Cambridge, 1985.

Mantzius, Karl. *A History of Theatrical Art.* New York: Smith, 1937.

Patterson, Michael. *German Theatre : a Bibliography from the Beginning to 1995.* New York: Hall, 1996.

Tydeman, William. *The Medieval European Stage, 500-1550.* Cambridge, UK: Cambridge University Press, 2001.

Wailes, Stephen L. *The Rich Man and Lazarus on the Reformation stage.* Selinsgrove, PA: Susquehanna, 1997.

Index

Ifans, Rhyss, 141
Intolerance (film), 108
Islam in Indian culture, 97–98; Muslim
  invasion of Spain, 119–120
Italianate ideals in France, 107–109, 112,
  113, 114, 118

Jodelle, Eteinne, 108
Jonson, Ben, 29, 139, 141
Julius Caesar, 33, 44, 46, 50, 53–54, 74
Julius Caesar (Shakespeare), 44, 46, 47,
  143

Kabuki, 103, 103–104, 105
Kean, Edmund, 149
King Lear (Shakespeare), 133, 140, 143,
  144, 146, 148, 149
Knittelverse, 156, 158, 162
Kurosawa, Akira, 148
Kyd, Thomas, 140, 158

La reine Margot (film), 108

LeComte, Valleran, 111, 115, 116
lighting, 27, 40, 75, 112, 135; lamps and
  candles, 74, 76
literacy, 2, 3, 12, 16–17, 24, 81, 86, 93,
  118, 138
Lisi, Virna, 108
Lope de Vega Carpio, Felix, 120, 122, 127
Lope de Rueda, 121
Lord Chamberlain's Men, 132, 137, 141,
  143
Luther, Martin, 67, 154, 162

Macbeth (Shakespeare), 137, 142, 143,
  146–147, 148, 149
MacDowell, Andie, 1–2
The Magic Flute (film), 76
Marlowe, Christopher, 53, 139, 140, 146,
  159
Menander, 22, 25, 27, 29, 49
Mesopotamia, 9, 11, 12–13
Midsummer Night's Dream (Shakespeare),
  105, 143, 161
mimesis (imitation of an action), 12, 17,
  18, 31–32, 34, 48, 60, 93, 98
Ming Dynasty (China), 86, 89, 90
Mirren, Helen, 148

Moliére (Jean-Baptiste Poquelin), 3, 29,
  118, 118, 159
Molina, Tirso de, 127, 159
Montdory (Guillaume des Gilberts), 113,
  115–116
Montfleury (Zacharie Jacob), 115–116
morality plays, 64, 65, 67, 151
movement in performance, 17, 24, 37, 40,
  52, 54, 61, 76, 77, 96, 98, 101, 102, 103
Murray, Bill, 1–2

Natya Shastra (The Science of the
  Theatre), 93, 94
neo-classicism, 46, 53, 77, 78, 79, 80, 81,
  82, 108, 109, 111, 113, 114, 115–116,
  118, 146, 147, 148, 159, 161, 162
Noh theatre and drama (Japan), 99,
  101–102, 104, 105
non-dramatic performers, 12, 48, 49, 54,
  59, 61, 65, 87, 112, 156, 162

Oedipus (Sophocles), 3, 22, 33, 34, 35, 39
Olivier, Laurence, 135, 149
orkestron (playing space), 39, 40
Othello (Shakespeare), 133, 137, 142, 143,
  146–147, 148, 149

Paltrow, Gwynneth, 135
Paulsen, Carl Andreas, 159–160
Pericles, 22, 41
Plato, 22, 25, 28, 30–32, 34, 53, 71, 92
Plautus (Titus Maccius Plautus), 52, 80,
  131, 140, 146
plot (*mythos*), 1–2, 28, 29, 32, 34–35, 36,
  52, 64, 79, 90, 97, 112, 135, 137, 140,
  142, 143
Plummer, Christopher, 44
Presley, Elvis, 80
Pulp Fiction (film), 35
pundonor in Spanish drama, 126, 127
Punic Wars, 43, 47, 48

Qin Dynasty (China), 12, 16, 47, 86

Racine, Jean, 116, 118
recorded history, 1, 2–4, 5, 10, 11, 14, 19,
  22, 29, 33, 41, 43, 45, 46, 47; oral
  history, 5, 11; memory, 1–2, 3, 11; time
  and chronology, 5–6, 7